ENDO

What I learned from Justin Donald in the first six months of studying his work earned me well over six figures in annual after-tax passive income. As a result, I am now a student of every word Justin writes, teaches, and reveals. Simply put, I consider Justin to be the #1 Lifestyle Investment expert in the world, and he gets my absolute highest endorsement.

—Ryan Levesque
Three-time Inc. 5000 CEO,
#1 National Bestselling Author of *Ask* and *Choose*

When it comes to growing and protecting my family's wealth, Justin Donald is the investor I've counted on. Having known Justin for over two decades, I can assure you that his track record as an investor is exceeded only by his character. His book *The Lifestyle Investor* combines both his years of experience and his impeccable integrity to create the must-read guide for cashflow investing.

—Hal Elrod
Bestselling Author of *The Miracle Morning*

Justin is a giver who shares his investing knowledge generously so others can win too. I recommend *The Lifestyle Investor* for anyone looking to grow their wealth, multiply their impact, and have fun in the process!

—Codie Sanchez
Investor and Founder of Contrarian Thinking

Justin values people more than profit and yet seems to win huge in both categories. That's rare in this field. I tell all my friends to learn from Justin. He's always honest, open, and trustworthy, which makes him the #1 pick for investing advice. His book *The Lifestyle Investor* embodies his years of experience and effective action—and if you want to learn the game of cash flow investing, this is your next book.

—Jon Vroman
Founder of FrontRowDads.com

Justin is someone who doesn't need to write a book or teach what he knows because he has invested well. Yet, with a generous spirit, he shares what he knows and leads by his example. He also makes sure nobody ever feels small or insignificant as he brings both the wealthy and those just starting out along for the ride. My clients who get to know Justin love him and his work. He is a value creator in my life and so many others. If you get a chance to learn from this man . . . take it. You will be glad you did.

—Garrett Gunderson
Multiple Time *Wall Street Journal* Bestseller
#1 *Wall Street Journal* and *New York Times*
Bestselling Author of *Killing Sacred Cows*

The Lifestyle Investor has become my investment Bible, and I recommend it to everyone!

—Jon Gordon
14x Bestselling Author of *The Energy Bus*

The Lifestyle Investor is a must-read book. It has completely changed the game for me and my family. I wish these concepts were taught in school, but they aren't. I am so glad that Justin shows us all how to make our money work for us in a simple and easy-to-follow way. I wish I would have read this book years ago!

—Pete Vargas
Founder and CEO of Advance Your Reach®

Justin Donald has found something that at first glance seems so simple, yet his ability to relate and then execute at a high level separates himself apart from a great many people. *The Lifestyle Investor* is a must-read for anyone who is interested in taking back their life and living it on their terms.

—Chris Pronger
NHL Hall of Famer and Olympic Gold Medalist

Justin offers up a common-sense approach to financial freedom. His book is not based on theory but on the practical applications he has utilized in his own life to elevate meaning and purpose across the spectrum of all that life has to offer.

—Casey Weade
Bestselling Author and CEO of Howard Bailey Financial®

Unlike a lot of teachers, Justin doesn't hold back the best strategies for himself; he shares them all to create a positive impact for you—and this book is no exception.

—John Ruhlin
Bestselling Author and Co-Founder of GIFTOLOGY®

Justin's book *The Lifestyle Investor* brings a how-to approach to investing in private deals and cash flow opportunities. You will get compelling value from his expertise and fresh perspective. As a person, I've seen Justin show up for his family and his followers. I am lucky to have him as a friend and business collaborator.

—Jim Dew
CEO of Dew Wealth Management®, Inc. 500 2022 and 2023

If you have the opportunity to spend time with Justin and learn from him, you're getting to learn from someone who has invested the time, energy, money, and resources to study and learn the best methodologies in the world of finance, tax, investing, and legal. We have an epidemic of financial illiteracy in our country, and Justin is tackling it head-on.

—Jeff Socha
Founder of Socha Capital

The Lifestyle Investor is a great read. It compiles Justin's years of knowledge and experience in an easy-to-follow format for anyone looking to start in the investing world.

—David Osborn
New York Times Bestselling Author of *Wealth Can't Wait*

If you're looking for fast, practical strategies to succeed in today's current financial environment, look no further than Justin Donald and his book *The Lifestyle Investor*. It's a must-read!

—Michael Hyatt
Founder and Chairman of Full Focus® and
Bestselling Author of *Your Best Year Ever*

Justin Donald takes the complicated topic of money and investing and makes it simple, easy, fun, and inspiring! *The Lifestyle Investor* is all about the American Dream, and it lays out the path to real financial freedom step by step.

—Mike Dillard
Founder of RicherEveryDay.com

Actionable, approachable investment advice to apply in today's ever-evolving markets . . . that's what you'll get when you read Justin's latest guide to cashflow investing. Justin doesn't hold back and generously shares his best strategies so that you can succeed no matter your goals.

—Roland Frasier
Investor and Founder of DigitalMarketer.com,
Scalable.co, EpicNetwork.com

If I had to summarize in one word what lifestyle investing and what Justin teaches have meant to me, it would be *freedom*. I spent over a decade in finance coaching with financial advisors from all over the United States, but much of what Justin taught me was new concepts I wasn't familiar with—concepts that allowed me to create a six-figure passive income within a couple of years. This allowed me to step away from a seven-figure career as an employee so I could build a business on my terms. As a married man with three children, I'm not sure I would have been able to make this move without the safety net that Justin helped me create with his Lifestyle Investing concepts.

The only thing better than what Justin teaches from an investing standpoint is who he is as a person. He's a husband and father first, and the whole idea of investing for the purpose of creating your ideal life is apparent in how he lives his by example. He's a person who serves others, and I'm excited he is sharing all of his secrets with the world in this very book you are holding in your hands!

—Brad Johnson
Co-founder of Triad Partners and Host of the
Do Business. Do Life. podcast

If you are looking for answers on how to successfully invest and gain the financial freedom that you deserve, then this book is for you. It totally cuts through the noise of the traditional investment world and gives you a glimpse of how a professional investor has been able to enhance his wealth and increase his lifestyle at the same time. This is something I believe we all want, although we don't all realize how attainable it really is. I personally worked over fifteen years to build a successful business, realizing it had become my life as opposed to blessing my life which is ultimately what I hoped for. I found myself living in fear, thinking there was no way out, and I was trapped, having to sell my time for money.

When I met Justin, and he shared with me the many lessons in this book, I realized there is another way. Within twelve months, all fear had subsided, and I walked away from my seven-figure job. This decision raised my standard on how to live a meaningful life, which ultimately gave me and my family the freedom that we deserve. I really couldn't have done this without Justin and the wisdom within these pages, I hope it does the same for you.

—Shawn Sparks
Investor and Author of *The Advisor Breakthrough*

Justin is a badass, plain and simple. *The Lifestyle Investor* is one of my all-time favorite books when it comes to thinking outside the box on how we look at investing, income, our money, and most importantly, how we think of these things as they relate to our most valuable asset, our time. Read this book right now, and then get ready to make a ton of positive changes to how you think about your personal, professional, and financial life.

—Darius Mirshahzadeh
Author of *The Core Value Equation*, Investor,
Award Winning CEO and Host of
The Greatness Machine podcast

When Justin chooses to do something, you can count on it being a very well-thought-out maneuver because he's thought out how to optimize the outcome. If you have an opportunity to work with Justin or learn from him, you will leave that experience a greater human.

—Brad Weimert
Real Estate and Business Investor, Entrepreneur,
Founder of Easy Pay Direct
Host of the *Beyond A Million* podcast

It is now possible to earn passive income, long-term equity, and achieve financial freedom while traveling the world, being fully involved in your family life and feeling fulfilled. Justin Donald's book *The Lifestyle Investor* teaches us how. And there is no one more conscious, experienced, and helpful to share this knowledge than Justin. Written for his daughter Savannah, you can expect ease in learning his smart financial strategies. I trust Justin fully and am grateful to be in his world for life!

—Amber Vilhauer
Owner of NGNG Enterprises, Inc.®

The Lifestyle Investor is the perfect guide for investing in today's ever-changing world, and you need a sound strategy for when it does. I highly recommend that you buy this book for your investing library. My favorite part is the 10 most important principles of cashflow investing . . . because when times change, you ALWAYS need a great strategy.

—Ken McElroy
Partner at MC Companies

The Lifestyle Investor is incredible. It compiles Justin's years of knowledge and experience in an easy-to-follow format for anyone looking to start in the investing world.

—Erik Huberman
Founder and CEO of Hawke Media®

I have built my life and businesses following a principle "Success Leaves Clues," and who better to follow than Justin Donald, who is one of the most successful cash flow investors and, more importantly, lifestyle investors. With this book, he doesn't make you hunt for clues. Instead, he lays out the step-by-step plan in great detail, giving you the roadmap you need to achieve your goals fast, so you can build the life of your dreams.

—Mark Moss
Host of the *Mark Moss Show*
Founder of Market Disruptor

THE LIFESTYLE INVESTOR®

THE 10 COMMANDMENTS OF CASH FLOW INVESTING FOR PASSIVE INCOME AND FINANCIAL FREEDOM

LIFESTYLE INVESTOR VIDEOS

Want to start your Lifestyle Investor journey quickly? Visit *LifestyleInvestor.com/Gift*. I'll walk you through a step-by-step system to reach financial freedom with cash flow investing and passive income.

INSIDER BONUS CONTENT

If you are reading this book on a Kindle or Kindle app, make sure it's the latest version. I'm frequently updating the online version of this book with more interviews, resources, and information based on the feedback you share, and I'm always adding new information from other investors, business owners, and clients I meet and talk to who are achieving financial freedom.

To get the latest and greatest online content, just open your app, click or press the "More" icon in the lower right-hand corner, and then press "Sync" so you'll always be up to date.

I appreciate comments and feedback, so head over to *LifestyleInvestor.com/Contact* right now!

THE LIFESTYLE INVESTOR®

THE 10 COMMANDMENTS OF CASH FLOW INVESTING FOR PASSIVE INCOME AND FINANCIAL FREEDOM

JUSTIN DONALD

ethos
collective

Published by Ethos Collective™
P.O. Box 43, Powell, OH 43065
EthosCollective.vip

Library of Congress Cataloging: 2020920778

Paperback: 978-1-63680-012-7
Hardcover: 978-1-63680-013-4
E-book: 978-1-63680-014-1

Disclaimer:

Dear Reader,

When I decided to write *The Lifestyle Investor* in 2020, I had no idea the global impact it would have. My original intention was simply to write a book for my daughter, passing on my passion for lifestyle investing with timeless principles and a proven formula for financial freedom.

In the three years since its release, I've been astounded by the reception this book has received. We hit #1 on the *Wall Street Journal's* bestseller list and *USA Today* list and *The Lifestyle Investor* is now in the top 1 percent of all books ever sold.

Yet the investing landscape evolves faster than the publishing cycle, allowing me to share all the new deals, insights, and wisdom I'm gaining on this journey. That's why I've prepared a trove of bonus content you can access here: *LifestyleInvestor.com/Gift*

Between this updated expanded edition and website bonuses, you'll find:

- Brand new deals I've completed using my 10 Commandments of Lifestyle Investing, with details on the opportunities I pursued and lessons learned.
- New resources, video excerpts, and wisdom from my Lifestyle Investor Mastermind education calls, summarizing some of our most valuable discussions on mindset, deal analysis, lifestyle design, and more.
- Cutting-edge strategies on due diligence, estate planning, asset allocation, and wealth management.
- Bonus chapters with my very latest insights on investing and tax strategy in our current economic environment (written after I submitted this updated manuscript to my publisher).

- A companion workbook with exercises and tools you can use while reading *The Lifestyle Investor* to capture your insights and bring them to life.
- Our Marriage & Family Planning Day tool, a go-to resource for Lifestyle Investor Mastermind members.

The principles in *The Lifestyle Investor* remain as relevant as ever. My team and I are also committed to sharing ongoing education that keeps you on the cutting edge. Our aim remains the same—to provide you with a roadmap to achieve financial freedom and live life on your terms. I hope these updates give you new insights and tools to accelerate your investing journey.

Thank you for your support. I wish you success in your pursuit of the Lifestyle Investor vision.

Gratefully,
Justin Donald

LIFESTYLE INVESTOR LEGAL DISCLAIMER

Neither this book nor any content presented by our organization is intended to provide personal tax or financial advice. This information is intended to be used and must be used for information purposes only. We are not investment or tax advisors, and this should not be considered advice. It is very important to do your own analysis before making any investment or employing any tax strategy. You should consider your own personal circumstances and speak with professional advisors before making any investment. The information contained in this book is based on our own research, opinions, as well as representations made by company management. We believe the information presented in this report to be true and accurate at the time of publication but do not guarantee the accuracy of every statement nor guarantee that the information will not change in the future. It is important that you independently research any information that you wish to rely upon, whether for the purpose of making an investment or tax decision or otherwise. No content in this book, on the website *(LifestyleInvestor.com)* or related sites, nor any content in our emails or related content, constitutes, nor should be understood as constituting, a recommendation to enter into any securities transactions or to engage in any of the investment strategies presented here, nor an offer of securities. Lifestyle Investor employees, officers, and directors may participate in any investment described in this content when legally permissible and do so on the same investment terms as subscribers. Lifestyle Investor employees, officers, or directors receive NO financial compensation from companies who appear in this book.

DEDICATION

This book is dedicated to the two most important women
in my life.

Jennifer, my beautiful wife—your love, support,
and steadfast belief in me encourages me
to pursue my potential.

Savannah, my sweet princess—you inspire me to learn,
grow, and share the wisdom I have gained so one day,
you can learn these lessons too.

I love you both more than words can ever describe.

Money is only a tool.

It will take you wherever you wish,
but it will not replace you as the driver.

—Ayn Rand

TABLE OF CONTENTS

FOREWORD
BY RYAN LEVESQUE

On March 23, 2019, I had a conversation that changed my life forever.

That conversation was with a guy by the name of Justin Donald. Everything changed when he whispered *four words* to me over lunch that I will remember for the rest of my life. These *four simple words* sent me on a journey that changed my life in ways I couldn't imagine—at a timescale faster than I ever dreamed possible.

And if you pay close attention to what you read in this book, the same could be true for *you*. Let me explain.

First, if you're like most people reading this right now, you probably have a dream to achieve financial freedom by generating enough passive, monthly investment income to cover your lifestyle expenses (and then some). In other words, to be in a position where you *no longer need to work*. Or right now you might be working a job and making decent money. Or you might own a *business* that makes decent money, but it's one that requires your time. Perhaps *a lot* of your time.

That second scenario is the exact position I was in when I first met Justin Donald. The day was Saturday, March 23, 2019. I was attending a retreat in Austin, Texas, as part of a group I had recently joined called *Front Row Dads*. A fantastic group devoted to being a better father, husband, and family man. It was at that retreat where I first met Justin.

After meeting for the first time earlier that day, Justin and I decided to have lunch together, the two of us. Talking about fatherhood and family, the conversation eventually led to the inevitable question, "So, what do *you* do for a living?"

Justin motioned me to come closer . . . "I'm a Lifestyle Investor," he whispered.

I looked around to make sure nobody was eavesdropping on what suddenly felt like a clandestine conversation. "*Lifestyle* Investor? What does that mean, exactly?" I asked.

He told me his story, and how he had reached complete financial freedom in his thirties. And how he did it *without* receiving a massive exit or inheritance but instead by taking an unconventional approach to *cash flow focused investing*.

"So, wait. You're telling me you generate 100 percent of your income through passive investments?" I asked skeptically. "Okay. So how would someone like me, in my position, get started to do the same thing?"

"Well, I'm happy to share, if you're interested," he replied. "How much time do you have?"

Now, before I go any further, I need to backtrack a moment. You see, I met Justin when I was in my mid-thirties, and I had just spent the better part of the last decade building a successful multi-million-dollar business. As a kid, I grew up working class and was the first in my family to go to college. After graduating, I went to work at a job making $42,000 per year, and a few years later, I was making six figures working for myself.

Eventually building a $10M+ per year business together with my wife that we started from a 500-square foot apartment with $5,000 we had squirreled away in savings. And even though I had traded working for *someone else* to working for *myself*, my wife and I were still working. And we were still working *a lot*.

Sure, we had more control, more freedom, and more *income*. Sure, we had good financial habits, lived below our means, and worked hard to continue saving for our future . . . But at the end of the day, we were still *working to make money*.

Money certainly wasn't working for us.

And with two young boys who were growing up faster than we could believe possible, the idea of being able to cover 100 percent of our family's living expenses entirely through *passive* monthly investment income—so we could take time off, spend more time together as a family, travel the world, and create memories together that didn't involve work—was *immensely* appealing.

But it also felt like a *pipe dream*. Not something possible for people like us, in our situation. At least not right then. Maybe in a few years, but not with everything else going on.

As Justin continued to go deeper and deeper into his story and share the details of *how* he did it, I began crunching numbers in my head, and it felt strangely *doable*. This wasn't about building a well-diversified portfolio using low-cost index funds across multiple asset classes, waiting for decades of compound interest to kick in. But it also wasn't about scrambling to put in all your chips on the latest IPO or hottest tech stock, either. In fact, it had almost nothing to do with investing in the stock market or *any* of the public capital markets, for that matter.

Now, as someone who had worked for the investment bank Goldman Sachs® in my early twenties, Justin's approach was, in a word, *unconventional*. But at the same time, it made *complete sense*.

When our lunch that day drew to a close, Justin posed a question that hit me like a sucker punch in the gut. He said, "Your kids will grow up before you know it. Why wait, when you could have the lifestyle you want right now and enjoy the greatest years of your life today?"

He was right.

I left that conversation with a renewed focus, a renewed sense of purpose, and a renewed sense of *urgency* to take immediate action. I decided to do whatever I needed to do to learn everything I could from Justin Donald and take massive action based on what I learned.

Now, a few months before that fateful lunch, my wife and I had sat down to set our five-year financial goals together as we had done, practically every year together since we had been married. We'd set an *aggressive* "stretch" financial goal to generate enough *passive* income (outside our business) to cover all of our family expenses *within the next five years*. In other words, it was our BIG "someday maybe" goal. Something I'm not sure either of us believed was even possible.

Fast forward to September 2019. Less than six months after deciding to learn everything I could from Justin and take massive action toward our target, we *had hit 53 percent of our five-year monthly passive income goal!*

I'll say it again: With Justin's help, we hit more than *half* of our *five-year stretch* financial goal in less than six months.

I'm talking tens of thousands of dollars per month, in *real cash flow* generated from 100 percent passive investment income. (And by the way, as crazy as this feels to be writing this, I'm expecting we'll exceed 100 percent of our five-year monthly passive income goal within the next twelve to fourteen months, if not sooner.) And we did it simply by following Justin's *10 Commandments of Cash Flow Investing*.

By investing in many of the *exact* deals Justin reveals *right here in this book*. And by taking copious notes and paying incredibly close attention to everything Justin shares.

When Justin writes, "It's not as hard as you think it might be, and it doesn't take as much money as you might think," he is right. But it *does* require the right focus. The right strategy. And most importantly, it requires the right *teacher*.

If there's one thing I've learned in my career in business and life—one thing I can describe as "the secret to success"—it all comes down to three simple steps. When there's an area of your life or business in which you want to improve:

Step 1: Seek out a mentor. Someone who has *done what you want to do*.

Step 2: Invest what it takes to *learn everything you can* from that mentor.

Step 3: Strive to *become that mentor's number one student*.

That's it. It's really as simple as that.

For me, in this particular area of my life, Justin Donald is my mentor. What I've learned from Justin has changed my family's life forever. And for that, I am forever grateful. So, I'll end by saying this, as clearly as I can: Read this book. Study everything Justin Donald shares. And most importantly, put what you read into action.

And the next time *you* go to lunch and someone asks *you* the question, "So, what do *you* do for a living?" maybe you'll be able to reply with those same four life-changing words: "I'm a Lifestyle Investor."

—Ryan Levesque
Three-time *Inc. 5000* CEO, #1 National Bestselling
Author of the books *Ask* and *Choose*
Featured in the *Wall Street Journal, Harvard Business Review, Entrepreneur,* and *NBC News*

FOREWORD
BY MIKE KOENIGS

What if you could wake up whenever you wanted, do whatever you wanted, and know that all your bills were covered? You could travel wherever and whenever you wanted and know you could have an amazing lifestyle? You could send your kids to the finest schools, wear great clothes, drive your favorite car, and live in the home and neighborhood you always wanted without fear of running out of cash? And what if you could do it all without having a regular *job*?

To most of us, that sounds impossible. But you're about to meet a master of cash flow investing for passive income and financial freedom, Justin Donald.

Justin walks his talk, and as soon as you read the chapter for Commandment 1, "Lifestyle First," you'll get a strong sense of what's possible, no matter what kind of investing climate you're in. Most importantly, you'll soon learn how to invest—*without requiring that you have money to invest.*

I met Justin on the island of Fiji a few years ago and was immediately intrigued by him. My first impression was that he seemed like a nice accountant or CPA-type. After getting to know him, I realized he was exceptionally smart and creative, lived a lifestyle I only dreamed about, and built it from practically nothing in record time. All that was packaged in a values-driven, disciplined, no-ego, likable person.

Before meeting Justin, I was a dumb investor, but I didn't think I was. I had investments in some stocks, mutual funds, and a whole bunch of startups going back almost 20 years. Unfortunately, nearly all were equity investments, and not one that I can think of had liquidated. In other words, I had been providing a whole bunch of people interest-free loans with no guarantee of future performance or profit. Dumb. Here I was, a successful serial entrepreneur with plenty of assets earned over 30+ years but with very little knowledge of what to do with them.

After one simple conversation with Justin that lasted about twenty minutes, he'd introduced me to some of the concepts that are now in this book for rethinking the way I would approach investing for the rest of my life. That included making sure I was generating monthly or quarterly cash flow, gaining equity, negotiating bonuses, negotiating what he calls sidecar agreements that produce even better returns because of enhanced terms, realizing the return of **principal** in a relatively short period, and fascinating ways to use existing investments or insurance policies to fund these new investments.

Along with that, he'd offered some interesting and fully legal ways to provide huge tax advantages. He also shared some of the most interesting ways to select hidden deals and opportunities most investors would never think about.

My only regret? I didn't meet Justin sooner. Suffice it to say, the way I think about investing and money changed in those few minutes.

In this book, Justin shares some unique strategies that enable him to make more money without having to invest or take more risks. He does this by stacking his systems and developing a unique mindset for finding unparalleled opportunities that would normally go completely unnoticed by typical investors. He'll show you how to leverage your resources and assets to build a unique portfolio that can pay you every month or every quarter to build and grow equity. You'll also understand what differentiates a great investor from an outstanding investor: mindset.

Justin built his net worth to tens of millions of dollars in just a few years using the exact strategies you'll learn in this book. And if you have any doubt whatsoever as to whether Justin, his methods, and his character are real, head over to his website and listen to, watch, and read a few of the testimonials from people who experienced actual results with his system. You'll quickly understand and see Justin as an amazing mentor and advisor to lots of people who didn't want to take 10+ years and risk millions of dollars to achieve what he has accomplished in a fraction of the time.

In short order, Justin has a system for investing and making money that flat-out works, no matter what level you're at in your investing career. If you ever get a chance to work directly with Justin, do it. He's incredibly busy with opportunities and professionals who want to study with him, but he never does it at the expense of his lifestyle or family.

The fastest way to become an exceptional Lifestyle Investor is to learn from someone who's doing it right now. Justin Donald is your guy. Enjoy this book—and make sure you check out Justin's free videos and resources on his website.

—Mike Koenigs
Serial entrepreneur, San Diego, CA

PREFACE

My favorite things in life don't cost any money. It's really clear that the most precious resource we all have is time.

—Steve Jobs

Welcome to my world! In this book, I've captured the most important concepts of how I invest. My goal in doing so is simple. I want you to become a Lifestyle Investor as well. This book will start you on your journey to financial freedom and the life of your dreams.

When I started investing, I was tired of trading my time for money. Learning there was a way to earn money that didn't require my time piqued my interest. As I continued my research and learned more, I discovered a community of people who regularly live the life I desired. I thought,

Why on earth am I spending so many hours working the way I am to generate the income my family and I live on?

I wanted to create independence from how I spent my time and the income I earned. From the very beginning, it was important that I could spend as much time as I wanted with my family and friends and live the lifestyle we wanted on our terms.

More than anything, my **mindset** was to buy back my time. I wanted to spend time with people I love, doing things that are fun and meaningful to us—from enjoying life in the moment (rather than someday) to taking care of our health to living with an abundance mindset and giving generously to people and causes that are important to us. What I've accomplished with Lifestyle Investing allows all that and more.

This book is about paying it forward and giving back. It's about sharing my experiences and lessons learned so you can achieve the lifestyle you desire. In line with my desire to give back and give generously, all my profits from this book are being donated to charities that help others improve their lives on the most basic levels.

When an article in *Entrepreneur Magazine* called me the "Warren Buffett of Lifestyle Investing," it made me realize how much time, money, and energy I'd invested in coaches, experts, events, masterminds, and travel to learn the strategies and framework to build my toolbox. It was at that point that my focus shifted to helping others achieve financial freedom.

My first step was to offer private coaching for investors, executives, and entrepreneurs. One of the reasons I started my private coaching group was because whenever I shared my vision for financial freedom, I usually heard, "I want that too." Then, when the demand for my coaching services became greater than the number of people I was willing to coach in a given year, my next step was to create the Lifestyle Investor Mastermind. This group setting provides coaching and interaction for like-minded people, and it's where I have learned and compiled the strategies, philosophies, and concepts that resonate with my clients.

While I no longer have clients working one-on-one with me, the Lifestyle Investor Mastermind has become a thriving group that shows members exactly how to implement the Lifestyle Investor principles and commandments in their lives in the shortest time possible. My goal is to move our members to cash flow generation quickly and avoid potential setbacks.

In the mastermind, I also introduce clients to the same experts and vetted deals I have access to. I teach them how to negotiate favorable terms to start generating cash flow immediately with an overall strong return. I teach them how to do this with the least amount of risk. And I show them how to do it all so they can avoid spending the twenty years it's taken me to understand and implement these principles and commandments. Many of these same strategies and concepts are included in this book.

LIFESTYLE INVESTING FOR YOU

This book is my next step to help you find your path to financial freedom through cash flow investing. It is the result of my previous study and coaching. You can do exactly what I've done if you follow the guidelines here. I call this book *The Lifestyle Investor: The 10 Commandments of Cash Flow Investing for Passive Income and Financial Freedom* because that title resonates with everyone I know. Everyone wants time compression. Everyone wants financial freedom.

The fastest way to get your time back is by investing in smart coaches and advisors who can compress twenty years of knowledge and experience into three, six, or twelve months. Reading this book is an important step on your journey.

If you're coachable and willing to open your mind to an expanded future for yourself and your family, you're in the right place, at the right time, with the right guide.

HOW TO USE THIS BOOK

Part One of this book contains some background information on who I am and why you want to consider Lifestyle Investing. I discuss the core principles you need as a **Lifestyle Investor,** along with unpacking the most common financial myths to help you reframe your mindset. Finally, you'll discover Murphy's Laws for the Lifestyle Investor. You don't want to ignore these laws.

In Part Two, you'll learn the **10 Commandments** of the Lifestyle Investor. With every Commandment, I include examples of real deals I've worked through. First, I'll explain the deal to you so you can see the opportunity and why I pursued the deal. You'll learn some of the background and why I felt the deal was worth investing in. To help you better grasp the cash flow investing concepts, at the end of each commandment, I discuss the mindset, structure, filter, and negotiations used. Finally, I'll sum up each commandment so you can take the principle of this chapter and apply it to your cash flow investing.

Part Three tells you how to get started on your journey—what your next steps are and why. It sets up to begin with my final thoughts.

Throughout the book, you'll find investing and financial terms. As each term is introduced for the first time, it is set in **bold**. Even though I give a brief description within the text for most of these terms, you'll find a more in-depth definition in the Glossary at the end of the book.

This book contains strategies culled from my extensive investment in coaching, education, and research. Much of the reputable source information is included in the Resources section. I hope you'll take time to study these valuable tools as well.

My suggestion is that you move back and forth as you read and digest the concepts and information in this book. They represent a lifetime of learning for me, and I wouldn't expect you to grasp them all by just reading from cover to cover.

Are you ready to begin your journey to financial freedom?

ACKNOWLEDGMENTS

Writing this book has been one of the most inspirational and creative things I have ever done. It is the culmination of the last twenty years of my entrepreneurial and investment career. There have been many lessons along the way and many people who have contributed to the content of this book. I am so thankful to everyone who played a role. It wouldn't have been possible without the help and influence of such an incredible team of high-caliber people.

Over the years, several friends have strongly encouraged me to write a book. Their consistent reminders warmed me to the idea. *John Kane, Ryan Levesque, John Ruhlin, Jon Vroman, Tim Nikolaev, and Hal Elrod,* thank you for your friendship, inspiration, and support through this writing journey. I value our friendship tremendously, and thank you for your persistence, encouragement, and belief.

Dad and *Mom:* Thank you for raising me in an extremely loving and grace-filled home and giving me the freedom and autonomy I desired to grow into the person that I am today. You always supported me in everything I ever did, and I thank you for that. You gave me choices and allowed me to learn from my mistakes. You gave me the space to grow wings and learn how to fly on my own. I owe so much of my success to each of you, and I thank you both for always believing in me.

Mike Koenigs and *Marissa Brassfield:* Thank you for your inspiration and creative ideas. You gave me vision and an exciting atmosphere and environment to create this great content and capture my story. You both saw something special and helped elicit that from me in a way no one ever has before. Not to mention, I have had some of the biggest laughs of my life spending time with you both. I am so pleased not only to have worked with each of you on this project but also for the tremendous friendship that we forged during the past year with all the time we spent together.

Amber Vilhauer: Thank you for your excitement and confidence in everything I have done, with regard to this book and also all the additional projects that are extensions of this book. You have been incredibly committed to delivering the highest level of service and support, and you have been a great collaborator and partner in many ways. Your work ethic is second to none, and you really shine in differentiating yourself from everyone else in your industry. I have loved every minute of working with you!

Kary Oberbrunner and his amazing team, including Kirsten Samuel, David Samuel, and Sarah Grandstaff: Thank you for all of your thoughtful insight, collaboration, and attention to detail. You are such an incredible team full of wisdom and creativity, and I feel blessed to have been able to work with each one of you. I have thoroughly enjoyed spending time with all of you, and I appreciate the influence you have each had on this book.

ACKNOWLEDGMENTS

Savannah: You inspire me, and so much of what I share in this book is for you to learn when the time comes. I marvel at how much of a learner you already are and how curious you are about everything. This book wouldn't be possible without you because you were the reason why I knew I had to put all my thoughts together in one place. I love you so much, and I can't wait for the time you grow up when you decide you would like to invest with me!

Jennifer: You have always supported me in everything I have ever done and have been a great source of encouragement every step of the way. You are truly my biggest fan, and that means the world to me. You have been such a strong figure in my corner through all the challenges and victories of my entrepreneurial life. Your discernment is truly a one-of-a-kind gift. I love you so much and feel incredibly grateful to be able to do life with you every single day.

PART ONE

THE CHALLENGE

WHO AM I, AND WHY SHOULD YOU LISTEN TO ME?

You have to learn the rules of the game, and then you have to play better than anyone else.

—Albert Einstein

I value and spend time learning from people who are world-class at their craft of investing. I read books and listen to podcasts by smart investors and people who have different philosophies that have worked for them. And as a Lifestyle Investor, I am intentional about my mentors, striving to be their #1 student.

Education is one of my biggest keys to success. I've invested nearly $1,000,000 in my education, attending boot camps and seminars and learning from coaches, my advisory team, and industry experts. To master the gamut of investments, I've studied real estate types, **private equity**, **public equity**, private credit (especially senior secured), distressed assets, operating companies, franchises, e-commerce, technology, syndications, funds, royalties, **collectibles**, **cryptocurrencies**, and more.

In short, I want to be skilled and knowledgeable across the board and stress-test my criteria to filter and select investment deals.

When I first started investing, I didn't know my criteria. I looked at deals subjectively—*this makes sense*, or *this feels right*. But over several years of educating myself and analyzing the types of investments I chose, obvious criteria emerged that simplified how I subconsciously, yet consistently, made decisions.

BEDROCK VALUES

I grew up in a working-class environment. My parents are both wonderful Christian people. In the family, they modeled values such as honesty and integrity. My upbringing established a bedrock of values on which I stand.

My mom worked full-time for more than twenty years as a secretary at the church we attended, earning about $27,000 to $30,000. A conversationalist, she consistently put people first. She taught me how to maintain strong connections, address conflict head-on, and put good relationships together.

My dad worked in sales for most of my youth, selling cars and appliances. I learned valuable lessons about work from him. He worked long hours and was often gone from 7 a.m. until as late as 9 p.m., six days a week, with an occasional shorter day. He wanted something better for me and didn't want me to work as hard. His example paved the way for my own success. His work ethic became foundational to mine.

My dad also taught me about goal setting. I saw how hard he worked to achieve his goals. He designed his monthly goals to hit his quotas and earn his bonuses. He shared those goals with me and how they broke down into strategic actions to achieve them. He taught me the essentials of goal setting and achieving my goals.

The values of other family members impacted me. My younger brother joined the army when he was eighteen years old and proudly served our country for seven years on several overseas tours of duty. I've learned a lot from him over the years about mindset, discipline, and courage.

WORK ETHIC

In seventh grade, I remember asking my parents for money. Their reply was, "You need a job. We're not going to be your source of income." So I started selling newspaper subscriptions door-to-door. I had a similar bonus structure to my dad's—I received a bonus if I achieved a certain sales number. I broke down what it would take per day to get there, and then I worked hard to achieve my goal.

Early on, I experienced a ton of rejection. Salespeople get a whole lot of "nos" for each "yes." Gradually, I built up an immunity to the word "no" to the point I didn't take it personally. Soon I became the top salesperson and retained that status through the end of high school. Depending on the time of year, I worked for four or five hours an evening, three or four days a week, earning between $250 and $500 per week. I loved having enough spending money to enjoy travel, entertainment, and experiences with my friends.

Because they were intrigued with how much money I earned, I recruited several friends to work with me. I soon had a crew who sold subscriptions for me, which gave me a taste for leadership and its margins. It was tough at first, and I learned not everyone was "a natural" at sales. Over time, however, I learned how to hire hard-working, talented people and develop a team that sold under me.

The sales pitch I'd developed was so successful that my boss asked me to script it out for the others to use as well. That was my first sales script, and I used it to train all of the new members on my crew. We laminated clipboards with some of the elements I'd incorporated into my script, including sales goals to earn scholarship opportunities. Once my team started using my language and scripts, I had much more competition because everyone's sales increased. Still, most days I still found a way to outsell them. (You can see a sample sales script at *LifestyleInvestor.com/Gift*.)

COMPETITIVE DRIVE

I've always been competitive in my pastime activities as well as my work. The thought of accomplishing something I haven't done before has been the most motivating factor, well beyond money or extrinsic rewards. My curiosity keeps me open to learning. I love the feeling of setting a goal, achieving it, and knowing I'm accomplishing my best.

Curiosity is imperative and keeps you open to learning.

My favorite games involve more strategy than luck. From card games like hearts, spades, euchre, gin, rummy, blackjack, poker, and racehorse canasta to board games such as Clue®, Risk®, and Stratego® to video games such as Mazecraze® on Atari®, Zelda™, and Mario Bros.™, my competitive drive gives me an advantage.

Competitive sports of all kinds have impacted my desire to succeed and give my best effort as well. By age six or seven, I played nearly every youth sport available in an organized league, primarily baseball and soccer, though I also played a decent amount of volleyball and basketball. Not being good at something wasn't an option. By being persistent, studying, and working to understand the aspects of a sport in which I didn't excel and playing and practicing until I did, I found success.

I loved the camaraderie of a team, but I hated to lose. One particularly painful memory from my youth is that I cried whenever I struck out in baseball. I'd return to the dugout with tears in my eyes. At first, I wasn't sure why I cried, but eventually, I realized that I felt like I had let the team down, which I never wanted to do.

FAMILY TIME

I'm a husband and a father. When my wife and I started a family, I didn't want to trade time for money. I knew I wanted to show up at every game, recital, and important activity in my daughter's life. When my daughter was young, I chose to work in a way that was not at the expense of relationships. I valued building a life that would give me and my family lifestyle freedom, and that's what I created.

Work hard when it's time to work, but not at the expense of relationships.

In the span of twenty-one months, right before my fortieth birthday, I had investments that drove enough **passive income** for both my wife and me to leave our jobs. I negotiated deals with over a hundred companies, multiplied my net worth to over eight figures, and established a family-centric lifestyle in less than two years. And then, two years later, I doubled my net worth again.

LIFESTYLE INVESTING WORKS!

I've now mastered low-risk cash flow investment principles, and I share my experience and strategies with entrepreneurs and executives around the world. In these pages, I share principles that center on creating passive income and significant wealth while being liberated from a day-to-day job.

Lifestyle Investing works. I've done it, many of my friends and clients have done it, and I know the roadmap for *you* to do it too. My system for investing and making money flat-out works, no matter what level you're at in your investing career. Check out the resources at *LifestyleInvesting.com/Gift*.

FIND YOUR PATH TO FINANCIAL INDEPENDENCE

My dad encouraged us to fail . . . It changed my mindset at an early age that failure is not the outcome, failure is not trying. Don't be afraid to fail.

—Sara Blakely

Over the years, I've studied people's mindsets—what makes them tick and what they desire in life. Additionally, I've gotten to a place where I understand what *I* want in life. That's important because what other people want isn't necessarily right for me. If I am clear with the outcomes I desire and am firm with my non-negotiables, managing my finances becomes more of a game. I can have the freedom to play. Once you reach that stage, you can play too.

To become a Lifestyle Investor and develop a successful **cash flow investing** lifestyle, you decide what that lifestyle looks like for you. What do you want in life? Why do you want it? How you answer these questions prepares you to work through the next three stages toward financial independence.

FINANCIAL INDEPENDENCE

There are different stages of financial independence. Each one is important and helps build momentum in creating the life you truly desire:

> Stage 1: Cover your bare minimum expenses to live.
> Stage 2: Maintain your current lifestyle.
> Stage 3: Live the life you've dreamed about.

How you move through these stages is up to you. This book is about how to do it as a *Lifestyle Investor*.

Stages 1 and 2 are the basics for an everyday, working person's life. To move into stage 3, however, you must face and evaluate your mindset. This mindset places limitations on how you look at investments, the value you give money, and how you allow money to affect your life. In stage 3, you're living life on *your terms* based on monthly cash flow, not annual cash flow. Financial independence lets you stop doing things you don't want to do and gives you the freedom to do what you want.

You can design your life to be what you want and live it on your terms. While money won't solve all your problems, it will solve your financial ones.

When you move into the stage of living life on your terms, you experience a total paradigm shift. You move from a scarcity mindset to abundance. Instead of grasping and scrimping with money, you realize it is a tool to accomplish your goals. In this stage, you understand that having a scarcity mindset is probably not the best and that living from an abundance mindset makes more sense.

> If you change the way you look at things, the things you look at change.
>
> –Wayne Dyer

CASH FLOW INVESTMENT

Many people make investments in businesses, effectively financing a zero-interest loan for an unknown timeframe for someone else. In doing so, they buy equity in exchange for believing that someday they're going to get their money back. That approach to investing is more of a gamble. It's not investing unless they have superior knowledge to understand and negotiate a wise deal. Otherwise, they're rolling dice and hoping to get the right number.

There may be a place for that investing approach for you. But I don't think it makes sense to invest in a way that doesn't achieve financial freedom first, or the proposed return is so low, or you won't see a return for ten to twenty years. The more significant part of my portfolio is geared toward generating cash flow. Not only do I expect a return of the principal of my investment, but I want cash coming in from it and as quickly as possible.

> Most people have the wrong mindset about money. Either they are conflicted about money and realize it, or they are conflicted but unaware.

Cash flow investing means some sort of cash comes in regularly—whether monthly, quarterly, or some other time frame. The goal is to have it flow in a way that you can live on it. For passive income, it's the idea that this money isn't based on work but on assets and other money working that don't require your time or (in many cases) anyone else's time either.

My goal is cash flow within the first month. For some investments, that goal isn't realistic. The first distribution might not be for a quarter or longer. But for new investors, it's optimal to invest in a way that provides some amount of cash flow immediately.

My end goal for each of my investments depends on the specifics of the deal and how **collateralized** the investment is—meaning how secure and safe the principal investment is. It also depends on how much I'm earning on that principal during the investment. If my return is high, I might be okay with having my principal remain in the investment longer because I'm earning a good return on that money. Most of the time, however, I like to get my principal back as quickly as possible because often my equity position would remain the same, even after my initial principal has been repaid. I want that principal back to reinvest in other deals.

For me, the ideal scenario is that I get the principal back in one to two years. Certain real estate investments might not return the principal as quickly, but they still could be inside a three-year window. That timeframe is acceptable to me but rarely longer. Real estate and debt investments are two of my favorites. I'll touch on them briefly here and in much greater detail later.

REAL ESTATE INVESTMENT

Location and structure are important when investing in real estate. Focusing on a good location can reduce risk. For example, you don't want to be an investor in a town with only one major employer. If that employer would go out of business, the whole town would suffer. If the whole town suffered, real estate would become less valuable, harder to keep occupied, and harder to sell.

I prefer investing in large cities with large populations and strong economic growth. I like to see a couple of key indicators that typically lead to having a strong occupancy, such as a market with a wide array of large employers, strong healthcare providers, and several good educational programs and universities.

The way you **structure** your real estate investments is also important. Look for deals that give you a lot of options for returns. For example, you can invest in certain real estate **asset classes,** which are groups of investments that behave similarly and are subject to the same market forces, to provide you with an opportunity to earn long-term equity while also getting a preferred return that generates cash flow. A **preferred return** is a profit distribution that is paid out to investors prior to the **general partners**, who run the day-to-day operations, being able to take any profits. So, you would have cash flow coming immediately.

Also, you want to invest in assets where principal comes back quickly, *and* you maintain your same equity position. This quick return of principal with immediate cash flow allows you to make other investments and create more equity positions and additional cash flow sources.

DEBT INVESTMENT

I'm a big fan of debt investments backed by collateral that pay a high interest rate with monthly cash flow. Often in this sort of investment, you can negotiate a kicker. A **kicker** is an additional perk that you negotiate into the deal, and often you can get it for free. Here are some examples of kickers with additional perks:

- Equity: a percentage of ownership in an asset
- Warrant: an option to buy equity in the future at a predetermined price
- Revenue share: a percentage of the total revenue that is paid out
- Profits interest: equity right based on the future value of a company

There are many different ways to create a kicker. I like to be flexible, stay creative with the process, and come up with ideas that best suit my family and me. These kickers may seem like small perks in the beginning, but there is a compounding effect that happens when you continue adding multiple kickers over time. If you choose to go after kickers, what ends up happening as an investor is you can get all your money out of each investment and still retain the kickers to participate in the long-term growth of the company or investment. And best of all, these kickers don't cost you anything extra to begin with.

The point of this chapter is that you can find your path to financial freedom by examining your mindset and choosing your investments wisely.

CORE PRINCIPLES AND CRITERIA FOR LIFESTYLE INVESTING

My #1 guiding principle for a successful life: Do the right thing; not the easy thing. In every moment of choice, choose to do the right thing over the easy thing, and your becoming successful is inevitable.

—Hal Elrod

F our core principles guide every investment I make. In Part 2 of this book, I explain each of my *10 Commandments* based on these principles and walk you through how they apply to each specific commandment. Right here, I want to introduce you briefly to each principle and each commandment.

PRINCIPLE 1: MINDSET

The best investment you'll ever make is in your **mindset** and personal growth. Nobody can ever take away your knowledge and education. From Warren Buffett to Benjamin Graham, Ray Dalio, John Templeton, George Soros, and John Bogle, each mastered their minds and fears to become incredible people to model. The same can be true for you.

I have invested a tremendous amount in my continued education, and I read over a hundred books a year because the most important investment in my portfolio is my ongoing learning and personal growth. My mindset on any given investment guides my choices.

PRINCIPLE 2: STRUCTURE

Do you want to know how to double your **return on investment (ROI)** with zero risk? Learn how to structure a better deal. **Structure** is the relationship between the specific investment terms in an agreement.

I'm highly attuned to **deal structures**. Almost every deal I invest in must produce predictable, recurring cash flow. Ideally, it produces cash flow *and* equity with a quick return of principal. What you'll discover in the chapters ahead is what I call my **Strategy Stack**—a way of combining multiple, non-obvious approaches to earn an even greater return with low risk.

PRINCIPLE 3: FILTER

What's the fastest way to determine a great deal or discern something you should run away from as fast as you can? Filters! **Filters** are criteria used to sort through and narrow down investment opportunities. Using filters to screen investments saves significant time and creates greater efficiency.

I've developed sophisticated filters and decision trees to determine whether an opportunity meets my criteria and should be acted upon. These filters often help me spot **invisible deals** (more on that later) and avoid overwhelm. The better my filters are, the more time I can spend evaluating high-quality investments.

PRINCIPLE 4: NEGOTIATION

Negotiation is a core part of my investment strategy. All opportunities are negotiable. Negotiating is not necessarily confrontational or adversarial. So never assume a term sheet is the final word.

I've created at least $7 million in additional net worth by negotiating unique and preferred terms. I'm regularly pulled in by investors and companies because I routinely stack multiple strategies to get increased returns through additional stock, warrants, advisory shares, and various other deal terms, often getting reduced fees and lower minimum investments as well. My goal for negotiating is to find terms that are a win-win for both sides. Because of how I negotiate, many companies and investment groups I have worked with in the past come to me first on future investment needs.

THE 10 COMMANDMENTS

For years, friends asked me to write a book to share my principles, commandments, strategies, and secrets to investing. At first, I didn't exactly know what those were, but looking back at all the deals I have done, I discovered a pattern and, with it, the criteria I have used for investing. In upcoming chapters, I will share one or more investment examples with each commandment to demonstrate how you can also apply each of these to your investments.

Before I get into the 10 Commandments, I want to mention the best deal I've ever done. It's produced the largest return of any investment I've ever made, it's something that anyone can do but most people don't know about or leverage, and it can single-handedly change the trajectory of your life.

Would you like to know what it is?

Head to *LifestyleInvestor.com/Gift* and download my Tax Strategy Playbook.

THE 10 COMMANDMENTS OF THE LIFESTYLE INVESTOR

COMMANDMENT 1: LIFESTYLE FIRST

Your investments are truly passive income rather than a factor of time spent in the business. *Passive income* means you're earning income while you're sleeping or offline.

COMMANDMENT 2: REDUCE THE RISK

Examine deal structures to minimize risk and maximize returns.

COMMANDMENT 3: FIND INVISIBLE DEALS

Watch emerging markets and unconventional investment opportunities, including new and disruptive technologies or companies in a reinvention phase.

COMMANDMENT 4: GET THE PRINCIPAL BACK QUICKLY

Can you get a return of your principal investment in one to two years? The quicker you get your principal back to invest again, the more your investments compound.

COMMANDMENT 5: CREATE CASH FLOW IMMEDIATELY

Can you negotiate cash flow monthly or quarterly? The more cash flow you have, the more it can support your lifestyle and eventually be used for additional investments.

COMMANDMENT 6: FIND AN INCOME AMPLIFIER

Negotiate preferred terms or sidecar agreements to amplify profit potential.

COMMANDMENT 7: PLUS THE DEAL

Investigate the perks and terms to optimize the deal for lower risk, greater returns, and long-term value.

COMMANDMENT 8: CUT OUT THE FAT

Eliminate any unnecessary fees, whether they're through middlemen, banks, or other financial institutions.

COMMANDMENT 9: USE LEVERAGE TO YOUR ADVANTAGE

Non-recourse loans are one strategy to protect investors if an investment underperforms. Sometimes, the benefits of working with a financial institution outweigh their fees.

COMMANDMENT 10: EVERY DOLLAR OF INVESTMENT GETS A RETURN

If you hire professionals to support you (i.e., your legal, tax, and financial team), ask them questions to educate yourself as you work with them. Make sure you learn what they are doing and why they think that is best. The goal is to walk away more educated than when you showed up to hire them.

Download a free copy of this resource at
LifestyleInvesting.com / Gift.

One of the biggest keys to success in investing is to have criteria—like my 10 Commandments—that guide your investment decisions. Your criteria allow you to invest based on a thoroughly thought-out process and not on emotion. If you have well-thought-out criteria, and your potential investments can satisfy each of those particular criteria, then you have a good indicator that you have a strong potential investment.

What you will notice as you continue reading is that most of the investment examples I use in this book apply to most, if not all, of the 10 Commandments and not just the particular commandment they are listed under. I don't always point it out, so be sure to look at each example to see how that particular investment fits each of the 10 Commandments.

WHY LIFESTYLE INVESTING IS THE ANSWER

The goal isn't more money. The goal is living life on your terms.

—Will Rogers

Perhaps you've reached that point in your life where you recognize or can acknowledge that being wealthy is inextricably linked to mindset, behavior, discipline, and point of view, not necessarily what's in your pocket or bank account. By learning my fundamental principles and the 10 Commandments of a Lifestyle Investor, you can move to the next level.

FREEDOM *FROM* AND *TO*

Most likely, you're reading this book because you want freedom *from* and freedom *to*— freedom *from* work and trading time for money and freedom *to* live life intentionally on your terms. You want to have more choices and the ability to do as you desire, when and how you want to do it, without restriction.

You want the ability to take time off when and as long as you want. You want the ability to send your kids to the best schools, buy the best brands and products, take extended vacations anywhere in the world, and buy your partner and loved ones' experiences and gifts without asking, "How much?" Maybe more importantly, you don't ever want to experience financial fears or a sense of "not enough" again.

If you're an entrepreneur who started a business because you wanted to create the freedom to buy your time back and stop working for someone else, you may have discovered that you have unintentionally become a slave to your business. You may be chained to a business that's producing only enough for you to cover your expenses or live your current lifestyle. Yes, you are your own boss, but owning your business can put you in and keep you in a different rat race from other means of employment. Is it a better-quality rat race? Sure, but it's still a rat race and constantly leeches your time. Even worse, it's covertly stealing your time from you, sometimes without you even recognizing it.

> How to grow as an investor: Be a sponge. Learn everything you can and implement one more thing tomorrow than today.

Real-life issues and problems come with being an entrepreneur, just as they do with being an employee in someone else's business. Unfortunately, many entrepreneurs never make it to a lifestyle of financial freedom or won't make it for a long time. Here's the good news: There's a way to buy your time back and cover your expenses. And once your expenses are covered, you can show up much better for your business *and* your loved ones.

JUST GOING THROUGH THE MOTIONS

If you're an employee in someone else's business, you may be just going through the motions of work and life, tied to a job or career you don't love but feel chained to because of the paycheck. Here's the good news for you. There's a different way to live on your terms and in a way that brings you passion, energy, vibrancy, and vitality. You do not have to wake up to an alarm clock when it's still dark outside, only to fight traffic to get to work for someone else who makes all the money at a job you don't really like anyway. Then do it all over again.

Every day you go to work for someone else, you're making them and their business or organization much more money than what you're making. To make it even worse, you're expected to be so grateful for this opportunity they've provided. After you pay your taxes and bills, the leftover money is all you have to live *your* life. I know this because I have experienced it. Most of us have been or still are handcuffed to that approach for earning a living either by a mental framework or habit and routine. Employment and earnings are on their terms, not yours. It's a broken paradigm. The way out is easier than you think.

It doesn't cost as much to cover your expenses as you think.

If you have a job that you love, a healthy relationship with your boss, and a strong 401(k), congrats to you, at least for now. You're an anomaly inside of a rigged game. You're in the minority. Nevertheless, the game is rigged.

A LIFE OF ENDLESS DEMANDS

I used to live in that broken paradigm. I'd set the alarm and get up at a certain time because I had responsibilities. I generally ran a conference call first thing in the morning, often at 6:00 a.m. or 7:00 a.m. If my day didn't begin with a conference call, I had to check in with whoever ran the operations to make sure they were running smoothly. Fortunately, I did not always have to be physically in my office all day, every day. Often, I woke up early and went right to the gym before work because I felt like it was the only time I had to work out.

In that life, everything was rush, rush, rush. I had no time to think. I went from thing to thing, meeting to meeting, with little or no time to decompress in between. Though I attempted to schedule my days proactively, I spent most of my time reacting to and solving problems. *After all,* I thought, *that was my job, wasn't it?*

After work, I'd arrive home exhausted. It was hard to juggle business demands and also be home for dinner. Though I made dinner the priority because being with my family was important, I constantly felt like I had work on my mind. I struggled to be fully present in other activities. Instead, I felt the consistent pressure that I could do more, was not accomplishing enough, and was potentially missing out on creating more income. Taking any time off meant double the work the next day.

The demands of a large sales territory were endless—weekday and weekend travel, board meetings, conferences, quarterly meetings, weekly conference calls, team functions, and office visits, among other obligations. The demands never ceased, even during the slow times. Then there was the summer. My wife was off from teaching, and my daughter from school, but it was my most challenging season for work. When my family was most available, I was the busiest, often working ten or more hours a day, six days a week. The cycle was never-ending.

Though not ideal, many positive things did come from this time in my life. I am thankful for the opportunities, growth, knowledge, skills, and amazing people I met. Many of these people remain some of my closest friends. This stressful period prepared and shaped my thoughts and choices about life. It forced me to align my lifestyle with my values.

MY LIFE ON MY TERMS

Now, instead of waking up and going to the gym before heading straight to work, I take some time to think, journal, and read. My faith is really important to me, so I spend time in prayer and devotion because they are a good foundation for how I want to show up in life.

By the time my family wakes up, I'm ready to hang out with them. We have time each morning to play cards, talk, listen, dance to our favorite music, or read a book together. I head to the gym after my daughter goes to school. I have mental self-care, daily quality time with my family, and then physical self-care. These times are the most important parts of my day, and I accomplish them before I do any required daily work.

Whole-body health is important to me as well. I stay informed on new studies and concepts, like intermittent fasting and eating primarily whole foods with each meal. Typically, I get a deep tissue massage each week and chiropractic adjustments as needed. I play volleyball at least one morning a week and trail ride one morning a week. The other days, I lift light weights, followed by some form of cardio.

When my workday ends, which can happen as early as I choose, my wife and daughter and I have a family dinner. After dinner, I spend as much time with my daughter as I can. After we put her to bed, my wife and I spend time together. The greatest benefit of this routine is the exceptional relationship my wife and I enjoy today. Becoming a "student" of my wife allows me to focus on her, our marriage, and our family, which fulfills her love language needs. That's how we do it.

As for my weekly schedule, I like to start and end my week in an inspiring way. I keep my Mondays open for thought-provoking activities. Fridays are reserved for fun events such as travel, family outings, date days with my wife, and spending time with friends. Tuesdays, Wednesdays, and Thursdays are when I work on my projects. I also schedule lunch or coffee times at least one of those days to meet with someone I can learn from.

I like to meet with people who pique my curiosity, which is imperative for me. As I mentioned earlier, curiosity keeps me open to learning. My goal is to meet one or two new people each week. If I can do that, I feel like I have had a successful week. Living in Austin, Texas, I find plenty of opportunities to continue growing and learning from creative entrepreneurs, investors, tech pioneers, other gifted professionals, teams, and companies. I look for inspiration, new learning opportunities, and other investors who do what I do so we can learn from each other.

Freedom of time, not freedom of money.

These days, when I travel, I bring my family with me so we can incorporate some fun family adventures together.

It creates a much cleaner, healthier, better dynamic for everyone. Also, my wife and I do quarterly overnights and annual weeklong trips to new and favorite locations to make sure we have a good connection and fun experiences. We schedule our family trips throughout the year for extended periods. Sometimes we vacation with another family or friends, but it's all centered on focused quality time.

My wife and I also think it's important that we each take a trip by ourselves. She has some annual girls' trips, and I have some guys' trips. We enjoy taking these trips so we can maintain strong relationships with our closest friends and family.

As an entrepreneur, I schedule two uninterrupted hours each week for technology-free thinking to proactively create the life I desire for my business, family, and personal life. The bottom line is that I take my spiritual, mental, and physical health seriously. My daily practices provide the energy to show up better for my family, friends, business partners, and work associates. A compound effect happens too. Creating and following empowering daily habits provides more clarity, wisdom, and time to process.

I love what I do because I get to choose what to work on, including who I work with and when those projects happen. I get a sense of fulfillment and satisfaction from learning and then teaching others. My lifestyle allows me to live life on my terms. Of course, it comes with a component of doing some work, but it's work I choose to do and enjoy.

More important than anything, however, is how I prioritize my days. I try to be intentional with my family time instead of working first and then trying to juggle everything else. I used to do what I needed for work and then tried to fit in everything else, including family time, working out, and relaxing.

Plan family first and work second.

That didn't work for me, nor did it create the vibrant life I wanted. Family comes first now, followed by my physical health and self-care. Before, I worked like a machine. All that mentally and physically consuming work came at the expense of my health, my family, and my life and didn't allow me freedom. Not anymore.

YOUR LIFE ON YOUR TERMS

Some people don't recognize they're a hostage, but it's only a matter of time. A new job feels good until it's not new anymore, and the reality of being in chains sets in. It's good to be grateful for a job, but it's also good to be smart about choosing the better and the best opportunities for a life on your own terms.

Here's another way to look at it. You don't *have to* have a job that provides income to live your lifestyle, and you don't *have to* have a lifestyle that meets or exceeds the income you're earning. Those mindsets create a real mental handicap that can keep you a slave to the business or the amount of money you make. The more you learn about choosing how you want to work, how you want to spend your time, how much you want to earn, and what it costs to live how you want to live, the more clarity you'll have about your decisions. Don't be held hostage by your day job or your business.

My mission is to help you buy back your time so you can proceed with intentionality on how, where, and with whom you spend that time. I want you to live life on your terms as well.

I believe anyone can make this shift. It begins with a commitment to gaining your life and time back. In the beginning, it's more of a mental shift than anything else. But once you flip the switch mentally, your behavior changes. You start taking actions to pave a clear path for the life you want to create.

It's about becoming a Lifestyle Investor, not the investor's lifestyle.

I'm looking for people who are open and willing to consider living life differently, who think that the status quo doesn't have to apply to them, and who are open to making choices to live on their terms.

I want you to experience autonomy and the liberating feeling of living your dream life. I want you to find the passion to create your ideal lifestyle *now*, not when you're retired. Retirement, Social Security, investments, nest eggs, and your health—none are guaranteed.

You could spend significant time neglecting your family to gain financial freedom, but when you finally do, your family might no longer be at your side due to death, divorce, or other unforeseen circumstances. You could chase something you consider important at the time that becomes the reason your family is no longer there with you. Why wait, when you could have that dream lifestyle now and enjoy the most fulfilling years of your life today *and* through retirement?

The information in this book will help you make a transition like what I described in my life if you apply it. Chances are, it won't happen overnight. It may take a year, five years, or even ten years; but at some point, you'll be able to step off the proverbial treadmill and create your success—and do so on your terms. Why not become a professional financial athlete now while you are young and have years to enjoy a new lifestyle of success?

Yes, you'll face hurdles to overcome, so good training is essential to win financial freedom. In my case, it wasn't until my investment income replaced my **earned income** that I could see how to buy my time back to focus on what I enjoy most in life. The abundance of time I bought back then allowed me to redirect my energy and focus on creating more income, all the while enjoying my personal life.

Today I don't *have* to work—I *get* to work. I wake up without wondering how I'm going to make money. The activity I choose to focus on doesn't have to produce income because my passive income exceeds my lifestyle.

TAKE CHARGE OF YOUR FUTURE

A gentleman who listened to an interview I did recently called me and wanted me to coach him. He said, "I've had a tremendous amount of success in many areas of my life, and by most people's standards, I have achieved great wealth and status in the business world, but I don't have your lifestyle." By now, you might be able to guess what I told him!

Though the possibility of upgrading your lifestyle may feel out of reach, it is doable. You control your future based on the decisions you make and the actions you take. In this book, you can expect to hear a different way to invest and live. It's not as hard as you think it might be, and it doesn't take as much money as you might think.

It's not about accumulating millions of dollars in a nest egg approach. Instead, it's about investing into assets one at a time that produce the amount of passive income you need to cover your lifestyle, whether you invest in these assets directly yourself or you invest through a partnership as a limited partner (LP) with an experienced team that professionally manages and operates these assets.

If you break down how much it costs to live right now with your current lifestyle every month, the amount needed to cover those expenses is probably much less than what you think it costs. It's inspiring and eye-opening to understand what it really takes to cover your lifestyle expenses and get out of the rat race for good. Take charge!

DEBUNKING THE MOST COMMON MYTHS ABOUT INVESTING

Risk comes from not knowing what you're doing.

—Warren Buffett

What I *used to believe* about money and what *I know now* are two different things. Before we go any further, pay attention to this: don't follow the crowd. The majority of people are in debt, not building wealth. My goal in this book is to show you how to become a Lifestyle Investor, no matter your current financial status.

If you're the kind of person who is comfortable investing in something and waiting ten or more years for a return on your investment, I'm probably not your guy. I focus on getting results fast and making money as rapidly as possible. I've found super-creative ways to discover out-of-the-box deals, negotiate unusually favorable terms, and generate cash flow in months instead of years while creating long-term equity. It's all done while focusing on reducing risk at every juncture. This approach, which I call my "Strategy Stack," is how I multiply my net worth and the net worth of the Lifestyle Investor Mastermind.

What I do and coach others to do is radically different from the traditional financial advice you may have heard. It's time to address six of the common misconceptions people have about investing.

MYTH 1: YOU WILL BECOME WEALTHY BY BUILDING YOUR 401(K), FOLLOWING TRADITIONAL INVESTMENT ADVICE, OR INVESTING IN THE STOCK MARKET.

These approaches for wealth building and retirement are flawed and outdated. Almost everything you've been taught over the years is now garbage. Throw it out. Qualified plans don't work. Social Security is going to run out. Medicare isn't sustainable. What if something happened and the economy was down right when you wanted to retire? What if half of your retirement income was wiped out? You wouldn't have enough time to build it back, and you would have lost way too much of your nest egg to ever recover during your retirement years.

Now, think about this. Why is the government giving you tax breaks now? It's because they're going to make their income on your savings later on when you retire, and they take a big chunk of your money. Most people look at the nest egg that they're accumulating without realizing that probably close to half of it will end up going to the government. The tax structure works for them, not you.

For anything the government says, "Hey, we'll let this compound in a tax-free growth vehicle, and you can pay tax up front on it," they limit the amount you can contribute (e.g., $6,500 in a Roth IRA or $66,000 in a solo 401(k) [in 2023]). You're limited because the government wants a piece of the growth—and they *will* get a piece of it. Oh, and the government can change the rules at any time. If they want the money early, they'll take the money early. If they want to push the retirement age back, they can. They are in control.

> It's difficult to get a man to understand something when his salary depends on his not understanding it.
>
> – Upton Sinclair

To become a Lifestyle Investor, you must change your mindset. You must think about investing differently. You can live life on your terms, but getting there will take a different approach.

CALCULATE ACTUAL RATE OF RETURN

Earlier in my investment career, I got quarterly and annual statements from my financial advisor and the investment and financial institutions I was investing through that reported a strong **average rate of return**, anywhere from 7–10 percent. For years, I never questioned these numbers and just felt good about how much I thought I was making. Then one day, because I wondered why I didn't have more money if the average rate of return was so high, I dove into the numbers.

Luckily, I'd kept a record of how much money I originally contributed into each investment, and I had statements showing my starting and ending balances. With that data, I realized that I could track how much I actually made rather than the average rate of return that was listed on my statement. I needed to calculate my **actual rate of return**, not my *average rate of return*. My actual return wasn't printed anywhere, so I had to do my own math.

To my surprise, my actual return was much less than what these institutions were trying to lead me to believe. In fact, at the time I checked my investments for the first time, doing my own math, I found out that I had actually lost money due to a bad stretch in the stock market—though my statement still said I had a positive *average rate of return*.

What these financial institutions were giving me in their reports was deceiving. They were using a smokescreen and distracting me from what I was actually making by telling me it wasn't as bad as it was. I was losing money, yet somehow, I had a positive average rate of return, which made it seem like I was making money.

The *average rate of return* is the only calculation many financial planners discuss because if you think you are making money through them, you'll keep your money with them and, they hope, add to it. That's a recipe that doesn't work for me. Commandment 7, "Plus the Deal," and Commandment 8, "Cut Out the Fat," elaborate on the flaws of relying on the average rate of return and help you understand what is happening with your investment.

You may already know this, but I want to point it out here: Financial planners still make money on your money even when you lose money. According to SPIVA's (S&P Indices vs. Active) 2019 year-end report, in the last fifteen years, the fund managers you pay to manage your investments do a worse job 95 percent of the time than if you invest in an index fund yourself. [1] In other words, you are

---

[1]   Berlinda Liu and Gaurav Sinha. "Spiva® Canada Scorecard." https://www.spglobal.com/spdji/en/documents/spiva/spiva-canada-scorecard-year-end-2019.pdf

paying fees to have someone manage your money when it's likely they won't make you more than if you invested it wisely yourself in the S&P 500 index. The reason? No one can predict the future, so you pay financial professionals to manage your investments, and statistics show that only 5 percent of the time they actually beat the market indexes. That rate is considered normal!

Make indexes your new normal, where you pay the least amount of fees to invest in the stock market.

401(K) FLAWS

Pension programs no longer work, so many companies have quit doing them. They are opting for 401(k) plans instead. Soon, people will realize that 401(k) plans don't work either. When it's time to cash in on their retirement income, the government will get a third or more, up to 40 percent or maybe even higher, depending on the tax rate and how much income they've earned from that accumulated nest egg.

If you have a 401(k), you must consider that this investment option traditionally has the highest fees of any other investment. You typically pay 3–4 percent, which doesn't sound like much until you realize that each percentage over time, depending on how much you make, can be millions of dollars. And mutual fund fees aren't much better and can often also charge over 3 percent in fees. That's real net worth that people are losing.

In addition to losing a large part of your nest egg in taxes when you draw it out, keep in mind that once you retire, you lose your three most significant tax deductions—dependents, mortgage interest, and business expenses. These deductions are likely a significant part of helping you earn the after-tax income you currently have become accustomed to, so maintaining that same lifestyle once those deductions are taken away will be harder to accomplish. Also, chances are, the taxable income rate then will be higher than it is today due to the massive amount of debt the US has accumulated.

SOCIAL SECURITY IS NOT SECURITY

On top of all of these factors is Social Security, which may not be around in the future. You're paying into a system that may not exist. Less people are paying into the Social Security system today than the number of people who collect on it currently, and the number drawing Social Security will continue to grow. The current financials released from the Social Security Administration say that Social Security is going to run out in 2035. This is not an opinion. People working in this government agency and managing these financials and the national budgets are the ones who are saying it's going to run out and is unsustainable.

What's worse, the financials released in 2020 by the Social Security Administration that projected the timeline for when Social Security will run out were released prior to the stay-at-home orders due to COVID-19. The newest estimates at the time of this writing have projected it could run out as early as 2032. The reality is that Social Security in itself is a Ponzi scheme. A **Ponzi scheme** takes new money to pay out a promised return to someone else. That scheme cannot possibly work as is, and it's going to fail. It's just a matter of time.

The framework of our financial system, from education to financial literacy, is outdated and broken. Unfortunately, it's based on a follow-the-herd mentality that says people just do what everyone else is doing. However, if what everyone else did worked so well, the distribution of wealth wouldn't be so lopsided. Trust me when I say the wealthiest one percent of the population is not investing in 401(k)s, in the stock market, and in qualified plans. There are a handful of anomalies able to do that, but the people living the lifestyle they desire are not clipping away at their 401(k)s to do so.

You can't become a Lifestyle Investor too early or too late.

NEST EGG STOCK INVESTMENT FLAWS

The whole idea of nest egg investing in stocks is a flawed concept. For most people, that's primarily or exclusively where their money is. Any time the stock market takes a hit, they lose a big stack of money. It creates a huge risk profile. Many people think they are mitigating risk by following professionals' advice, but what they're really doing by having all their money in the stock market is putting all their eggs into one basket—the US economy and US companies (or their respective countries).

When inflation is happening, the dollar isn't going as far. Through quantitative easing and continued stimulus packages, our government is increasing the amount of **fiat currency** being pumped into our financial system. *Fiat currency* is money that is not backed by a physical commodity like gold but has still been declared as legal tender by a government (i.e., the US dollar). All this money printing dilutes the value of the dollar and also penalizes people who save money, making their money much less valuable.

Most people aren't getting pay increases at the rate of inflation, so both their purchasing power and overall net worth are shrinking.

During times of inflation, and even in normal times, one of the best places to invest is in cash flow-producing assets. The value of the dollar decreases with extra money being printed, but the value of assets, and especially cash-flowing assets, increases because they appreciate in tandem with the supply of money being added into our financial system. As you add value and increase profitability in cash flow producing assets, they appreciate twofold. So not only do you get the cash flow they produce that keeps up with inflation, but you get asset appreciation and a hedge against the devaluation of the dollar in a physical asset. In other words, when the monetary supply expands, your assets expand.

There's no guarantee that the US is going to remain the superpower that it currently is or that the massive stimulus packages aren't going to have long-lasting negative effects at some point. There's no guarantee that the economy is going to be stronger when you retire. There's no given that, if you take a hit, you'll have enough time to recover.

Look at all the drags slowing down the growth and compounding of your investments—you've got inflation, **volatility**, taxes, and fees for anything and everything out there. The amount of fees being paid to financial advisors is a total drag on your wealth accumulation and exponential growth. If you're not focused on enhancing your financial literacy and you're leaving the decision-making up to others, in most cases, they're going to do what's best for *them*, not what's best for *you*.

Here's a summary of what I've said to debunk Myth 1. Conventional financial education says to save money in tax-advantaged vehicles and invest in the stock market and hope it works out. It's all about the rate of return, and it's all product-based—*this product or that product is what's going to get you there.* Your plan needs to be more holistic. There are many different ways to skin a cat. Run from anyone who tries to sell you a single product-driven strategy.

Run, too, from any plan that is average-rate-of-return-driven because the average rate of return doesn't matter. The average rate of return is a slippery, manipulative, and slimy phrase to make people feel good about not making money and a smokescreen so people won't realize they're not making as much as they think they are. What matters is the *actual* rate of return because that's real money.

MYTH 2: YOU CAN'T SPEND MONEY FREELY TODAY AND GROW YOUR WEALTH AT THE SAME TIME.

Money and wealth typically don't result from a nest egg accumulation approach in which you build a nest egg of millions of dollars, draw from it when you retire, and live a happy life. This strategy relies on endless hope. *Hopefully,* you'll be able to accumulate this huge amount of wealth, and *hopefully,* by the time you do, the stock market will be in good shape, and *hopefully,* you will be able to retire in a good season for the economy. If all these hopes are fulfilled, *hopefully,* you'll be in good health and physically well enough to enjoy retirement.

Notice how many what-ifs and conditional statements are the basis for the way the average person invests. The reality is, if you distribute from your nest egg and doing so takes down your principal, then at a certain point, your nest egg is going to deplete to zero.

Yes, the goal is to build up that nest egg, never touch the principal, and live off the interest. That goal, however, hinges on the belief that you have investments that will continually generate enough interest to live on—something that, in fact, can change at any given moment. Your returns could change, the market could change, and the cost of living will certainly change.

CALCULATE YOUR MONTHLY COST OF LIVING

What makes more sense is to consider how much it *costs you to live* from a monthly cash flow standpoint rather than an annual income standpoint. Look at what it costs you to live on an annual basis, and then break that number down to what it costs you to live on a monthly basis. That total is the amount of income you need to earn to cover your monthly expenses. This is an actual strategy that relies on numbers you can figure out and doesn't revolve around hope or unknown income in the future.

Here are some important questions to ask yourself:

- How much does it cost me to survive at a bare minimum and cover all my basic monthly expenses (mortgage/rent, food, utilities, transportation, etc.)?
- How much does it cost me to live my current monthly lifestyle?
- How much does it cost me to live the monthly lifestyle I aspire to live?
- How can I create an income to cover those lifestyle costs without using my time?
- Most importantly, how can I cover my bare minimum basic monthly expenses to survive on passive income alone?

Answering these questions can provide some clarity on the next steps you can take to create the lifestyle you want today that doesn't rely on income from your job or your business.

Once your expenses are covered, one of two things can happen. You can enhance your lifestyle. If you choose to do that, you'll want to increase your income. Ideally, you can do so through passive investments and owning assets and not through earned income. The other thing that can happen, once your expenses are covered, is you can take your extra cash flow that exceeds your expenses and reinvest it into additional investments that continue to produce income.

CONCENTRATION RISK

As you start to create your passive income, take the necessary steps to diversify your cash flow across many different asset classes, sectors, and industries. Should something happen that negatively impacts one of those areas, you won't suffer as much loss because you will not have all your cash flow concentrated in that one area. This strategy mitigates **concentration risk,** which is the risk when too many investments are exposed to the same economic forces.

During my journey to financial freedom, I worked hard to keep my family's expenses the same for a long period of time so that as our income increased, our lifestyle didn't consume that extra income. As a rule, I'd take whatever income was above and beyond our cost of living and invest it in a variety of new ventures and investments that generated even more cash flow.

Starting out, I was conservative with the investments I made. I focused entirely on investments that produced cash flow. Once all our expenses were covered, I became more liberal with my investments. This strategy has allowed us to live a great lifestyle, and it also has given us the ability to be generous with our income as well.

Once our expenses were covered, I felt comfortable venturing out of the box a bit to see if there was anything I could improve upon or hadn't yet considered from an investment standpoint. I started meeting with and learning from other experts and professionals who shared additional strategies and investment opportunities that could help me reduce risk and increase returns, as well as help me diversify asset classes.

My risk tolerance shifted. Financial freedom had given me more options of where to invest. For example, I had saved for stock market investing and equity investing (especially **angel investing**—discussed later) until I was sure my cash flow was more than enough to cover my lifestyle expenses. Those investments are riskier than highly vetted real estate rentals (directly or through a fund) or senior secured credit funds that produce predictable cash flow.

I now like to use the extra cash flow that I earn above and beyond my lifestyle expenses to invest in **equity investments**, stock market indexes, other stocks I like, and other options I consider to be riskier than strong cash flow producing assets. Those options include investing in operating companies and creating unique terms, structures, and one-off deals, something I do frequently today.

Once you have your basic lifestyle expenses covered with passive income, you can spend more time figuring out the different investment vehicles you may want to add to your portfolio. Great questions to ask yourself are:

- What gives me the best return with the least amount of risk?

- What emerging markets should I consider that didn't exist that long ago?
- How can I diversify my investments, even across other cash-flowing opportunities?

As you can see, my philosophy on investing is different than most people's. Here it is in a nutshell: focus on passive income first to cover all expenses, and then diversify that passive income to have multiple income streams so you aren't reliant upon just one asset for income. After that, stock market index investing is the cheapest way to invest in the stock market, having the lowest fees. Invest for the long term into the stock market because emotional investing causes loss over time. And avoid buying and selling at inopportune times and during times of crisis, which could wreak havoc on your portfolio.

Investing in operating companies and structuring unique agreements to gain cash flow as well as participate in the upside is another strong investment opportunity that can become part of your passive income strategy both before and after your expenses have been covered. Reserve straight equity investments until all your expenses are covered because these tend to be the riskiest investments of all. **Seed round** investments, which are the first round of funding for a startup, pose the greatest risk. These investments can be very lucrative, but the odds are not in your favor; typically, if there is a big payout, it won't be for decades. I only allocate a small portion of my portfolio investments to them—typically 1% of my net worth, and this capital only comes from the cash flowing investments I have already made. This way, if a deal goes bad, I only lose the surplus of that cash flowing deal, which will have another distribution in the next month or quarter.

Whenever you make a riskier investment like seed round investing, be sure the funds come from the cash flow produced by passive investments—and that the income exceeds your lifestyle expenses. If the investment doesn't work out, you lose only the cash flow from that asset as a one-time distribution, not the actual principal you could be earning cash flow from.

This hierarchy of investing has proven to be a critical component in the success of my investment strategy, and I will explain each type of investment in more detail in the pages that follow.

MYTH 3: THE BEST INVESTMENTS ARE TRIED-AND-TRUE CHOICES YOU'VE ALREADY HEARD ABOUT.

Fifteen years ago, there was no such thing as single-family home rentals as an asset class. Around twelve years ago, they became an official asset class and one of the fastest-growing asset classes in the US.

The cannabis, CBD, and hemp industry is taking off right now. It is one of the fastest-growing industries in the US.

The music industry has royalty investment opportunities that are now more prevalent than ever before and with easier access for investors. They've always been there, but now there are new ways to monetize effectively and track those royalties, especially with the boom that is happening and the lower barrier to entry on both the artist and investor side.

There are more opportunities to invest in original production content (think shows, movies, music, etc.), which is a brand-new booming category that a decade ago was basically limited to only HBO and a few other producers. Now, there are many competing companies offering fantastic investment opportunities, and the barriers to entry are much lower.

Many other emerging markets exist from international opportunities. Most people only look into the country where they live, but there are opportunities outside our borders in countries that most people don't even consider. If you educate yourself or find people who are educated about them, opportunities are everywhere.

Technology is another market with investment opportunities. They can be hit or miss, but there are always new, innovative, and disruptive developments worth paying attention to. Financial technology, or Fintech, is blowing up. **Software as a service (SaaS)** is taking off. Crowdsourcing and **crowdfunding** are becoming more popular and mainstream. E-commerce, in general, is revolutionizing the way people shop and conduct business. Even the trend of marketplaces is becoming the norm for where people shop.

Healthcare and senior living are other sectors with booming opportunities. Hotel conversions to condos and apartments are in high demand. Industrial distribution centers and warehouses are growing tremendously with the boom of e-commerce.

The list goes on and on, and that's my point. All these new, booming, and emerging markets have opportunities where most people aren't making the time or don't have the confidence to look.

MYTH 4: YOU CAN'T UPGRADE YOUR LIFESTYLE WITHOUT SACRIFICING PROFIT.

Lifestyle inflation is a threat to long-term financial freedom. Let me say that again in another way. Nothing is a given.

Being a Lifestyle Investor means that while your income increases, your lifestyle doesn't increase linearly. Those I've trained, coached, and developed understand this rule. Your lifestyle doesn't change dramatically until you have enough repeatable investments to sustain your desired lifestyle change. Remember, you become a Lifestyle Investor more than you live an investor's lifestyle.

When I get extra income, I am free to choose whether or not to improve my lifestyle because I've already bought another asset that produces the income to cover that expense. For example, if I want to get a new car, I'm methodical in my approach. Instead of spending my money to purchase that car, I know that it's smarter to buy another asset that produces the income to cover the car payments and expenses of owning it *before* I make the car purchase. If I just spend the money on a car, I lose that total amount of principal to something that does not generate cash flow.

A car generally isn't an asset; it's an expense. It just makes sense to put the principal to work to earn the extra cash flow that will cover the car's expenses and liabilities. This approach also gives me the opportunity to earn even more cash flow on the principal I invested when the car is paid off. When I mention this strategy to clients, they are blown away. "You can do that? I've never even thought about that. But how would I do that?" To me, it's a smarter way to make that purchase.

Home improvements are also a good example of where you can cover your expenses in advance by buying assets that produce income. The extra income allows you to pay for new furniture, home remodeling, or even a bigger or more expensive home.

My family's current home is in a hotter market than our previous home. This home cost twice as much as the last one, but I bought an asset that produced the income to cover more than twice the cost of the mortgage before I purchased the home. We didn't upgrade our home until we'd upgraded our real estate portfolio, which covered the income needed to upgrade our home and cover that new mortgage. The new home was then a safe, smart investment.

Buy an asset that scales in the future. Be proactive.

Anytime my family wants to increase our lifestyle, buy something new, upgrade our home, do a remodeling project, or whatever, I want an income-generating asset producing the cash flow that will cover the new expenses. The same strategy applies to travel. We've taken many trips around the world, visiting numerous countries along the way, and were able to cover those expenses with cash flow from investments. During our last trip to Europe, we spent six weeks visiting several countries in the Mediterranean and traveled along the different coastlines. Everything was 100 percent covered by cash flow from another asset we purchased.

Another tip: when you have the right tax strategists on your team, vacations can be treated as board meetings as long as you take minutes to prove what you've done.

Another way to utilize this strategy is to create new cash flow whenever there are business upgrades or growth opportunities. I've done this in several businesses. Here's how you can do it. Let's say you need to invest in your business in order to create more scale and overall growth by adding more employees, increasing marketing, buying more specialized equipment, or building a bigger office space. If the business profit supports these added expenses, you can have the business purchase a cash flow-producing asset to cover the new expenses. If the business profit doesn't fully support the increased expenses, you may need to take out a loan.

Here's the twist. What if that loan was to yourself? You can invest personally in cash flow-producing assets that cover the additional expense of scaling the company and have the loan paid back with interest. This is a win-win scenario for both you and your business. Plus, you accomplish it while buying more cash flow-generating assets.

MYTH 5: MOST INVESTING EXPERTS GIVE GOOD ADVICE.

Did you know that the vast majority of people in the financial services industry don't operate under fiduciary responsibility? **Fiduciary** responsibility means that whoever is investing your money has an obligation to do what's best for you. Because many financial planners don't have to do what's best for their clients, only something that's good or that they *think* is good, they typically do whatever is best for *themselves*.

Also, the advice you get from these advisors is often biased because they have incentive to act in a certain way that may not be in your best interest. They'll then invest in products to inherit extra bonuses, commissions, or kickbacks. Unfortunately, this behavior is extremely common in the financial services industry. Countless news articles and publications have uncovered this behavior over the years.

I want to say it again: *Financial freedom does not come in the form of IRAs and qualified plans.* Financial freedom generally doesn't come in the form of any books touting these methods. Many professionals who've become rich in the financial services industry didn't make their clients much money, but they had a large number of clients who made money for *them*. Most experts in financial services or investing don't make their money based on the principles they preach; they make it by selling an idea they didn't follow. Dave Ramsey and Suze Orman are two examples. They make money from their "platforms"—selling financial products and services from their TV and radio programs.

By the way, these experts do a masterful job of helping people get out of debt. Unfortunately, they don't teach people how to create *wealth*. And they're also not skilled at creating a wealth mindset because their mindset is scarcity.

"Don't buy that latte; that latte worth $5 today could be worth *this* amount in fifty years if you save that money instead." It's a total scarcity mindset.

> Don't live out of a scarcity mindset. The better you feel about my life today, the more opportunities you have.

If you want to be a Lifestyle Investor, don't focus on following the norm because you aren't after normal. The average person doesn't know what they're doing with their finances. Whenever you see what most people are doing, run in the opposite direction because most people don't have it figured out. Why copy a bad example?

Do copy the people who do have it figured out and have the lifestyle you want. Copy people who have accomplishments you respect and practice what they preach when they are teaching what they've personally done versus how the market trends. Get a financial coach who is transparent with their earnings and who has *recently done* what you want to accomplish.

MYTH 6: YOU NEED A LOT OF MONEY TO START CASH FLOW INVESTING.

In this book, I share a variety of investments. The most important thing for you to know is that *all the strategies can work for you no matter what you have to invest.* How you decide to get started may depend on your knowledge, risk tolerance, and investable capital. The good news for you is, I have a number of strategies to use as a starting point.

Also, whether you are an **accredited investor** or not makes a difference in certain investments. An accredited investor is an individual or business entity that is allowed to invest in certain investment opportunities based on satisfying at least one requirement regarding their income, net worth, or professional experience. For an individual to be accredited, they either need to have a net worth of $1,000,000 or have an annual income of at least $200,000 per year for the last two years (or $300,000 combined annual income if married).

The **Securities and Exchange Commission (SEC)** has these requirements in place to identify sophisticated investors who have a reduced need for the protection of regulatory disclosures. Basically, the SEC tries to protect uneducated investors against fraudulent and manipulative investment practices.

What most people don't realize is that a tremendous number of investments exist that don't require becoming an accredited investor. Investment requirements vary based on the type of investments and the sector. For example, a lot of real estate investments don't require being an accredited investor.

An important decision you need to make is whether you prefer to make a direct investment versus investing in a fund that has a collection of investments. If the investment is a strong opportunity, then it makes sense to go into the deal directly. Sometimes, however, it's nice to remove some of the risks by adding multiple investments. That way, if one of the investments goes bad, it can be offset by the other investments that go well. (I will cover these strategies in much more detail in the chapters ahead.)

Another decision to make is what platform you are using. Several platforms, including CrowdStreet and Fundrise, among others, are crowdfunding-based. Non-accredited investors, as well as accredited investors, can participate. These platforms create plentiful opportunities and are a nice option for people looking for smaller investments starting with as little as $1,000. They have good deals to find if you do the research and dig through them. Not all investment offerings on these platforms are great, but if you learn how to evaluate investment opportunities, there are plenty of good deals. I've invested in deals through some of these platforms, so I am a believer in them for *the right deal*.

Besides crowdfunded platforms, there's also standard **syndication**, which is a partnership between several investors to combine skills, resources, and capital to purchase and manage a property they otherwise couldn't afford. If you're looking into that sort of investment where there's an operations team, look at how much experience they have. Find out and take into consideration how much they charge in fees. Some people don't know that there can be fees hidden in the **private placement memorandum (PPM)** documents, so you do need to read the fine details. I will cover syndications in more detail later in the book.

IF YOU HAVE $50,000 OR LESS TO INVEST . . .

One option besides investing in index funds is to invest in real estate. I like real estate in general because intrinsic value is built already into real estate, and it won't go zero like stocks can. Real estate has value, so it can be used as collateral to get a bank loan for purchase. This asset class can be easier to finance than other investments, such as businesses that don't have collateral to pledge.

Investing in real estate rentals is attractive to a lot of people because it often produces cash flow right away. It includes investing in single-family homes, mobile home parks, apartment complexes, industrial distribution centers and warehouses, and self-storage units, as well as other real estate options. When you find the right deal, it will cash flow on day one. It is a little riskier if you are a new investor, and some real estate won't produce cash flow immediately, so make sure whatever you invest in does have cash flow.

Senior credit funds are another interesting option. You can have a **first-lien position** on real estate or other collateral, so it is much less risky than other investments. These funds also produce consistent and predictable cash flow, typically on a monthly basis.

There are plenty of other good first investments if you have $50,000 or less, but I've highlighted a handful that I know can work.

IF YOU HAVE MORE THAN 50,000 TO INVEST . . .

I remember when I made my first investment of just over $50,000. It kept me up at night. I thought, *Oh my goodness, what if this fails? This is a lot of money. I could lose it all.* But what I wanted to do was stop the limiting beliefs in my mind. So, I thought, *You know what? If there's any way I'm going to learn, it's going to be when I have my money in the deal.* After doing that deal, I was much more confident in the next deal and didn't lose sleep over it. I understood the process better and had an education of what happened—the experience really mattered.

My advice to you, if you feel the way I did, is to remember that most people also feel the same way when they start investing. You have an opportunity to educate yourself. Your task is to do your **due diligence** on the front end to determine if you are investing in a good deal. If you're unsure if it's a good deal, run it by people with expertise in that area. Have some good advisors around you.

While you're in the process of learning, consider **diversification** as a strategy. If, for instance, you want to invest $250,000, you could invest in several smaller deals of $50,000 each. Diversifying your investments like this is a good idea if you don't have expertise in a particular asset class. Essentially, diversification prevents you from putting all your eggs in one basket.

There's no doubt that the more money you have, the more opportunities become available. For example, some of the strongest investments I've seen also come with a higher minimum investment (e.g., a $250,000 or $1 million minimum). Because the minimum investment is high doesn't mean any investment offering below it isn't a good deal. On the other hand, a number of additional deals and investments with improved terms exist at these higher numbers.

When you start investing, these numbers might look impossibly large, but with practice and education, they get easier and easier and become more familiar too. My experience and education have allowed me to invest more than what I used to be comfortable with.

Once you start investing and learning as you go along, investing becomes easier. You're less emotionally involved and tied to the outcome.

MYTH 7: THE UPCOMING GENERATIONAL WEALTH TRANSFER WON'T IMPACT ME.

The largest transfer of wealth in history is upon us. Over the next ten to fifteen years, Baby Boomers are projected to pass down over $100 trillion in assets to younger generations. To put this sum into perspective, it's larger than the entire current economy of China.

This unprecedented shift will reshape philanthropy, investing, entrepreneurship, and more. But most importantly, it represents a once-in-a-lifetime opportunity for financial freedom. With preparation and foresight, this wealth transfer can be a catalyst to achieve your lifestyle goals.

Don't assume this will only impact the ultra-wealthy. Here are realistic ways to capitalize on this historic opportunity:

- Invest in sectors like senior care, medical technology, and transportation that will boom from this demographic tidal wave.
- Explore commercial real estate and other investment opportunities related to aging life care management. Demand for these services will surge exponentially.
- Research causes you care about and get involved. Major donations are expected to these areas.
- If you have aging parents, help them put legal protections in place to safely transfer wealth. Learn about their investments.
- Build relationships with affluent yet aging business owners looking for business partners and liquidation partners to eventually pass the torch.

The odds are high you'll intersect with the transfer in some way. Take steps now to educate yourself on the impact and potential opportunities. The decisions you make today will determine whether you're a benefactor or a bystander.

MURPHY'S LAWS FOR THE LIFESTYLE INVESTOR

I really believe it's better to learn from other people's mistakes as much as possible.

—Warren Buffett

Every investor makes mistakes and loses money at some point. However, if I can prevent you from making one stupid investing mistake—like the one I'm about to share with you—I can save you hundreds of thousands or millions of dollars of your money. But more importantly, I can save you years of your time. After all, this book is about *becoming* a Lifestyle Investor.

In the military, most soldiers see some variation of **Murphy's Laws of Combat** in their barracks as they go through basic training. I originally found this information on a Reddit post. Some of the comments by men and women who served in the military said one or more of these laws even saved their lives in armed combat. You can find hundreds of these so-called "laws" online, but I picked twenty of my favorites for this list.

MURPHY'S LAWS OF COMBAT

1. Friendly fire—isn't.
2. Field experience is something you don't get until just after you need it.
3. No matter which way you have to march, it's always uphill.
4. Odd objects attract fire. You are odd.
5. If it's stupid, but it works, then it isn't stupid.
6. Try to look unimportant; the enemy may be low on ammo and not want to waste a bullet on you.
7. Never share a foxhole with anyone braver than yourself.
8. Never forget that the lowest bidder made your weapon.
9. There is no such thing as a perfect plan.
10. Five-second fuses always burn in three seconds.
11. The important things are always simple; the simple are always hard.
12. Incoming fire has the right of way.
13. No combat-ready unit has ever passed inspection.
14. No inspection-ready unit has ever passed combat.
15. If the enemy is within range, so are you.
16. The only thing more accurate than incoming enemy fire is incoming friendly fire.
17. Things that must be shipped together as a set aren't.
18. Things that must work together can't be carried to the field that way.

19. Anything you do can get you killed, including nothing.
20. Professional soldiers are predictable; the world is full of dangerous amateurs.

Whether you are or were in the military or not, you can see some of the wisdom in these laws of combat. The danger of ignoring them, it turns out, can be deadly. They have led me to develop my own set of laws I call *Murphy's Laws for the Lifestyle Investor*.

THE DANGER OF IGNORING THE LAWS

I'm going to tell you here one of the greatest investing mistakes I've ever made to prevent you from falling into the same space. Do you remember the Ponzi scheme perpetrated by Bernie Madoff and discovered in late 2008? I got caught in a Ponzi scheme that cost me almost a million dollars.

A few years ago, I heard about an amazing opportunity. I'd always wanted online real estate and found out about a company that built websites that would generate passive income from multiple income streams, including advertising revenue, affiliate revenue, and e-commerce revenue. It was said that it would ultimately build an audience list, and I would wind up with not only income but an asset that could be sold. The deal seemed awesome because it paid 20 percent per year on my money. Plus, when the site sold, I would get to split the amount with the company 50–50.

Sounds productive so far, right?

Better yet, the investment required no work on my side, just capital. One of my good friends had invested in the company back in 2012, another in 2014, and the company had never missed a payment. From every perspective, it looked like a sure thing.

Let me give you the bad news first. I wound up investing $300,000 and made $60,000 the first year, exactly as promised. The business never missed a payment. Then, when the site was sold, my profit was $200,000. I chose to reinvest that money plus another $100,000, effectively doubling down. At that point, I was in for $600,000 (my original investment of $300,000 + $200,000 from the sale + another $100,000).

I had another year and a half of returns that paid me a total of $200,000. Since everything to that point had worked like clockwork, I made yet another investment of $200,000—for a total of $800,000.

I have a very thorough due diligence checklist that my team, including my attorney, goes through before I make an investment. When I shared this deal with my attorney, he immediately tried to convince me not to get involved. He said, "It looks too good to be true." Sadly, I went ahead anyway.

And so began what I call Murphy's Laws for the Lifestyle Investor: The Checklist That Shall Not Be Violated.

MURPHY'S LAWS FOR THE LIFESTYLE INVESTOR: THE CHECKLIST THAT SHALL NOT BE VIOLATED

1. If it looks too good to be true, it probably is.
2. If anything feels creepy, it probably is.
3. Beware of name-droppers and name-dropping.
4. The important things are always simple; the simple are always hard.
5. When in doubt, review the Principles and 10 Commandments of Lifestyle Investing.
6. Beware of abnormally high returns, regardless of how much you would like it to be your reality.
7. Beware of dying industries.
8. Beware of dying markets and cities.
9. If there is only one major employer in a city or town, it's probably too risky to invest there, no matter how good the deal looks.
10. Investing in something just because your friends did, without doing any research yourself, isn't smart.
11. Don't invest in something without considering how much it will cost for you to own and operate it.
12. Do your due diligence! Don't trust their numbers. Remember, they are the ones that want to sell. Compare your notes with fellow investors to ensure you're hearing consistent information.
13. Research customer reviews online.
14. Run background checks on sellers and partners.
15. Get legal advice. Professionals will see things you don't.
16. Make sure other experts like the investment.
17. Interview several investors who have been long-time investors.
18. Beware if there are no long-time investors.

19. Never meet a person on their own battlefield. In other words, don't go to battle with an attorney who can drain you both energetically and financially.
20. Let the party you are buying from underestimate you; get your ego out of the way, and don't act smart.
21. Never sign a contract without reading it first, and have your attorney approve it.
22. Never assume the contract you're signing is the same one you approved; people can insert sneaky clauses at the last minute.
23. Know which opportunities are built by professionals; those are usually predictable. Some are built by amateurs; those are dangerous. You need to know who you're dealing with.
24. The bank doesn't care where the money comes from as long as it's legal.
25. Sometimes the best investment you'll ever make is the one you don't do.

Download a free PDF of this Murphy's Laws resource at *LifestyleInvestor.com / Gift.*

Let me give you a few specifics to fill in the blanks. My attorney said, "It looks too good to be true. It looks like a Ponzi scheme." He was creeped out by the deal simply because of the way the company's legal counsel worded the contract.

Eventually, when the deal fell apart and the auditing began, I found out these facts:

There's a gift in this mistake. I'm a fool for losing the money. I'm a greater fool if I don't learn the lessons.

- The company lied about having third-party auditing, and the prestigious firm they said did the auditing.
- They were an Inc. 5000 Fastest Growing Company for several years, and they continued to sustain their status with fraudulent financials.
- The founder was constantly name-dropping several online celebrities who were involved as investors and consultants to add further credibility.
- Eventually, when the company missed a payment, the owner wound up going down for paying investors with incoming investment money, which made this whole deal a Ponzi scheme.

Unfortunately, the owner was given bad business advice. The legal contract I signed—and all the investors signed—stated that the company had discretion for how they could use incoming investor money—a portion would go to paying a guaranteed return, and a portion could go to "other expenses" they had. Part of their expenses included payouts to the older investors. Although the owner maintained that he didn't know it at the time, paying old investors with new money is against the law. As my attorney and I started uncovering more, we found out that the banks the company used should have known what was going on because the warning signs were present all along.

Ultimately, the owner scaled too quickly and spent too much money. He brought on a CFO and CEO too late to make meaningful changes. It was a twenty-seven-year-old business that worked—until it didn't.

I'm limited in what I can say at this point, but the owner is probably going to go to prison for a long time. The average sentence for a business Ponzi scheme is eight to twelve years (according to my anecdotal online research).

There is a happy outcome to this story, at least for me. It turns out a Ponzi scheme is 100 percent tax-deductible according to the IRS, much more advantageous than writing off a typical business loss. The way the deal was structured, I received accelerated **depreciation**, which circumvented what would otherwise have been a large tax bill the year I invested. I can't disclose any more details because of the ongoing investigation at the time of this writing.

Here's the moral of the story. Never let your ego and fear of losing money cause you to do illegal things that can land you in jail or ruin your relationships, reputation, or marriage. You can always earn back money, but you can irreparably destroy your reputation in minutes.

Here's the gift of learning from this financial mistake. I'm a fool for losing the money. But I'm a greater fool if I don't learn the lessons inherent in the deal gone bad. Surround yourself with people infinitely smarter than you. Heed their advice and protect your risk. You may lose a battle, but make sure you win the war.

My goal is to give you the guidance and support you need so you don't make

Surround yourself with people infinitely smarter than you. Heed their advice and protect your risk. You may lose a battle, but make sure you win the war.

stupid decisions that cost you money and so you can protect yourself using the strategies and commandment stack to reduce your risk and make a good return. If you've lost money in the past, it's not your fault—you didn't have the right guide with the appropriate toolbox to help you reach financial freedom.

2024 UPDATE: THE DANGERS OF IGNORING MURPHY'S LAWS FOR THE LIFESTYLE INVESTOR

In the 2020 version of *The Lifestyle Investor*, I wrote about the danger of ignoring **Murphy's Laws for the Lifestyle Investor** and talked about one of the greatest investing mistakes I've ever made—getting caught in a Ponzi scheme that cost me almost $1 million.

It's "The Checklist That Shall Not Be Violated" for good reason. Recall the first law: "If it looks too good to be true, it probably is." Or the sixth law: "Beware of abnormally high returns, regardless of how much you would like it to be your reality."

By reader request, here is the update on that terrible deal and its aftermath that I couldn't publish in the earlier book.

AN ELABORATE RUSE

As I was writing *The Lifestyle Investor*, the owner was being tried for criminal fraud after independent investigations from the Federal Bureau of Investigations and the Securities and Exchange Commission. The court had appointed a receiver to take control of remaining assets, and profit shrank to a minimum.

I was called in as a key witness by federal prosecutors to testify against the owner in court. I worked with the prosecution team and federal agents to hand over the incriminating evidence I had gathered: recorded phone conversations, video calls, email correspondences, financial statements, screenshots, and more.

Lifestyle Investor Lesson: Keep a meticulous digital paper trail. Archive all communications involving financial and business deals.

During the trial, I flew into Chicago to take the stand. I was grilled for over an hour, not including a lunch break in the middle of my testimony.

The owner's legal team tried aggressively to rattle and discredit me. They questioned my credibility, character, and motives in an attempt to poke holes in the information I provided.

I stuck to the facts and timeline of events without getting defensive or emotional. Even when I was frustrated by their tactics, I knew I was on the side of truth and didn't let them rattle me.

It was an interesting experience to look in the eyes of a guy who made so many poor choices and flat-out lied to hundreds of people.

After deliberating, the jury found the owner guilty on all seven charges of wire fraud—each punishable by up to twenty years in federal prison. His sentencing is scheduled to take place in 2024.

While justice was served in this case, nearly 500 investors also affected by this scheme are in the same position as me: *learning the hard way.*

A SILVER LINING EMERGES

In mid-2023, I received an email noting that there would be a distribution from what was recovered by the receiver that took over. Though these receiverships often spend substantial money on forensic accounting, there was still some underlying value in the assets. We've received an initial 10 percent distribution, with a second disbursement due in the future. The key takeaway is that even disastrous deals can have a silver lining if intrinsic value exists. By investing in companies with tangible assets, you secure a senior position to recoup losses if things unravel.

> **Lifestyle Investor Lesson:** Seek companies with tangible assets securing senior creditor status to get repaid, even in worst-case scenarios.

Though it took several years in this case, we're finally seeing some money returned.

It pays to think through worst-case scenarios and ensure adequate remedies are in place. Staying focused on value positions you best in any outcome.

A SHIFT IN MINDSET

Here's another really good lesson that I've learned. I used to make investments thinking, "This is a really good deal. Let me see if I can prove otherwise." But the reality is that most deals are actually *not* good deals. Even the good deals can turn bad in certain economic seasons.

> **Lifestyle Investor Lesson:** Enter deals with
> intense skepticism, scrutinizing weaknesses until
> they're proven a wise investment.

So now I enter every deal thinking, "This deal is likely not good unless I can actually prove otherwise." Instead of entering a deal thinking, "I want to invest in this—let me see if there's any reason not to," I now assume it's a bad deal unless I can poke holes and find truth that makes it a good deal.

This mindset shift in how I evaluate deals has helped me say no to more deals and spend less time on ones that aren't worth pursuing. It impacts my filtering process, so I can more quickly filter opportunities.

HARD-LEARNED LESSONS FROM A CAUTIONARY TALE

With time and reflection, I extracted invaluable insights from this catastrophe:

- Our minds can rationalize away even the brightest red flags when we want something. I ignored expert warnings and my own intuition.
- My perspective has changed on how I approach deals. Instead of assuming a deal is good, I now assume most deals are flawed and scrutinize them intensely.
- Trust must be complemented by rigorous due diligence.
- A good reputation takes a lifetime to build but moments to destroy. One bad decision can undermine years of goodwill.

- The choice to do right when it's uncomfortable defines who we are.
- Mistakes and failures can be our greatest teachers if we extract the lessons. My responsibility now is to share my learnings with humility.

SAFEGUARDS AND BEST PRACTICES TO MITIGATE INVESTMENT RISKS

Based on the hard lessons I learned, here is a checklist of safeguards and best practices you can implement to mitigate investment risks moving forward:

- Rigorously vet every deal with qualified experts who offer unbiased counsel, even if it means losing the opportunity. Slow thinking beats speed.
- Do not ignore red flags or suspend disbelief regardless of how promising an investment appears or who is involved. Trust facts over emotions.
- Assume most deals are bad from the start and scrutinize them intensely before considering investment. This perspective allows more objectivity and prevents you from being seduced by superficial strengths.
- Foster a contrarian culture on the team and make it okay to critically challenge each others' assumptions to avoid groupthink.
- Maintain meticulous records should issues arise later, requiring investigation or litigation. An impeccable paper trail protects all parties.
- Develop contingency plans to rapidly respond when investments show early signs of issues. Nimble course correction can save so much frustration later on.

- Remain hyper-vigilant of blindspots fueled by ego or greed, as they can make it easy to miss crucial warning signs.
- Hold yourself and your partners accountable to the highest ethical standards, especially when stakes are high. Reputation lost is nearly impossible to restore.

PART TWO

THE COMMANDMENTS

COMMANDMENT 1: LIFESTYLE FIRST

My definition of success is to live your life in a way that causes you to feel a ton of pleasure and very little pain—and because of your lifestyle, have the people around you feel a lot more pleasure than they do pain.

—Tony Robbins

(As of this writing, I no longer coach one-on-one. All my advisory activities take place through the Lifestyle Investor Mastermind, a community of Lions and my trusted, vetted financial experts.)

Let me tell you a story about my first Lifestyle Investor Lion. Lions are my high-net-worth private investor clients who coach with me one-on-one over the course of a year. Each Lion receives personal coaching on a high-level investment strategy that includes mindset, deal structuring, deal filtering, and negotiation with real investment opportunities. My goal is to help each Lion build a portfolio of investments that mirrors my own, providing cash flow with the least amount of risk that is lifestyle-compatible.

After a year, each Lion has the knowledge, wisdom, and understanding of how to stack strategies that provide the highest return on investment. More importantly, during that year, each Lion gains access to my huge network of over twenty years of relationships with professionals who specialize in creating unique structures to protect their assets and provide high-level tax strategy and advice. These Lions also gain ongoing access to deals that are often invisible or difficult to access without an introduction. As I mentioned earlier, I call this exclusive group the Lions Network.

My first Lifestyle Investor Lion now wakes up when he wants to wake up and hasn't used an alarm clock in years. He has no boss or job that demands his time. He spends the first hour of his day reading, praying, meditating, and journaling. (Last year, he read more than 150 books.) Then he spends an hour working out. At age forty, he has chiseled abs, and his wife of almost ten years still thinks he's hot.

After his workout, he reviews his eight-figure portfolio and seven-figure bank accounts and reflects on his lifestyle vision. It includes family vacation goals consisting of two months of travel and international trips (one to Europe and another to the Caribbean). It also includes him taking at least two business trips with ultra-high-net-worth individuals who've become close personal friends. Over the next two hours, he joins video calls with the CEOs of his most recent investments, takes a leisurely lunch, and quits his day at 2 p.m.

He and his wife have customized an educational solution for their daughter that includes homeschooling and private instruction, so he is available to spend time with her. He and his wife also can spend hours together, walking and talking. The three of them have regular family meals. After they've tucked their daughter into bed, he and his wife enjoy a bottle of wine to connect and reflect.

This Lion chooses to work three days a week, takes three- and four-day weekends, and knows he could stop working for years if he wanted. And he has an abundance of *time to think*, which he uses to listen to inspiring podcasts that help him strategize for the long term and then journal his insights. He now earns more in his sleep in the first week of the month than he used to in a month's worth of fifty- to seventy-hour workweeks. (Back then, he was a high-income earner with a multiple six-figure income!)

Today, my client has total agency in his life. He has the freedom to choose how he spends his time, both with his family and friends and pursuing his passions and purpose in life. He pursues mental, physical, emotional, and spiritual growth by placing his relationships and overall health first. He has given his wife the freedom to pursue her passions. At any time, if he and his wife choose to stop sending their daughter to one of the best private schools in the United States, they have the ability and time to homeschool her. They do not live a conspicuous, flashy lifestyle. No one would guess his net worth by just looking at him and his family.

Not only does he have the same friends from twenty-plus years ago, but he also has access to a whole new level of relationships with multimillionaires and billionaires. He and his wife tithe to their church and give generously to several philanthropic organizations every year. His life is filled with choices and freedom. He could buy whatever he wants for his family at any time, but what drives him is making an impact, connecting, giving back, and making a difference.

The first benchmark to financial freedom that he set for himself was to make it possible for his wife to stop working. She was a talented high school business teacher, but as a family, they wanted a higher-quality and more flexible lifestyle. She was earning $36,000 a year, so he knew he needed to invest in an asset that produced that same amount of income. Technically, he could invest in an asset that produced less income than $36,000 a year because her after-tax income was much less than that. Plus, investment income is taxed at a much lower rate than earned income as well.

He broke down what he needed to make per month, and then he decided to buy a mobile home park. This first purchase nearly covered her salary, and it was enough that she didn't need to work anymore. It was a smooth transition for her to step away from teaching to spend more time as a family, travel, and do other things all the family wanted to do. It bought her time back and created that freedom of time in her life. Then he did the same thing to replace his income just a few years later.

Full disclosure: My very first Lion was me. I had to live the Lifestyle Investor vision before I felt comfortable teaching it or sharing it with someone else. My rule is never to take financial advice from someone who isn't currently doing what I want to do and experiencing the lifestyle I want to live, so I had to live it first.

Most people live a reactionary life. My goal? Live proactively and intentionally.

For me to have total confidence in my ability to coach and teach everything you're about to read in this book, it's critically important that I live by example—and *recency* matters. If I were writing this book ten or twenty years after my last failure and I hadn't recovered, I wouldn't trust myself to give you good advice. Plus, I'd never work with a financial coach who isn't earning more than me.

THE FREEDOM FORMULA

Before you go any further listening to me, take a moment right now to do this **Freedom Formula** exercise. Check your highest priorities in each Freedom Formula category to help you design your perfect lifestyle.

TIME + MONEY + RELATIONSHIPS + IMPACT = LIFESTYLE INVESTOR FREEDOM

Freedom of **Time**: What's important to you?
❑ Time to wake up when you want ❑ Time to exercise and get in shape ❑ Time to pray and meditate ❑ Time to journal and reflect ❑ Time to homeschool your children ❑ Time to listen to inspiring podcasts and read inspiring books ❑ Time to strategize and do long-term thinking, planning, and goal setting ❑ Time for family dinner and uninterrupted quality family fun

---

Freedom of Time: What's important to you?

- ❑ Time to vacation several times a year (or even more based on your dreams)
- ❑ Time to travel for months at a time
- ❑ Time to take a class or learn something you have wanted to learn

---

Freedom of Money: What's important to you?

- ❑ Choosing to work or not work for years at a time
- ❑ Buying whatever you want, whenever you want
- ❑ Writing a giant check or making a frivolous purchase without noticing the balance in your bank account
- ❑ Seven-, eight-, or nine-figure net worth
- ❑ Seven figures or more in liquid assets
- ❑ Anytime, anywhere vacations
- ❑ Extended worldwide travel in the nicest hotels and homes anywhere in the world for as long as you want
- ❑ Paying for any professional or service to *buy more time*
- ❑ Giving generously and freely
- ❑ Using money as a tool to accomplish more dreams and goals
- ❑ Creating a trust fund for family, friends, or others

Freedom of **Relationship**: What's important to you?

- ❏ Taking courses or classes to connect more deeply with your spouse and children
- ❏ Working with people who inspire you
- ❏ Choosing who to spend time with on a regular basis
- ❏ Scheduling dedicated quality of time with the five to ten most important people to you
- ❏ Scheduling epic experiences with the people you love most in your life
- ❏ Pursuing relationships with anyone that elevates you or any social status or ability to connect with influencers
- ❏ Courage and confidence to connect with "celebrities"
- ❏ Building relationships with "ambassadors"—individuals who can influence influencers and help you gain access to affinity groups and organizations
- ❏ Participating in your children's hobbies or sports teams, Parent-Teacher Association, or other groups
- ❏ Media—Increasing your visibility online, in media, and in the press so that you can share your message and easily connect with more people
- ❏ Elevated groups—Joining high-level professional groups such as The Lifestyle Investor Mastermind, Tiger 21, EO, YPO, Strategic Coach®, Genius Network®, or Front Row Dads to meet and connect with high-functioning, high-performance individuals who can mentor you and help you grow

---

Freedom of **Impact**: What's important to you?

❑ Doing inspiring, energizing work
❑ Supporting a nonprofit, 501(c)(3), or charitable organization
❑ Being able to directly help people in need
❑ Mentoring students eager to learn
❑ Setting up a foundation
❑ Volunteering to serve your church, community, career groups, or charities
❑ Establishing a grant fund for a school, university, or charitable group
❑ Donating your expertise
❑ Pursuing your passion without factoring in money
❑ Being able to give back or support an organization dedicated to animal advocacy, ecological conservation, or other causes that benefit the planet
❑ Artistic expression that positively affects an audience or group that matters to you

---

You can download a free PDF of this resource at *LifestyleInvestor.com/Gift*.

Notice that the Freedom Formula begins with time. If you had the ability to buy more time, you would have the life you've always dreamed of. That's what being a Lifestyle Investor is all about. It's owning your time and buying more time and freedom to do whatever you want to do, whenever you want to do it, with whomever you want to do it with, for any reason, as well as using your unique gifts in a way that brings the most passion in your life.

Your next step is to write a brief paragraph based on your values, considering the model of the Lion lifestyle I described earlier. What does your perfect day look like? If you had days like it for the rest of your life, would you feel like you were living your "happily ever after" life?

After you've written that paragraph, here's one more exercise. I call this my "Freedom From" and "Freedom To." If you could do one thing that would move you closer to your happily ever after, what would it be? Use this space to describe your Freedom Vision.

(If your book is in hard copy, write in it so you can look back at what you decide is your perfect life. If you are reading on a digital device, use the note-taking feature so it's saved there.)

YOUR FREEDOM VISION WORKSHEET

Date: Time: Location:

_____

_____

_____

_____

_____

_____

_____

_____

_____

_____

_____

_____

_____

_____

_____

_____

_____

_____

_____

_____

_____

_____

_____

Download a free PDF of this resource at *LifestyleInvestor.com/Gift*.

Are you pleased with what you've written? Hopefully, today represents the first day of the rest of your life as you become a successful Lifestyle Investor. You've discovered your Freedom Vision. Now it's time to find out what you need to do to achieve it.

The first step to becoming wealthy and becoming a Lifestyle Investor with the ability to live life on your terms is changing your mindset.

ADOPT THE MINDSET

I'm a huge advocate of personal and spiritual development. If it weren't for pursuing this work personally, I wouldn't have the lifestyle freedom, money, or the ability to share my system with you now. But I do, and I can. It all begins with adopting the *Lifestyle Investor* mindset.

Wealthy people *think* like wealthy people. They have disciplined behaviors and thinking processes, and they practice the habits of wealthy people. People without wealth are the opposite. They're stuck in a cycle of undisciplined behaviors, wrong thinking, and bad habits. They don't see or understand the nuances and distinctions that wealthy people do.

My stories in this book are one resource for you to use to begin to think like wealthy people think. Please refer to additional tools in the Resources section of this book.

The Lifestyle Investor mindset includes believing in and acting on the discipline that each investment must truly represent passive income in which your earnings don't depend on the time you spend working. Adopting this discipline means your income becomes fully independent of you and happens whether you're asleep or on vacation.

We've all heard the adage that time is money. Most people believe you have to be working in your business to make more money. The truth is, even outside the realm of passive income, it's still not the best protocol or value to follow inside a business.

Another myth is the idea of building your nest egg and living a frugal life. You can't even go to Starbucks to get your latte because you've got to save every extra penny you can to build a bigger nest egg.

Both of those are total myths, wrong ways of thinking that keep you from becoming wealthy.

When you change your thinking to make *lifestyle* your priority, you will approach every element of a deal differently than a conventional investor. When you stack my strategies and commandments together, your investments can offer you additional levels of freedom and income.

One example is learning how to structure loans properly. Instead of going for a conventional bank loan where I put 20 percent down, and the bank covered 80 percent, I actually negotiated a deal with the owner/seller of a mobile home park to finance it. We talked about it, and he felt comfortable with me putting 15 percent down with him, which was my goal. I wanted to get a better deal than if I used a financial institution.

The out-of-pocket cost on the first park was a down payment of $65,000. I then bought a second park with the same loan structure and a down payment of $75,000. My family lifestyle at the time cost $110,000 a year, so both of those down payments combined covered a little more than our annual lifestyle expenses, which is relevant because my first goal was to have twelve months of living expenses saved just in case we ever needed it.

As I mentioned earlier, I first wanted to replace my wife's $36,000 of income. The cash flow from the $65,000 down payment on the first property nearly accomplished it. I typically enter into deals where the cash flow is immediate, so we were cash-flowing positively the first month. It's important to note that although the number needed to cover our lifestyle at that time was $110,000, we could've covered our bare minimum expenses for about $52,000 per year. Knowing that, I made sure the cash flow from my second deal, combined with the amount from the first deal, would cover those bare minimum expenses. It did.

As a Lifestyle Investor, I often tried to prepare mentally for worst-case scenarios, so I would have a good plan in place in case my family needed it. In this case, if I became injured and couldn't work, I knew we'd be covered and could survive, even if it wasn't at the same level as our lifestyle that we had become accustomed to at that time.

WEALTH OPTIMIZATION

Let's talk about the concept of **wealth optimization**. When I look at wealth, my mindset is to take a holistic approach. First of all, I don't look at wealth as only money. Money is one component of wealth. A healthy physical body, emotional state, and spiritual strength are all parts of wealth. So are relationships and purpose. Therefore, when I look at wealth, I want to optimize every component of it.

Being in a good place financially, which is a big component of wealth, buys your time back to do other things. You can make sure you're mentally and physically strong, intellectually growing, and stimulated. You have the time, space, and finances to eat the right food (which could include buying organic or having your meals prepared for you). You can schedule regular adjustments, acupuncture, or massages for your physical health. You can give attention to your emotional and spiritual health. All these components work in tandem with each other.

When you think specifically of wealth creation and wealth building from a financial sense, there's a holistic way to look at the overarching picture. Most people look at the little snippets they've learned from someone who probably isn't even educated holistically or even qualified to share high-level strategy, and the information they get is mostly propaganda. Most of the information comes from Wall Street and banks that cultivate and curate the content and education going through our universities and colleges. These sources steer people to give *them* money.

The people at the institutions teaching you to invest have the same mindset as the information sources that want your money. Once you give these sources your money (i.e., banks), they make a multitude of money on it, give you low returns, and pay themselves first, regardless of whether they're making *you* any money. It's crazy. And if you continue this insanity of giving them your money without results, you're as guilty as they are at perpetuating this craziness.

I have two snippets, tried and true, about *lifestyle first* and how much time is involved in earning a return. First, some investments require no time at all. They are truly what most people are looking for once they learn they exist. Second, in some cases, it may make sense to invest a little time at the beginning to supercharge your return.

When I first started investing, I was willing to invest a little time at the beginning to get a higher return. Now, my investments don't take any time—they are truly passive invest-ments—and I'm willing to take a lower return in exchange for my time. One reason I bought mobile home parks is that they have the highest **cash-on-cash return** and the lowest commitment of time in the real estate rental space.

Starting out, it made sense for me to spend the five extra hours a week it took to run the rental business myself. I needed to learn how to do everything anyway so at some point I could replace myself. By running the business myself at first, I was able to make a much stronger return than if I paid someone else to run it for me. Eventually, I hired some amazing people that I love to work with and trained a team to take over all operations. In doing so, I knew I would make a smaller return than running it myself, but I also knew my end goal was to buy back my time. My director of operations is a wonderfully amazing woman who has worked with me for over fifteen years now and does an infinitely better job running my real estate portfolio than I ever used to do!

If your objective is the highest rate of return, and you're willing to invest a small amount of time in the beginning, investing into some sort of real estate rental, like mobile home parks, is one of the easiest ways to start lifestyle investing. Being willing to invest a little time in the beginning is an important mindset and discipline so you can become consciously competent at finding the balance that's right for you.

Sam Zell's unwavering belief in mobile home parks was another major factor in my decision to invest in this asset class myself. When I think of Sam, I picture the man most people would consider the greatest real estate investor of our time, hands down. He accomplished something incredibly rare - becoming the largest owner in three major real estate asset classes simultaneously: commercial real estate, apartment complexes, and mobile home parks. But what really caught my attention was his conviction in mobile home parks. Sam bought his first park in 1983 and later told me it was the single greatest investment he ever made. He spent a decade acquiring more parks before taking his portfolio public as Equity Lifestyle Properties (ELS) in 1993, and it remains the largest in the industry to this day. Even when he sold off his commercial and apartment portfolios to Blackstone right before the 2008 financial crisis, making a fortune, he held onto his mobile home park investments.

As a fellow Chicagoan who also got his start in real estate, I've always found Sam's journey incredibly inspiring. His book and the conversations I had the privilege of having with him before he passed away in 2023 have been deeply influential in my own life and career.

If you have more money and don't want to spend time in the beginning, here's an example of how you can leverage both your time and money to create true passive income as a lifestyle investor by using hard money loans. The example shows how each of my principles of investment comes into play.

EXAMPLE: HARD MONEY LOANS

A **hard money loan** is a loan that is secured by real property. Often, it is considered a last resort loan in the event that someone can't get bank financing. Many people use these loans as a short-term **bridge loan** or construction loan before they refinance a property with long-term financing. Hard money loans typically originate from individuals or companies and not banks, so they have a higher interest rate and a shorter duration than a typical loan. There are also hard money lending funds with professional operators. The fund model spreads out the risk over many assets, which reduces the risk even more than lending on a single asset.

MINDSET

I am a big fan of mirroring others who have a successful process. It's part of my Lifestyle Investor mindset. If someone else can do it, then I can too. I have a few highly successful friends who have done hard money lending most of their careers, so I've modeled their approach and terms to do hard money loan deals. This approach allows me to earn a great return in a safe investment that requires little to no time, so I can genuinely put lifestyle first.

I like the short duration of the hard money loan with a high interest rate and **points** (or fees) charged on the front of the loan. These investments, when structured correctly, have little risk but a high return, especially when secured in high-growth cities and vibrant housing markets. Plus, due to the short time frame and front-loaded fees, I am able to easily structure additional loans to compound my return.

STRUCTURE

The right structure is essential to a good deal. Here are some of the specific terms I use to create a strong return and protect my investment so I don't lose money:

- Six- to twelve-month loan
- **Balloon payment** at the six- to twelve-month term (repayment of the loan)
- Monthly interest-only payments
- 10–12 percent interest
- 2–4 points (2-4 percent of the loan) either paid upfront or at the end of the term
- Investment backed by collateral that is at least two times greater than the loan (in most cases, it's collateralized by the **deed of trust** on the property, and you assume ownership of the asset and can sell it if the borrower defaults)
- Use experienced operators and real estate professionals with a proven track record to avoid a **default**

FILTER

Remember, a filter uses criteria to sort through and narrow down an investment opportunity. While it might sound negative, what's most appealing about a hard money loan deal is that if the borrower defaults, my investment becomes infinitely better. My hope is that the borrower doesn't default, but the deal is structured in a way that is very attractive to me if they do. If they do default, my investment improves exponentially. I can take possession of the asset that it's collateralized against. As you can see, my investment terms create a double-win scenario where no matter what happens, I earn a solid return, which is my favorite type of investment.

NEGOTIATION

Here is my principle of negotiation at work. When I make the deal, I negotiate more collateral than the value of the loan. If a borrower defaults, I come out ahead with another real estate asset greater than my investment. I also like to negotiate a high point total, such as 4 percent, to be paid on the front of the loan to reduce the risk of the deal. Additionally, I like to charge a high interest rate, such as 12 percent or greater, and to have a short duration of the loan term. These elements of the deal are to ensure that I gain my principal back within a year or less with strong cash flow for my monthly payments.

I only release half of the loan amount in the initial installment until certain criteria are met. After those criteria are met, I release the rest. This approach helps minimize the risk involved and also makes sure the borrower uses the capital in the way they are supposed to do to ensure that the loan performs well.

THE DEAL IN REVIEW

Commandment 1 is "Lifestyle First." It is important to me that all my investments enhance my lifestyle in some way. Not only do I want to have strong cash flow from most of my investments, but it is also important that my investments don't require much, if any, time. This commandment enables me to earn income that is independent of my time.

To follow this commandment, I look for investments such as hard money loans (and variations of hard money loans, including lending funds and highly collateralized business loans) that give me more freedom of time without sacrificing a high return. A hard money loan is just one of many investments that satisfy "Lifestyle First."

COMMANDMENT 2: REDUCE THE RISK

Rule No.1: Never lose money.
Rule No.2: Never forget rule No.1.

—Warren Buffett

What if you could go to Las Vegas, gamble, and lose a game of poker, roulette, or blackjack but still walk away with positive cash flow? Does that sound impossible? When you invest and know how to negotiate using my **Strategy Stack,** a way of combining multiple non-obvious approaches to earn an even greater return with low risk, you'll discover opportunities to win in a way that you come out cash flow positive, even if part of your investment fails.

Warren Buffett's first two rules of investing sum up this chapter nicely. The hard part is implementing those rules and preventing yourself from violating them when you get emotionally involved in a deal and let fear or becoming overwhelmed get in the way of discipline, experience, and wisdom. If you lose money, you have to work twice as hard to replace it. Plus, you have the **lost opportunity cost** of what that money could have been earning.

One goal of reducing risk is to have your principal investment and any potential downside associated with it protected from loss. Another goal of reducing risk is to have so much leverage that whomever you are investing in or lending to realizes that they have so much more to lose than gain if they default, and so they will do whatever it takes to honor your agreement. In other words, if you lend a company $500,000, but you collateralize the loan with assets that are worth $10,000,000, then the owners will do whatever it takes to pay you back because they won't lose a $10,000,000 asset over just a $500,000 loan.

One of the facts about investing is that there's no such thing as a sure thing. Eventually, you're going to lose money. However, when you apply the principles and commandments of being a Lifestyle Investor and understand how to stack the strategies, you'll dramatically decrease risk and your downside. Let's begin with a list of strategies to reduce risk.

WAYS TO REDUCE RISK

- Educate yourself on investing and on the particular investments you decide to do.
- Collateralize the loan (ideally, at least two to three times the loan amount, just to play it safe).
- Be creative with all the different ways you can collateralize loans, such as using real estate, accounts receivable, inventory, equipment, intellectual property, stock, and notes receivable.
- Have strong legal documents that protect your risk and secure the terms.
- Make sure you have a **senior secured** position or **first lien position** on the asset (this means you are first in line to get paid back and are in the safest position in an investment).
- Improve proposed terms to be favorable to you and reduce some risk right out of the gate.
- Find a way to get points or fees paid to you upfront.
- If lending, limit how much of the loan someone has access to by using performance metrics that need to be hit first in order to release portions of the total loan amount.
- Put covenants in place that act as a guardrail to prevent deterioration of value; if the business starts to slip, you can change the terms of the agreement for immediate repayment of your loan.
- Use a **personal guarantee** as a way to secure an investment in which if the other party defaults, you have the right to go after other assets they have to get your investment back.

- Try **stock pledges** as another great way to secure an investment and increase the likelihood the contract terms are honored.
- Add a default interest rate provision into your contract so that if someone defaults, there is an automatic increase to the interest rate.
- If you are the borrower rather than the lender, use **non-recourse** debt so that in the event of a default, no one can come after any of your assets except the asset associated with the default.
- Accelerate the distribution schedule as a way to increase the speed with which an investment or loan is paid back in order to get your money out of an investment in a much quicker time frame.

Download a free PDF of this resource *at LifestyleInvestor.com / Gift.*

LIFESTYLE INVESTOR MASTERMIND PREVIEW: DUE DILIGENCE

Conducting proper due diligence is essential to reduce risk and enhance returns. Inside the Lifestyle Investor Mastermind, members gain exclusive access to experts that I'm constantly meeting in my network. Our Mastermind calls are an opportunity for all of us to learn together from these world-class specialists.

In January 2022, the leadership team from Venturi Private Wealth presented on The Art and Science of Due Diligence. Chris Schelling specializes in vetting alternative investments in private equity, and I was thrilled to soak up his "6 Ps" formula alongside my Mastermind members. Here's a preview of his system:

Performance begins and ends the evaluation. While past results don't guarantee future performance, they provide perspective on outcomes, skill, and total return. Look at alpha generation as a sign of investment acumen. Consider risk-adjusted returns like the Sharpe ratio. And remember, total return is the ultimate goal.

People focus on the team behind the investment. Assess trustworthiness by looking for integrity, ethics, and transparency. Review competence via track records, education, and relevant expertise. Ensure alignment of interests through co-investment, compensation incentives, and other skin in the game. Analyze stability by learning how long they've worked together and their dynamics. And consider diversity of perspectives and backgrounds.

Philosophy reveals foundational principles and investment beliefs. Look for consistency versus drastic changes over time. Understand differentiation: what makes their philosophy unique? Assess believability: is it grounded in reason? And ensure philosophy aligns tightly with process.

Process demonstrates repeatability, scalability, adherence to philosophy, and risk controls. Walk through a deal lifecycle to understand their approach. Examine how investment decisions are made—is there a checklist? Review risk management protocols.

Portfolio offers perspective on concentrations, liquidity, risk profile, and fit with philosophy and process. Check sector exposures, ease of liquidating holdings, and the alignment of actual risk versus stated risk appetite.

And **Price** is at the center of it all.

The Ps provide a principles-based framework to conduct thorough due diligence.

This was a small taste of the exclusive training Lifestyle Investor Mastermind members receive to expand their knowledge and reduce risk. Be sure to visit *LifestyleInvestor. com/Gift* for a video excerpt from this masterclass.

As I share in Commandment 8: Cut Out the Fat, one of the biggest ways I reduce risk in my investments is by investing in relationships that provide me access to specialized expertise and wisdom that is nearly impossible to find or replicate on my own. If you want to take your investing knowledge and results to the next level, the first step is to book a free strategy session with my team at *LifestyleInvestor. com/Strategy* to explore which of our courses or Masterminds are right for you.

EMPLOY DIFFERENT RISK STRATEGIES

You could look at a deal and say that the default terms are what they are; someone has come to you with terms, and it's your choice to invest in it or not. Sure, some deals are that way, but most deals are not. It's a myth that investing, in general, is really risky. You only hope that it works out, or you decide it's so risky that you don't even get in the game. Don't automatically accept the terms. Be creative to reduce your risk.

Good investments are not that difficult to negotiate once you're educated. You can't just hope for the best results. You need to do enough due diligence to feel comfortable with most investments out there, and then you need to structure your investments properly.

I liked my first mobile home park deal because it was a seller-financed situation. It was a non-recourse loan, which means if I defaulted in any way, the seller didn't have the right to come after my other assets. He could get his property back, and he'd get to keep the down payment and the interest. For me, I knew if everything went wrong and I totally screwed up the deal, I wouldn't risk the rest of my assets.

I like seller-financed deals because of this non-recourse aspect. But I also like them because the process is much cleaner and quicker. You don't have to go through all the underwriting and jump through all the hoops that you would with a bank. When you can establish good relationships and have good credit, a bank can be helpful, but I try to avoid them if I can. If a seller will do a ten-year note at 5 percent interest, amortized at twenty or twenty-five years, that is a very attractive deal. I don't have a whole lot of skin in the game, so to me, that's a true win-win. (I discuss non-recourse loans, **seller finance**, and other lending options in much more detail in Commandment 8: Cut Out the Fat.)

I'm going to show you a couple of real-life examples and deconstruct how they came together and how each investment works. I want to give you an idea of what a super low-risk investment looks like when you apply my principles, commandments, risk reduction, and the Strategy Stack all together. As I mentioned at the beginning of this chapter, my Strategy Stack is a way of combining multiple non-obvious approaches to earn an even greater return with low risk.

The example that follows might be a bit technical for you, but one of my objectives in this chapter is to show you in detail what a typical low-risk deal might look like. You'll learn how to use a system that consistently produces measurable results as long as you keep your emotions out of the way, stick to the fundamentals, and find creative ways to stack these strategies.

My intent in sharing this is for you to start recognizing how you can examine any deal—no matter how simple or complex—in such a way that you can always stack the odds in your favor. That means you can walk into a situation that might look like a gamble but always walk away with money in your pocket.

EXAMPLE: CANNABIS/HEMP/CBD INVESTMENT

One of my favorite investments right now is a senior secured credit fund that specializes in lending in the cannabis, CBD, and hemp industries. Since banks can't lend in these industries, this fund produces some incredibly high returns for its investors with monthly distributions because the fund can charge high interest rates to these companies borrowing the capital. Additionally, the fund can collateralize each loan many times over because the people who own these companies have no other options for getting capital, and they would rather pay a high interest rate with collateral than give up equity in their company. They'll do what they need to do to scale their company. It presents a perfect storm for an investor in a unique season of abnormally high returns in a high-growth sector. Eventually, interest rates will drop down to normal levels once this industry is federally legal.

Some of the states that have legalized cannabis restrict the number of licenses they'll give out, so these licenses become more valuable. You might have one company that has a $3 to $5 million loan, but they've pledged their license as collateral. That single license will sell anywhere from $10 to $60 million. Owners of these companies will often personally guarantee these loans and even set up a third-party escrow account where they pledge stock to automatically convey if they default on their loan. So there's very little risk of a default, which is good for the investors.

MINDSET

The emerging cannabis, hemp, and CBD industries are one I'd been studying for a while, and I concluded that I wanted some sort of exposure to this market as long as it was legal and ethical. Because it's a relatively new space, there are still unsophisticated investors and deals available that are ideal for my strategies. Also, these industries are **uncorrelated** to the overall economy, which means it is expected to grow for many years to come even if the overall macroeconomic conditions enter into a recession. (Having **non-correlated** investments in your portfolio is important so that you have defensive positions that do well even if the stock market or your other investments go down.)

This particular investment came from my network, and the co-founders of the business are friends with my attorney. My law firm did all their subscription agreements and vetted them, so I felt very comfortable with this investment option and my strategy. Additionally, the industry as a whole has been seeing growth in the 25 percent plus range quarter after quarter, so the returns looked to be exponential. Additionally, the investment was through a fund, which helped mitigate some of the risk.

STRUCTURE

Here is the structure of the deal:

- 8 percent preferred return (actual returns are 15 percent)
- Distributions paid monthly
- Total projected **Internal Rate of Return (IRR)**: 20–30 percent
- Two-year hold on capital, but can take money out in the event of an emergency with notice

- Ability to participate in equity and warrants negotiated in certain deals
- Opportunity to co-invest on many deals outside the
fund to gain more exposure to certain companies
with even better terms.
- Ability to go public for a three to four times multiple
above and beyond the projected returns

FILTER

This investment was offering one of the highest overall
risk-adjusted returns I'd seen for a senior secured credit
fund. The investors were in the most secure position in the
investment and first in line to be repaid if anything ever
went wrong, yet they still earned a high return. Plus, each
loan was collateralized, often by five to ten times more than
the loan value. Additionally, this investment has a two-year
lockup on the principal investment. After that two-year time
frame, the principal can be returned or remain in the fund.
Most investment opportunities similar to this one have a
much longer lockup period than two years.

Because some of these ingredients are not yet federally
legal, banks aren't allowed to lend in this space, which has
created a high return for the companies that do lend in this
market. Also, these companies are highly vetted. They aren't
even considered unless they're working with one of the 600
regional and local banks in the US that allow cannabis,
hemp, or CBD companies to have a bank deposit account
with them to verify their financials.

Because these companies are highly vetted and extremely
successful, they have large amounts of collateral to pledge,
such as land, real estate, equipment, other assets, accounts
receivable, stock of membership interests, and even the
cannabis license itself. Many of these short-term loans come

with equity and other warrants that improve the deal. There is a lot of downside protection in this investment, plus strong monthly cash flow and the ability to have big upside returns.

NEGOTIATION

I negotiated a **sidecar agreement** with preferred terms for anyone in my Lifestyle Investor Mastermind who invested. A sidecar is effectively a bonus addendum or an additional agreement with special terms for an investor or group. (I discuss sidecar agreements in much more detail in Commandment 6: Find an Income Amplifier.) I also negotiated a **right of first refusal**—the ability to be the first person the fund managers ask to co-invest on the many deals they do outside the fund.

THE DEAL IN REVIEW

The Warren Buffett quote that opens this chapter perfectly sums up the concept of Reduce the Risk: Don't lose money. If you can set up an investment with my Strategy Stack, you can generally negotiate great terms and reduce the risk at the same time. Examples include earning high-interest payments with regular distributions, having a balloon payment at the end of a short note term, finding creative ways to have the borrower personally guarantee the deal, and getting paid as a vendor or advisor, too, among other strategies.

Many of my students and clients have successfully shifted their investing mindset from being equity investors to becoming cash flow investors. An equity investor is someone who risks capital for an eventual payout, but most of the time, the deals are basically zero-interest loans for an indefinite period of time, which is incredibly risky. Cash flow investing is better overall because it reduces the risk.

This next example is a perfect blueprint for reducing risk that you can use as a model in your next negotiation. It is a super-low-risk investment in which you can apply my principles, commandments, Strategy Stack, and risk reduction all together.

CANNABIS/HEMP/CBD INVESTMENT - 2024 DEAL UPDATE

2024 UPDATE SUMMARY:

- Private credit cannabis deals averaging 15 percent plus cash flow
- Projected 30 percent plus IRR once funds are fully realized
- Leveraged valuable licenses and assets for security
- Among largest investment allocations
- Compelling passive income source

I first got into the cannabis, hemp, and CBD space a few years back when a friend introduced me to an investment group. This group was run by some really sharp investors who had both a private credit fund for cannabis companies as well as an equity fund.

Given that cannabis was still in the early growth stages and companies couldn't access traditional financing, the opportunity for private credit lending at attractive interest rates was enormous. The equity side also seemed promising if we could get in early with the right companies. So, I decided to invest in both their credit and equity funds, which gave me exposure across multiple companies in the space.

Over the last few years, private credit investments have been knocking it out of the park. Despite the challenges in public markets for cannabis stocks, these private debt deals have consistently delivered over 15 percent in annual cash flow back to me and the other investors.

Many of the companies we lent to are profitable, have valuable licenses and other assets and have continued to thrive. We've even had some single off-balance sheet direct lending deals that have produced over 30 percent returns in less than twelve months.

While the upside of the equity deals is still unknown, if this performance keeps up, I expect we could see total internal rates of return in the 30 percent plus range once the funds are fully realized. For a relatively new high-growth sector that faced regulatory uncertainty, the private lending side has been a home run.

Given the outsized returns and the fact that these investments comprise a significant portion of my overall portfolio, cannabis remains one of the most attractive areas I'm focused on. I expect it to continue playing a prominent role in my holdings, given how well it has performed.

The private lending cannabis deals exemplify "Lifestyle First" investing. The hands-off debt structure requires no time from me operationally. I simply collect my 15 percent plus annual cash flow returns and am projected to see total IRRs around 30 percent plus over time. This passive income gets generated predictably without ongoing active involvement.

KEY INSIGHTS:

- Private credit cannabis deals have consistently delivered 15 percent plus cash flow.
- Private lending proved more resilient than public equity cannabis investing.

- Valuable licenses provided security on debt investments.
- Profitable companies and valuable licenses provided security on debt investments.
- Expected 30 percent plus overall IRR once funds are fully realized.
- Cannabis remains a top investment focus, given strong returns.

EXAMPLE: AMERICAN AIRLINES FORMER HEADQUARTERS

I had an opportunity to invest in American Airlines' former headquarters in Dallas, Texas, through a commercial real estate company in Austin which I have made several investments with. The former headquarters is a premium-grade, high-end campus comprising three buildings totaling 1,388,727 square feet, along with two structured parking garages. Its estimated construction cost in the late 1980s of almost $490 million can be contrasted with today's replacement value of over $400 million. American Airlines outgrew these headquarters and elected to build a new two million square foot campus. The sale included a lease-back of two of the three buildings for six months while construction finished on their new campus, reducing the investor's risk of holding costs for the duration.

While the building was fully marketed, there were few value-add office operators willing to take on the heavy lift associated with re-stabilizing large corporate campuses. The general partner was able to negotiate a discounted purchase price of $57 per square foot—12 percent of replacement cost. The low basis afforded the general partner the ability to offer compelling lease terms compared to market rates.

During due diligence prior to closing, the asset was soft marketed to find premier tenants that are some of the largest and most well-respected companies in the US. Because very few large commercial block spaces were available in the entire Dallas-Fort Worth market for tenants seeking space in excess of 200,000 square feet, the deal was even more attractive. The site had not just one but three buildings that could meet those prospective tenants' needs. This pre-closing strategy allowed the operator to sign a lease within six months of closing for one of the three buildings, reducing the lease-up risk on the remaining two buildings.

MINDSET

I had the opportunity to buy a high-end Class A campus of three buildings in one of the strongest markets in the US for just $72,950,000, which was an extremely discounted rate. These buildings are what Fortune 100 companies, government agencies, and high-level security clearance defense contractors use as their headquarters. The opportunity was unique to participating investors because of the market timing and closing in April during the 2020 stay-at-home orders. Several other factors helped me acquire this asset quickly and at a great price.

STRUCTURE

Here is the structure of the deal:

- 10 percent preferred return
- Return of capital projected to be two years or less
- Projected return of 3.5–4.5 times the initial investment
- Investment projected a four- to five-year time frame (I was confident with the demand and pricing, it would be much shorter)
- A $250,000 investment was estimated to return between $875,000 and $1,125,000 in 4–5 years

FILTER

This property was a top-quality asset, in one of the best markets in the US, at a great price, and with plenty of opportunity to add value and increase profit. The buildings had qualities that made them attractive to tenants that required security clearance, which increased lease terms and real estate values. Big-name tenants were found with government backing before the deal was completed.

The general partner has a great reputation and over six hundred individual investors that have never lost money in over twenty-eight years of investing in real estate with this company. The partner also has a historical **internal rate of return (IRR)** of 32 percent with an average hold time of just over four years, with investor principal typically being paid back in one to two years.

NEGOTIATION

During due diligence prior to closing, the general partner immediately began negotiating with two of the largest government defense manufacturers and contractors, one of the largest hospital groups and healthcare systems with dozens of offices, one of Silicon Valley's largest companies, and one of the largest e-commerce companies in the world to rent the available space. This move reduced my risk even more. In addition, the general partner offered all new investors a **put option** that allowed me (and all of the other investors I brought into the deal) to get back all of the amount invested within thirty days—at any time, for any reason, and with no expiration of the put option for the duration of the investment.

The founder and president of the commercial real estate company personally guaranteed the investor put option with his own assets, so even if this investment failed, he'd still own the liability and pay investors with his own money. I was also able to verify that he had the liquid net worth to be able to cover 100 percent of the put options if all investors redeemed their put options at the same time.

THE DEAL IN REVIEW

If this were an ordinary deal with an ordinary investment group, the group would probably collect some money, pay some interest, and get their money back in five to ten years. For this deal, however, the general partner structured it so investors would get their initial investment back in one to two years and have a 400 percent plus return on their investment. Also, investors had put the option in place to get money back at any time if there was anything about the deal or timeline that they didn't like.

What many people forget is that there are thousands of ways to negotiate a deal, so you don't violate Warren Buffett's Rule No. 1 and Rule No. 2. When you follow the principles and commandments and add as many elements in my *Strategy Stack* as possible, you are positioned well not to lose money.

AMERICAN AIRLINES HEADQUARTERS - 2024 DEAL UPDATE

2024 UPDATE SUMMARY:

- Acquired Class A buildings at deep discount to replacement cost
- Experienced two-plus-year COVID delays, but fundamentals still strong
- In final stages of major new leases
- Projects expected to stabilize by 2024
- Strong returns expected despite extended timeline

A few years back, I invested in the three massive headquarters buildings in Dallas, Texas. American Airlines had built these iconic headquarters but then outgrew them and moved into a giant new modern campus.

These buildings were architectural masterpieces—Class A trophies spanning over 1.3 million square feet in total. Since they were no longer of any use to the company that built them, it gave us the chance to scoop them up for a small fraction of their replacement value, around $57 per square foot.

The opportunity was incredible, given the buildings' premier quality and location in the thriving Dallas market. The strategy was to lease to new corporate tenants wanting amenitized space at affordable rates.

The plan was to have the buildings re-tenanted within three years or so. But no one could have predicted what came next—the COVID-19 pandemic.

Everyone was shocked when COVID caused a two-plus-year delay. Companies went remote, and commercial office demand plummeted. Despite headwinds, momentum resumed with major leases to marquee tenants. The timeline extended but projected stabilization by 2024 bodes well for returns.

Recently, the delays have started paying off. A major lease was executed with Bell Helicopter for several floors of one building. Another building is in final negotiations with a huge defense contractor. Despite COVID, tremendous momentum has begun again.

While the timeline extended, the fundamentals remain strong. Given the extremely attractive basis we acquired the buildings for, I'm confident this project will deliver excellent returns to all the investors. The buildings are projected to stabilize by late 2024, and we expect to exit within a few years after that.

The risk on this deal was reduced substantially by acquiring iconic Class A buildings at a mere fraction of replacement cost. The world-class assets in a thriving market, scooped up for pennies on the dollar, significantly lowered chances of issues arising from unexpected COVID delays. Even external shocks couldn't undermine such an attractively priced portfolio in an incredibly resilient area.

KEY INSIGHTS:

- Unforeseen external events like COVID do happen, which can significantly delay timelines.
- Quality assets in strong markets will attract tenants eventually.
- Maintaining conviction amid uncertainty is key.
- The low basis acquired gives flexibility to deliver returns over a longer hold period.

COMMANDMENT 3: FIND INVISIBLE DEALS

The sky is filled with stars, invisible by day.

—Henry Wadsworth Longfellow

I t seems like everyone is looking for a sure thing in an investment, a leg up, a way to find free money—usually through a stock tip or an insider tip that's hopefully legal. But it's absolutely the wrong way to think when you're looking for an invisible deal. The best way to find an invisible deal, instead, is to find a distressed business that's unprofitable because it hasn't been able to get rid of dead weight, baggage, or a part of the business that's obsolete. That invisible deal is only invisible to insiders who've been looking at the business the same way (or the wrong way) for too long.

Recently, I had an opportunity in my investor network to buy Dress Barn®, an extremely recognizable, publicly traded retail brand business that had been suffering for years. The big opportunity was a result of their flourishing online presence, which had impressive sales. They had warehousing, manufacturing, packaging, marketing, and stable teams, but the business was floundering significantly due to brick-and-mortar retail dragging down their margins and profits.

Dress Barn's parent company, Ascena Retail Group, is the largest specialty retailer for women and girls in the US. Even though they once owned several well-known retail brands, they were focused on physical retail presence and weren't innovating with the times and growing their e-commerce presence. At the time of the deal, they were on the brink of bankruptcy and eventually did file for Chapter 11 bankruptcy protection.

Through my investor network, I negotiated an amazing invisible deal that even industry insiders didn't know was happening until the deal was done. It consisted of breaking apart the online from the brick-and-mortar retail and acquiring the brand. I was able to negotiate amazing terms for myself and a group of other investors I helped assemble.

The final deal allowed us to take over the brand and all intellectual property, decide how much inventory we wanted to buy at a discount, establish new relationships for inventory, continue relationships with the best suppliers, get rid of all liabilities and lease commitments, and access the entire customer database (nearly eight million customers) and all the buying behavior and customer data.

The prior management had emotional attachments to the old business and the way things had been done for so long that they'd become myopic. Their loyalties and habits prevented them from cutting back and seeing the opportunity. This simple but invisible deal was quite easy to manage. We got rid of the dead weight and focused on the new, profitable money.

One important fact that anyone going through a downturn needs to understand is that it's better to be smaller and highly profitable than huge and unprofitable. We investors knew it. We hired thirty of their best employees of the nine thousand they had working for them at the time.

The new ownership group was filled with really smart, experienced online marketers who knew how to take the online brand and multiply the traffic and income through leverage, advice, and predictable growth. And because I strategically choose my investors and partners with specialized knowledge, we hold an added unfair advantage that we bring to every deal.

As an outside investor, one thing I've learned that drives me is to make sure I have a significant amount of consistent **"deal flow."** By seeing hundreds or even thousands of deals a year, I'm able to scrape the cream off the top. And because I've built a substantial network of investors and private clients who want access to high-quality, low-risk deals, together we have a secret, unfair advantage in practically every market and industry.

AGGREGATED BENEFITS

I present dozens of deals inside my Lifestyle Investor Mastermind that are vetted and compared against hundreds of other potential opportunities, and we only invest in the ones with the lowest risk and highest rate of return—with an added focus on a return of the principal investment in the shortest period of time.

Here are the aggregated benefits to the investors that we were able to negotiate in these deals:

1. **Monthly Cash Flow:** With an investment as low as $50,000, each investor receives a monthly cash flow of 20 percent interest, which is $833 per month on a $50,000 investment.

2. **Kicker**: Investors receive a **cash bonus** of up to 20 percent of their investment, varying based on the size of their investment paid at the end of the note term.

3. **Principal**: At the end of either a one-year, two-year, or three-year note term, all the investors receive 100 percent of their investment capital back.

4. **Free Equity:** In this case, the equity kicker is called a kicker because it's free. Most of the time, investments are in straight equity, so each $50,000 equals a certain amount of equity. Principal is repaid, plus equity of up to 3 percent per million is gained, depending on the particular deal (0.3 percent per $100,000). So, an investor who puts in $250,000 receives 0.75 percent equity for free.

Let me break this deal down for you so you can see what would happen over the course of two years if you were one of the investors. To make the math easy, let's say you invest $1 million into the deal (even though the minimum investment was $50,000).

Each month, you would receive a dividend check of $16,666.67, which will total $200,000 annually ($400,000 over a period of two years). At the end of two years, your money is entirely out of the deal. There's no more risk, but you'll still receive an additional 20 percent cash bonus, or

$200,000. You'll also receive equity in the form of founders' shares representing 3 percent of the business—without paying an extra penny. Assuming the business would be acquired for $100 million five years from now, that equity represents $3 million in *additional* profit (plus 3 percent of the dividends every year until the business is sold or if it chooses to distribute rather than reinvest the profit for growth to create a larger exit price).

Additionally, if something would go wrong with the deal, you've negotiated the first lien on the intellectual property as collateral, which is a strong position, especially since the brand was bought for pennies on the dollar. The brand and intellectual property would be really easy to sell and at least get what you paid for the brand, if not considerably more. Also, being in a debt position rather than an equity position would mean you would get paid back first before anyone else, so your risk is much lower than if you had invested directly into equity.

Making $600,000 on a $1 million investment over a period of two years with the opportunity to potentially make an additional $3 million *with no added risk*—since it's all "house money" at this point because you have over 100 percent of your money back—*seems* like a pretty good deal to me. And remember, this is a retail brand that most people would think is on its way to the graveyard. But, in reality, it's scaling rapidly through pure e-commerce versus the business being hamstrung by its existing brick-and-mortar operations. *That's* what I call an invisible deal.

I love doing what I do. At any given time, I have ten to thirty deals in my mastermind, where we vet these deals together after I have done a preliminary round of vetting myself. When I'm working with my Lions, I get to go out and find amazing deals like this one, negotiate incredibly lucrative terms, and then bring them into opportunities that are much better than deals most people invest in that typically only align with one of my commandments for investing. As the Mastermind has grown, I'm now getting access to deals members are bringing to the table. Truly invisible deals!

TWO GUIDING PRINCIPLES OF INVISIBLE DEALS

Here are two guiding principles that I look for in finding invisible deals.

1. Pay attention to emerging markets or unseen opportunities outside the mainstream.

This principle can be applied to new technological innovations or companies currently in a reinvention phase. I also like new technology that is superior to whatever is currently the status quo and will disrupt and transform the way an industry operates moving forward.

Specifically, in real estate, I like to gain access to off-market opportunities from the many relationships I already have in the space. For example, the rise of single-family homes or single-family rentals wasn't even an asset class a little over a decade ago. Hearing about it and being on the cutting edge of investing in that asset class has paid huge returns for investments I've made.

2. Pay attention to what's going on with trends in the economy: what's strong and what's not.

Be up to date on shifts taking place, like e-commerce, for example, which has become one of the leading industries in the world. Also, industrial distribution centers are going to be more in demand because businesses need more space to store their inventory and get it closer to the customer. The most expensive cost of getting their product to the customers is that last mile. If you pay attention to what's going on in the world, you can identify many more new trends emerging, such as these.

For example, in 2022, the US government passed the CHIPS and Science Act into law, which includes $52 billion to incentivize semiconductor manufacturing. These chips power everything from smartphones to cars, computers, and artificial intelligence systems. Companies like Intel, Micron, and Taiwan Semiconductor Manufacturing Company have all announced plans to build new semiconductor factories.

I'll share more about my approach to investing in artificial intelligence at the end of this chapter.

INVISIBLE DEAL CATEGORIES

Here's a list of the several categories of invisible deals I've seen that investors are likely to participate in because these investments resonate with them. I frequently get involved in investments like these through syndicated deals, or I create investment opportunities and assemble investor groups from my Lifestyle Investor Mastermind.

Invisible Deals Smart Investors Seek

- Exclusivity deals—closed deals you must be personally recommended into
- Pay-to-play deals—deals that you only have access to because of previous investments or you have paid some sort of a fee to allow you to take part
- **Off-market** deals—Investments that have not been advertised publicly for sale, meaning there is often no competition or much less competition to buy these assets

---

- Institutional deals—investments that are typically reserved for institutional investors, but with the right connections, can be made available to an individual investor or group
- Unconventional investment opportunities—terms, structures, and industries that are uncommon and often overlooked
- Government incentives, which include government contracts with preferential terms and grants that act as extra investment dollars that aren't added to the capitalization table, so investors aren't diluted
- Emerging markets—markets that are on an uptick that may not be common knowledge
- New frontiers—new ideas or industries that will likely become mainstream in the future
- Trend focused opportunities—strong investments based on the current economic climate and market trends
- Disruptive opportunities—companies or industries that challenge the status quo and create more value than what's currently available
- Deal flow networks—massive groups of investors who see hundreds or thousands of deals a year
- "Ecosystems"—smaller groups of sophisticated and experienced investors who love sharing what they have learned and the investments they are making

Following is an example of an invisible deal and the application of my principles and commandments to it.

EXAMPLE: STELLAR

Stellar is a single-family home maintenance company in the home rental space for large institutional owners such as REITS, private equity groups, and large property management groups. This company has its own proprietary software, which helps differentiate it from everyone else in the industry.

MINDSET

I listen to many podcasts, and one of my favorites is "How I Built This." It stimulates my thinking and causes me to think deeply about entrepreneurial endeavors. I also network with a lot of successful business owners who scale businesses quickly and produce strong profits. Additionally, one of my goals is to keep an eye out for emerging markets and consumer trends that might have huge opportunities associated with them.

At the time of this deal, the single-family home rental space was one of the fastest-growing markets in real estate, and the demand for reliable maintenance for the largest acquirers of single-family homes was a true need that no company had successfully scaled to meet. The obvious unmet need meant a big opportunity was available to get involved in this industry and at least get a piece of the action and also, on a larger level, potentially disrupt the way maintenance was being performed at scale.

STRUCTURE

One of my investments with Stellar was to provide them with a credit line because they couldn't do so themselves. My two partners in this deal are brilliant and hardworking people with a tremendous vision for the future; however, one had bad credit and couldn't get a loan, and the other had no credit and couldn't get a loan. I didn't have to invest any money directly into this business except to set up a revolving line of credit for them, one that would be repaid each month when the balance was due.

I did some advising on this business and helped with hiring, training, developing teams, and creating recruiting protocols, among other things. Plus, I was able to leverage my network to offer connections that would help Stellar scale much quicker. In the early years, I also helped make sure Stellar had the proper insurance in place to protect against anything that could have a huge negative impact on the company.

FILTER

I liked the risk profile on this investment because my down-side risk was minimal, and the potential for an exponential return was very strong. The most I could lose was my max line of credit, which I had capped at an amount I was comfortable losing; however, if this investment worked out as I thought, the returns would be exponential. I also like investments where I have strong operating partners, and in this case, two very strong operators were in place who I knew had impeccable work ethic.

NEGOTIATION

This investment was unique because rather than being an equal one-third partner, as the operating partners originally proposed, I negotiated my equity position down to just 20 percent. I knew I wasn't going to work as much or as hard as my partners, and that level fit my lifestyle investing principles. I wanted to protect my time and make sure this business opportunity didn't have a negative impact on my family, which is always my top priority.

THE DEAL IN REVIEW

The two partners were very excited about my proposal to take less equity, and that was a huge benefit because I didn't feel like I had to commit as many hours as they did. I acted primarily as a **capital partner** at first and then helped build many of the systems they currently have in place. I was then able to step away again indefinitely and trust that the company was in good hands.

This investment was a home run. The company performed well enough early on that I was able to take distributions that totaled more than my risk exposure of the maximum line of credit I was responsible for to ensure I never lost any money on the deal. It ended up being a multi-million-dollar deal, and the company continues to grow today.

Stellar has become an industry leader in the single-family home rental space. The largest Texas Venture Capital firm, S3 Ventures, based out of Austin, along with Brick and Mortar Ventures, based out of San Francisco, co-led the **Series A** round with a $10 million investment—giving Stellar a post-money valuation of $43 million. In 2022, Stellar raised a $20 million Series B round led by Weatherford Capital to grow its operations even further.

STELLAR - 2024 DEAL UPDATE

2024 UPDATE SUMMARY:

- Provided credit facility to enable small companies to scale
- Grew into a large tech-enabled services firm
- Multiple funding rounds increased valuation exponentially
- Proprietary software was a competitive advantage
- Being reliant on large clients poses risks

Several years ago, I co-founded a property maintenance company alongside two partners. We saw a major opportunity given the booming rental home market. Though profitable, we couldn't get traditional financing to scale quickly on our own credit, so I provided an initial revolving credit facility.

I believed this maintenance company had huge potential given the booming rental home market and their proprietary software that differentiated them from competitors. My partners were extremely hard-working, and I offered strategic advice to help them expand.

Since then, this company has rebranded and absolutely exploded in growth. They've raised both Series A and Series B venture capital rounds from tier-one firms like S3 Ventures and Navigate Ventures.

This propelled their valuation to over $90 million and took them from a services business to a technology-enabled company. Their software and data analytics capabilities proved pivotal in driving this transformation.

Under the guidance of institutional VC investors, they've professionalized operations and expanded nationally. Their tech emphasis also opened up partnerships with companies they previously just serviced.

The speed of their rise has surprised even me. However, growing so fast and being so dependent on large customer contracts puts them at risk if those relationships change. Overall though, Stellar exemplifies how technology can reshape and revalorize traditional businesses.

Stellar exemplifies "Finding Invisible Deals." I provided alternative financing to allow a small company with proprietary technology to scale. This enabled them to transition into a large tech-enabled services firm that top VC investors now see tremendous upside in.

KEY INSIGHTS:

- Pivoting into a tech-enabled model led to exponentially higher valuation.
- Prestigious VC investors provided operational improvements and expertise.
- Proprietary software strengthened competitive positioning.
- Risks being overly reliant on a handful of big customer contracts.

2024 UPDATE: AI GROWTH INVESTING - MAXIMIZING RETURNS IN AN ERA OF INTELLIGENT MACHINES

Over the last decade, I've become convinced that artificial intelligence can revolutionize and reconfigure how businesses operate and pave the path to the creation of trillions of dollars in new wealth. Since *The Lifestyle Investor* was originally published, AI has exploded onto the scene.

The AI market is projected to reach $407 billion by 2027, a significant increase from its estimated $86.9 billion revenue in 2022. This astounding five-year projection underscores the vast potential of AI over the next decade.[2]

Of course, new technology also brings significant uncertainties and risks. Investing in unproven startups carries the danger of betting on the wrong horse, as many AI companies will inevitably fail or run out of cash. That's why I've developed a balanced strategy to gain exposure to AI's growth while mitigating risks in a way that follows my commandments and principles.

At the heart of my approach is a clear, deliberate strategy: I invest in both big industry leaders and smaller, agile newcomers. This strategy is like having one foot in a stable place with established leaders and the other foot ready to adapt and benefit from nimble, innovative startups. It helps me manage risk while maximizing potential rewards at different stages of business growth.

I've invested in the biggest three AI companies and also in smaller AI startups. This way, I'm ready to benefit from both established giants and innovative newcomers.

---

[2] Katherine Haan, "24 Top AI Statistics and Trends in 2024," Forbes.com, April 25, 2023, https://www.forbes.com/advisor/business/ai-statistics/

Some of these smaller startups are likely to be bought by big companies, including the ones in my portfolio.

For example, I invested early in OpenAI® as a leading natural language pioneer and Anthropic for its human-aligned AI systems. I've also invested in the Canadian AI company Cohere®. This gives me exposure as they compete for market share at the top of the food chain. I also backed smaller companies like a leading open-source company working on creative AI applications and another that is applying AI to data labeling for companies like Nvidia, Samsung, and the US Army and Air Force.

My approach to AI investing isn't just about making big bets on what companies and industries will benefit most from the technology in the next few years. It's about thoughtfully moving through the implications of AI while being smart about managing my risks as an investor based on the growth cycles of my portfolio businesses. (I'll share more about this below as I break down how I think about venture capital investing.)

It's easy to get distracted from your own investment principles when a technology is in a hype cycle, as AI has been. Did you know that total spending on AI systems was forecasted to reach $97.9 billion in 2023, up from $37.5 billion in 2019? From 2018 to 2023, the AI sector was predicted to grow at an annualized rate of 28.4 percent.[3] This highlights the near-term momentum in AI investments, but to me, it also shows the importance of forward-thinking investors who can see beyond this wave and anticipate the inevitable dips, spikes, and corrections.

---

[3]   Jeremy Bowman, "Investing in AI Stocks," *The Motley Fool*, updated November 25, 2023, https://www.fool.com/investing/stock-market/market-sectors/information-technology/ai-stocks/.

I'm convinced AI represents a step change in innovation that will influence the future of almost everything we do. By carefully selecting investments, I'm positioned to see extraordinary returns.

That's the art of spotting outliers early. I spend time researching demographic changes, consumer preferences, and other factors that signal potential trends. Then, I analyze if a niche today aligns with mainstream movements ahead.

For example, AI exploded as processors advanced exponentially. And as Silicon Valley honed the technology, I identified leaders plus newcomers with differentiation. This balances established giants with next-gen upstarts.

Another seismic shift is the great wealth transfer from baby boomers to millennials, estimated at over $100 trillion. So I examine what millennials value. How do their habits and preferences differ? Companies catering to these changing dynamics will ride an economic wave.

From niche-to-mainstream trends to demographic/generational shifts, I concentrate capital where outsized growth should follow. This systematic approach to identifying future outliers, ones that will lead the change in new business models, core systems, and everyday processes, is crucial for lifestyle investing.

WAYS TO RIDE THE AI WAVE

Now that you've learned how I developed a balanced investing approach to capitalize on the rise of AI while mitigating risks, it's time for you to create (or optimize) yours. Consider these strategic points below and use them to craft your own AI investing principles.

- **Investigate AI's Potential:** Recognize that AI represents a significant wave of innovation with the power to transform industries and generate vast wealth. Study it so you can discern marketing hype from reality.

- **Diversify Investments:** Instead of concentrating on just a few AI startups, diversify your investments. This approach spreads risk and increases the potential for returns.

- **Big and Small:** Consider both established industry leaders and agile newcomers. Investing in big companies and smaller startups offers a balanced strategy, combining stability and innovation.

- **Acquisition Potential:** Promising AI startups may be acquired by larger companies earlier than in other tech sectors as large companies fight for market dominance in an exploding market. Position yourself to benefit from these opportunities.

- **Focused Sectors:** Invest in AI sub-sectors where a region leads globally. In the US, areas like natural language processing have strong long-term potential.

- **Early Stage Access:** Gain access to promising startups by partnering with angel groups and incubator programs, allowing you to invest at an early stage.

- **Long-Term Perspective:** Aim for a long-term investment horizon, holding AI investments for five to ten years to maximize potential returns and ride the inevitable early corrections and dips.

- **US Dominance:** With the passage of the 2022 CHIPS and Science Act, the US is investing $52 billion to strengthen AI-adjacent sectors like semiconductor and electronics manufacturing. Top AI players like OpenAI and Anthropic are based in the US, and will likely benefit from this legislation and the commercial investment it catalyzes.

- **Risk Mitigation:** In addition to a well-balanced portfolio approach, keep your eyes open for regulation and legal precedents in the AI space that may affect how companies deploy AI locally and globally. The "Wild West" innovation environment we're seeing now won't last forever.

As always, do your own research, follow your investment principles, and conduct thorough due diligence on each AI investment—no matter how exciting or promising it sounds. This is not the time to outsource your critical thinking.

COMMANDMENT 4: GET THE PRINCIPAL BACK QUICKLY

It isn't sufficient just to want. You've got to ask yourself what you are going to do to get the things you want.

—Franklin D. Roosevelt

Imagine if you could buy a house for $500,000, get all of your money back in two years, and be able to reinvest that money into another house while still benefiting from the equity from the previous house. Now imagine continuing that cycle. It'd be like compound interest on steroids.

What if you could do all of it without the complexities of owning, buying, and selling each of the homes? I've already talked about how much I love real estate, but when you are the owner, a lot of issues arise that you need to deal with. What I'm going to share with you right now is a powerful strategy that'll allow you to have all the benefits without the risk, and all in a short period of time without all the work involved.

Let me describe a perfect deal. You invest money into this deal, you get all your money out in less than two years, and you retain equity so that when the asset is sold, you make additional money, generate cash flow during the holding period, and have the ability to take tax deductions for an extra kicker (or free money). I love free money. How about you?

The big challenge a traditional investor has versus a Lifestyle Investor is the complexity of building and scaling a team. It's easy to get into a circumstance where the cost of a team, all the overhead, and your time can exceed the profit you'll make and the risk you have to take.

QUICK PRINCIPAL BACK DEALS

Let me illustrate how a **Quick Principal Back** deal works and why you can create all the benefits I just described with very little risk. The goal of this strategy and the commandment is to get your money back within one to three years rather than five to ten, as with most investments.

Let's say you are able to invest $100,000 in a property worth $15 million but purchased below market value for just $12.75 million due to it being a private off-market deal. If anything goes wrong with the investment, you have a strong likelihood of not losing money because of the discounted purchase price. In the first year, you receive a 10 percent preferred return on your money, paid quarterly—that's $2,500 per quarter and $10,000 per year. In this particular deal, at the end of a year and a half (if not sooner), you get all of your $100,000 principal back.

It gets better. A return of principal is not taxable—you're only paying taxes on the $10,000. But not really. Because this deal is a real estate investment, you receive accelerated depreciation, which allows you to show a loss on your taxes. You also receive equity in this particular investment, which in this case, amounts to 0.75 percent.

I actually made this investment one year ago, and the property is already worth a little over $21 million due to rehabbing the property, filling vacancies, and raising rents to market rates. So, my 0.75 percent is worth $158,250 in equity.

I hear all the time that it's unreasonable to expect a fast overall return on investment and a quick return of principal, so it's not what most people look for. It doesn't even register to them that there could be a better way to invest than just investing in a traditional real estate deal that takes a long time to see a return on their investment. Also, in those deals, their money is going to be locked up for an extended period of time.

Another thing I often hear is, "I hope that I see it in this decade," or "I may never see it again, but this *seems* like a good investment." That thinking perpetuates the myths that reflect a lack of education about the options that actually exist. Yes, there are plenty of investments where you can invest now and may never see that principal again; and there are plenty that may take a decade or longer to see the principal because you have to wait until a company has some sort of a **liquidity event** (if you're investing directly or for equity). The truth is, several other ways exist to invest where you can still have equity while receiving cash flow now.

My clients and I are in several deals right now that return our principal investments at the one-year mark. Some are real estate deals, and some are debt deals. Some of them are unique structures investing in operating companies. A few of them are in the final month or two of the term before the principal is paid back in full. Other deals have already paid back the principal in full, so now we have no risk at all in the deal and are just participating in the upside. Investments structured this way are some of my favorite investments. They fit the model of a Lifestyle Investor.

THE VELOCITY OF MONEY

Something that's really important to me is allowing money to move—the velocity of money. Two of my commandments specifically address it. Commandment 4, "Get Principal Back Quickly," and Commandment 5, "Create Cash Flow Immediately," are important because both of those criteria create velocity of money. You can take your cash flow payments that come in on a monthly or quarterly basis and reinvest them. You can get your principal back and reinvest it.

Ideally, whenever you invest principal in the first place, you want to try to get some form of equity in return. It allows a portion of your investment to continue to compound over time, and then you get to participate in the upside, even when you have all of your initial investment out of the deal. So, you have "house money" that continues to compound on an ongoing basis. In other words, you have a tremendous amount of upside in your investments but zero risk once your principal is out. You know this. We've already covered it.

Let's take the return of principal investment one step further to really see the impact on the velocity of money. The way most people invest is in long-term deals where money is either locked up, and they can't touch it, or they know they aren't supposed to touch it for more than a decade at a time. Examples include stock market investing through both retirement accounts and buy-and-hold strategies for the long term, venture capital funds, new real estate developments that don't have cash flow and may never have cash flow, and equity investments that won't produce a return for decades. In each of these scenarios, your money is not being fully utilized; it's just sitting idle. You hope you get a good return, but you won't know for a while.

Instead of having money tied up for ten years and waiting to see how strong the return is, I'd rather take that same money and invest it in five or more deals with one-year and two-year terms that produce cash flow immediately and can buy me some sort of equity position, so I have upside in several deals. Let's say I structure each of the five investments to get the principal back within two years. Doing so allows me to invest in five different opportunities during the ten years most people have their money tied up.

Notice the outcomes, especially as they relate to velocity of money. I have earned cash flow the entire time, I have de-risked the investment because I have my principal out of the deal, and I have been able to get some equity even though all my money is out. On top of all of that, I can participate in any big exits over the long haul. What's more, I've used the same strategy with the same money for all five deals since I'm reinvesting the same principal that is returned to me on each investment.

Taking the short-term and long-term potential into account, I am confident that my return on those five investments is going to significantly outperform the return of a single investment held over that same ten-year period. In the one-investment approach, all eggs are in one basket. In my approach, I am able to compound my income and returns because I put that money to use again and again.

Now, let's look back on the Dress Barn deal from the previous chapter. The business was sold in a fire sale, more of a liquidation event. The deal was structured around a one-year note paying a 20 percent interest with a monthly distribution. At the one-year mark, a balloon payment took effect for the return of the principal. This deal perfectly illustrates how you can earn a great return on a company that provides strong monthly cash flow; get your full investment back in a year; maintain long-term equity; and then reinvest that same capital in another deal to do it all over again.

This next example also perfectly illustrates these points and explains how you can get your principal out of an investment quickly and repurpose it.

EXAMPLE: PRIVATE MULTIFAMILY SYNDICATION

I have invested in many multifamily private syndications through the years with various operators. One investment syndication, in particular, has 2,600 apartment units in several states, $39.6 million in capital under management, $225 million in assets under management, 427 total loans, and over $51 million in funded loans. Investing in a private syndication that has a strong track record and strong operators local to that market is an easy way to invest in real estate without the complexities of traditional ownership. If you're interested in learning more about investing in syndications, be sure to watch a free training I did with franchising specialist Erik Van Horn at *LifestyleInvestor.com/Gift*.

MINDSET

Always meet the influencers who are in the middle of maximum deal flow. Finding the right opportunity and taking the time to meet in person is critical to me in my research and decision-making process regarding new investments.

I had just attended an investment conference, met many smart investors, and made it a point to connect with many of the investors and syndicators who spoke during the event. I'm proactive about meeting anyone who I think would be a great fit for my network or who I'm just interested in getting to know better and learning what they specialize in. I tracked down this syndicator after he spoke, developed a relationship with him, learned his areas of expertise, and did some research to figure out if a deal with him would be a good fit for me.

STRUCTURE

Here is the structure for this deal:

- 10 percent preferred return
- Quarterly distributions
- Return of principal in 1.5 years (I had previous deals where my principal was returned in just one year)
- Refinance proceeds at that 1.5-year mark **pro-rata** to the investment (all tax-free because of how it is coded)
- Equity payment each year in perpetuity for the percentage of equity owned
- Equity proceeds if the property is ever sold
- Long-term appreciation
- Depreciation passed on to investors
- Annualized return of 41.35 percent in 1.5 years

As I reviewed this deal related to my desire to get my principal back quickly, I knew this particular investment was a solid addition to my portfolio because of the associated great return yet low-risk profile.

FILTER

The secret to learning how to filter is to spend your time around smart investors who are actively making and not losing money and in the midst of a large volume of deal flow. This particular investment was in a strong market. It was a value-add project, which in this deal meant that the operators were going to take an existing property that was already performing well, improve it, and be able to charge higher rent.

Occupancy was already over 90 percent, so demand was strong and in a market without much competition. I also liked the fact that I would get my principal back quickly and still have equity in the investment for the long term.

NEGOTIATION

Private multifamily syndication deals are often difficult to get into, so I worked hard to move myself to the front of the line by developing relationships with the best general partners and operators to have access to their exclusive deals. My relationships allowed me an opportunity to invest before the general public and bring some of my friends into the deal as well.

I had already developed a healthy relationship with this particular syndicator (and many other syndicators as well) by offering massive value above just investing. Because of that relationship, my network and I had earned the opportunity to invest in all future syndications before they were offered to any other investors. It was a massive perk for my network and me. I also negotiated preferred terms for my group, something I routinely do for many other investments.

THE DEAL IN REVIEW

In this particular real estate deal, I received a preferred return of 10 percent paid quarterly until my principal was returned with a target of less than eighteen months (it ended up being close to a year). Once the property was refinanced, my principal returned, and I made my pro-rata percentage of the proceeds of that refinance tax-free. Also, even when my principal was returned along with an over 41 percent return, I still had long-term equity in the deal. In fact, I'm going to have equity into perpetuity because this group likes to buy and hold, so I'm getting the best of all worlds.

I have equity I didn't have to pay for that will continue to appreciate, and I got my principal investment back quickly. More importantly, I'm getting that equity without locking my money up and with some cash flow today. At some point, if they do decide to sell, I will make my pro-rata percentage on the sale as well.

PRIVATE MULTIFAMILY SYNDICATION - 2024 DEAL UPDATE

2024 UPDATE SUMMARY:

- Executed business plan and refinanced quickly to return principal
- Many syndicators used risky bridge/variable rate loans
- Vetting debt terms helps reduce downside risks
- Working with experienced general partners is key

Real estate syndications allow investors to participate in large commercial properties that would normally be inaccessible. I've invested in a number of great multifamily syndications run by top-tier general partners.

One syndication I invested in owned a portfolio of apartment communities across several states totaling around 2,600 units. The business plan was solid, and the markets had strong tenant demand.

Within eighteen months, they successfully executed their value-add business plan and refinanced the portfolio. This enabled them to return my entire principal investment plus deliver an annualized return exceeding 40 percent over that short hold period.

While this particular syndication excelled, others have faced challenges in the current rising interest rate environment. Many syndicators relied too heavily on short-term bridge loans or variable-rate debt.

As their loans expire and need to be refinanced, they are unable to find attractive financing, causing deals to unravel. Thankfully, I steered clear of deals using those risky loan structures.

A decade ago, I had friends aggressively pursuing syndication deals using short-term bridge loans and variable-rate debt structures. They implored me to pursue the same high-upside strategies.

In the bull market of the last decade, those risky structures paid off handsomely for them. However, I maintained the discipline to invest only in deals using fixed-rate, long-term financing. Maybe I sacrificed some return, but I also avoided calamity when markets shifted.

As expected, when their bridge loans expired, the turbulence of rising interest rates detonated those deals. They faced disastrous outcomes—some experienced total losses, some are marginally surviving after years of being locked up. Unlike them, my approach insulated me from any blow-up risk.

My criteria allows me to earn consistent, healthy returns across economic cycles without threat of loss. Some call that boring. I call that sustainable and critical for enduring turbulent times. I have conviction that rigorous analysis and finding the right partners means no regrets in any decade.

The market conditions underscore the importance of working with general partners who have experience across economic cycles and understand financing. Taking the time to understand the debt terms can help prevent nasty surprises and preserve your investment.

A key focus in any syndication is "Getting My Principal Back Quickly." I target sponsors able to execute business plans and refinance within twelve to eighteen months to return capital, so it can be redeployed sooner. Anything longer, and I'd rather invest in a fund for diversification.

Even though these types of partners are scarce nowadays, it's worth the diligence to find them. The rewards can be tremendous when you land partners capable of navigating turbulence and delivering solid executable deals. Maintain conviction during uncertain times—with rigorous analysis, you can find the right teams.

KEY INSIGHTS:

- Many syndicators used risky variable-rate loans or short-term bridge loans.
- These loans can blow up deals when they become due in rising rate environments.
- Working with experienced general partners is crucial.
- Vetting financing terms is important to reduce downside risk.

COMMANDMENT 5: CREATE CASH FLOW IMMEDIATELY

I'm a cash flow guy.
If it doesn't make me money today, forget about it.

—Robert Kiyosaki

When you think about mobile home parks, what's the first thing that comes to mind? If *wealth* isn't one of your first thoughts, keep reading.

Not too long ago, my wife woke me up, saying, "You're never going to believe what happened." She'd just received a call from her parents with a horrible report. A special unit of the SWAT team dressed in hazmat suits had just shown up at a mobile home park in her hometown in the southern Midwest. It turns out that the SWAT team had been casing the park based on a report that a meth lab was in it. The story was all over the news, on the radio, and on the front page of the city's largest daily newspaper.

I felt like someone had kicked me in the gut. It turns out that I *owned* that mobile home park. The last thing I needed was negative public relations.

First, the good news. Upon further investigation, the police and SWAT team didn't discover a meth lab at all. No problem and no drugs. The bad news is that the news media never made a retraction or reported the good news. What was done was done. Other good news. Over the next three months, the park added five new tenants. Maybe the old saying, "Any public relations is good public relations, and any marketing is good marketing," came true in this case.

Why am I telling you this story? Sometimes the best and easiest income and the simplest deals aren't obvious. This story illustrates how I've made millions of dollars in real estate, specifically, in mobile home parks.

MOBILE HOME PARKS AS REAL ESTATE INVESTMENTS

Before you think to yourself, *People who live in mobile home parks must be difficult to deal with,* hear me out. Mobile home parks are a great investment. Here's the first reason why. When you know what to look for and craft a smart deal—one with a low down payment and immediate cash flow—and you can do seller financing, it means no banks.

Gain the maximum return with the least amount of investment.

In my case, I put down only 15 percent, or $65,000, on my first mobile home park. It immediately produced $2,000 net every month, or $24,000 per year. This asset secured a cash-on-cash return of 36 percent in the first year. A **cash-on-cash return** is the return calculated solely on the actual cash invested in the deal from the down payment. In this case, it was the return on the investment before improving the property and increasing rent.

My second mobile home park, which I negotiated from the same seller, had another down payment of 15 percent—$75,000—and immediately produced $3,375 per month, which was $40,500 per year, or a 56 percent cash-on-cash return.

Cities typically don't want mobile home parks and often try to redevelop them into other forms of real estate. There are only forty-four thousand mobile home parks in the United States, and approximately one hundred per year are rezoned and redeveloped into more valuable properties. That means they are a limited resource.

Because mobile home parks are real estate rental properties, they fall into an IRS class allowed to utilize accelerated depreciation, which means you don't get taxed on all the profit you make. Also, you can buy mobile home parks at the highest cap rate in real estate, which basically means that they produce the best returns at the lowest price; and on top of that, they have the lowest risk. Plus, if you need to use a lender, a mobile home park is an asset class that has one of the lowest default rates in all real estate, so it is relatively easy to get a conventional bank loan if a seller finance opportunity doesn't exist.

PASSIVE INCOME AND THE IRS

An interesting fact to keep in mind on your journey is that **earned income** is the highest taxed income in the United States (and most other countries). In other words, the income you earn from your job or your business is taxed more than any other income you earn. **Passive income**, on the other hand, is one of the lowest-taxed incomes. Often, depending on the investment, many ways exist to substantially reduce the amount of passive income that is taxed, including depreciation and deductions. It is even possible to completely eliminate taxes altogether on your passive income.

Do you know that the IRS has a "passive investor" designation that exists if you don't have any earned income and all your income is derived from investments? Passive investors actually pay the lowest percentage in taxes legally.

Most people look at the IRS tax code as a bunch of rules telling you what you can't do. If you study the tax code, it can guide you to certain investments the government wants you to make based on the incentives in place. One of the reasons I like real estate in general, and especially real estate rentals, is because the government wants adequate housing for its citizens. It incentivizes anyone who wants to invest in housing, among other investments, by giving tax benefits not available if you just work for someone else. If you follow the tax code and what the government wants you to do with your income, you can save a lot of money and help your country at the same time. I could write a whole book on tax strategy alone; for some of my favorite strategies, head to *LifestyleInvestor.com/Gift*.

Your risk is reduced further because you have multiple tenants, so if one or two tenants miss a payment or get evicted, you don't feel the pain the way other investors feel it when they have a single tenant who doesn't pay rent. Even when evictions are necessary, due to the inexpensive rent and limited space, the parks fill up quickly. For most tenants, a mobile home park is more desirable than renting an apartment because they have a yard, land, more living space, and no neighbors upstairs or sharing adjoining walls.

Many mobile home park owners are unsophisticated and cash-poor, so it's easy to walk in, make simple and basic improvements that increase the value of the property, and implement incremental rent increases, which is almost all profit. For an investor, mobile home parks offer a great buy-and-hold strategy and are easy to flip, especially when you know how to find a right-fit buyer. Let me break down another one of my mobile home park investments as an example.

BUY TO FLIP

My third mobile home investment deal was a bigger deal than my first two parks. I found this mobile home park and negotiated directly with the owners, a husband and wife who wanted to retire. We decided the value of the property, which also included twenty-eight homes and a large workshop, was $960,000. I was able to split the deal into two parts, with the bank financing the land itself and the homes being sold separately, which were considered personal property. The bank valued the thirteen-acre parcel of land at $800,000 with a $160,000 down payment at 4.5 percent for a ten-year loan amortized for twenty years. My payment was $4,000 per month.

Next, I negotiated the twenty-eight homes to an extremely reasonable $155,000, which is about $5,535 per home for homes that were worth anywhere between $10,000 to $20,000 per home. Additionally, I was able to negotiate a zero-dollar down payment on a ten-year note that was amortized at thirteen years and interest-free. That monthly payment was just $1,000.

Here's where things got really exciting! The property cash flowed immediately, and after some initial improvements and a rent increase, it was profiting $14,000 per month. At the end of the first year, my cash-on-cash return was 105 percent, producing a total profit of $168,000 on a down payment that was just $160,000.

I sold the property for $1.2 million exactly one year and one day later, which produced $240,000 in profit plus the $168,000 cash-on-cash return from the first year for a grand total of $408,000 in profit in just one year. Because I timed the sale for one year and one day, I was able to avoid **short-term capital gains tax** that would have occurred if I sold it in less than a year, which is taxed at ordinary income tax rates. **Long-term capital gains tax** is discounted to just 15-20 percent, depending on your tax bracket.

THE 1031 EXCHANGE ADVANTAGE

I have more good news about real estate investing. There is a way to reinvest the profits into more real estate to avoid owing a long-term capital gains tax: It's a financial tool called a 1031 exchange you can use to your advantage. With the proceeds of the single park sale, I purchased two additional parks and doubled my monthly cash flow by using the same model.

1031 EXCHANGE

A 1031 exchange gets its name from Section 1031 of the US Internal Revenue Code, which allows an investor to "defer" paying capital gains taxes on an investment property when it is sold as long as another "like-kind property" is purchased with the profit gained by the sale of the first property. In essence, an investor can avoid paying capital gains tax indefinitely on selling investment property by continuing to utilize this strategy.

There are two big lessons you can learn from this example. The first is that when you understand and combine principles and commandments, it multiplies your profit and reduces your risk. You can find a plethora of ways to negotiate amazing deals, as I did in this one.

The second lesson you can learn relates to what I did to educate myself on how to invest in mobile home parks. learn how to do mobile home investing. I hired and paid a mentor who taught me the tricks of the trade and how to structure a basic deal, one that I expanded as I grew my skill set. Unfortunately, my mentor didn't bring me any deals, which I would have loved, because he was busy running his own business.

Now, my Mastermind members love working with me because my team and I find deals, help them structure and negotiate those deals, and find creative ways for them to reduce risk, increase cash flow, quickly return the principal, and avoid tax consequences. I decided to start coaching and teaching because if I would have had someone share strategies and principles like these with me twenty years ago when I started investing, I know I would have built a significantly larger and more profitable portfolio and in a much faster timeframe.

PRIVATE REAL ESTATE FUND INVESTING

In the last chapter, I discussed investing in a private multifamily syndication, which is an example of a direct real estate investment where you invest directly into a specific deeded property that you own (e.g., house, apartment, mobile home park, storage unit). In that example, I acquired an ownership interest in an entity that directly owns this asset with a goal of producing cash flow immediately.

Here, I am going to discuss investing in private **real estate funds**, which like the last example, many people may not realize is even an option. Investing in a real estate fund is an example of an indirect real estate investment because you are not investing directly into an asset but rather buying shares in a fund or trust that owns many assets.

Real estate fund investing can be done in the public markets on the stock exchange as well using **real estate investment trusts (REITs)**, but I prefer investing in private real estate funds because there is less volatility and often much more cash flow and a much bigger overall return. (I discuss investing in funds in more detail in the next chapter, Commandment 6: Find an Income Amplifier.)

EXAMPLE: PRIVATE REAL ESTATE FUNDS

I met an operator who also is a great investment analyst in an investment group I'm part of, and we really hit it off. We have many mutual friends, and he is highly regarded by everyone. He is much more analytical than I am, so we make a good team. Plus, I knew I could trust his market research based on his results and his reputation. We started analyzing investments together, figuring that if we independently like a deal and it passes both of our vetting processes, then it's likely a good investment.

This operator has shared a bunch of his deals with me, and I have done the same. So far, our approach of two minds being greater than one has worked out exceptionally well. We have invested in many private real estate funds in various asset classes with some exciting returns.

MINDSET

I've invested time as a real estate operator and learned all that it takes to be a strong operator, so when I started investing in other people running operations, I knew what to look for. I also am a big fan of fund structure in general.

If a fund owns a hundred properties and one of them doesn't perform, there won't be much impact on the overall return because the other ninety-nine properties are likely to perform well. If I directly invested in only that one property, however, then I would be in a position to lose money. Investing in a fund is a great way to minimize risk and diversify your investment across different locations, sizes, and property types, among other factors.

STRUCTURE

I have invested in several fund structures over the years with varying terms, including these examples:

- Preferred return: 8–10 percent
- Monthly distributions (sometimes quarterly distributions)
- Internal rate of return (IRR) of 15–25 percent
- Return of principal in two to three years

- Profit split after return of principal (splits vary on each deal and can range anywhere from 80 percent to the investor and 20 percent to the fund manager to an even 50 percent split; these splits are often represented as 80/20, 70/30, 60/40, and 50/50)
- Depreciation passed on to investors pro-rata (no taxes on a good amount of the profit, and often, with accelerated depreciation where you can take a larger deduction in the beginning, potentially not any taxes on it)

FILTER

I like the consistent monthly or quarterly cash flow of this investment as well as it being one of the safest ways to invest in real estate because so much risk is mitigated with having many properties in the fund. The key here is only investing in funds that have proven general partners and local operators who have a long track record of experience and success in operating that specific type of real estate. I also make sure the financials are very strong and reasonable for the market and asset class.

The funds I invest in have operators with a tremendous amount of experience and strong financials that conservatively show how I will earn great returns. I also like to invest in funds that have a selective process for the assets they purchase and specialize in asset classes that are generally recession-proof.

NEGOTIATION

Even when investing in funds, I often negotiate many of the terms. Some funds have exclusivity, and it's difficult to access them. Plus, they often have high minimum investments.

Everything is negotiable. I negotiate lower investment minimums based on what I feel comfortable investing, not what the fund minimum may be.

I also like to negotiate preferred terms when I have the leverage of having a large group of investors who also want to invest. These terms include waiving fees, paying a higher preferred return, and improving the profit split. Additionally, I like to negotiate to gain access to future funds opened before they are available to other investors and become oversubscribed. In the next chapter, I will explain in much more detail how I secure preferred terms utilizing sidecar agreements.

THE DEAL IN REVIEW

To create cash flow immediately, you've got to use all of the above principles, especially Filter. It is incredibly important to vet deals not only based on the financials and asset classes but also by the general partners and operators who run them. Successful investors realize that having an experienced general partner and strong operator is as important as having strong financials. One without the other is not a good deal. You really need to have each.

Additionally, it is important to recognize that sometimes the most non-obvious and even undesirable investments produce the best cash flow. Mobile home parks and industrial warehouses are perfect examples, and these assets are often purchased in private real estate funds. At first glance, they may be unattractive and perhaps even just weird-sounding investments; however, they often require a small down payment and have minimal risk (especially if you are buying them cheaply enough). Financing is often done by the owner—if they are not institutionally owned—and it's easy to make improvements, which immediately increases cash flow. In many cases, few improvements need to be made.

In an up or down economy, low-income housing, such as mobile home parks, is a great investment. Everyone needs a place to live, and they are the most affordable housing in a town or city. Likewise, industrial distribution centers are a great investment. With the e-commerce boom, there is more of a demand than ever for industrial distribution centers. To top it off, these investments are real estate, so there are massive tax benefits. A smart investor with the discipline to focus on investments in asset classes such as these can make a substantial fortune in good times and bad.

PRIVATE REAL ESTATE FUNDS - 2024 DEAL UPDATE

2024 UPDATE SUMMARY:

- Funds allow greater diversification across assets/ locations
- Poorly structured debt amplified risks in some funds
- Conservative fixed-rate loans reduced blow-up risks
- Success hinges on an experienced fund manager
- Provides steady cash flow distributions

Given my positive experience with real estate syndications, I began making investments in private real estate funds focused on specific property sectors like industrial, multi-family, self-storage, and so on.

The fund model allows for greater diversification across more assets and markets compared to doing individual syndication deals. It also provides access to professional fund managers and operators I wouldn't invest with otherwise.

While the funds delivered excellent returns initially, some have faced challenges recently. In particular, funds using floating-rate debt or short-term bridge loans have struggled as rates increased rapidly.

As I covered with syndications, I had friends aggressively pursuing funds using floating rate structures, imploring me to pursue the same high upside strategies.

While they benefited in the bull run, I maintained the discipline to invest only in funds using fixed-rate, long-term financing without major payments coming due. Maybe I sacrificed some return, but I also avoided calamity when markets shifted. Trying to maximize leverage works wonderfully when rates decline but can be disastrous in rising-rate environments.

Now, as their loans needing refinancing have detonated those funds, my more conservative approach has insulated me from blow-up risk across economic cycles. This turbulent environment has reinforced the need to partner with experienced managers who have navigated prior cycles. I'm thankful for having avoided those risks by focusing on fixed-rate structures and seasoned managers.

The funds I invested in utilized conservative long-term fixed-rate loans without major near-term maturities. This insulated them from the unprecedented rate increases that torpedoed highly leveraged strategies with excessive floating rate exposures.

I have conviction that rigorous analysis and finding the right fund managers means no regrets in any decade, even if that means taking a more measured approach in the short term.

Additionally, I prefer to invest in funds with a targeted specialty rather than attempting to diversify across too many asset classes. For example, I would invest in an industrial fund focused solely on that sector rather than a mixed-use fund attempting to balance industrial, multi-family, self-storage, and more. I've found niche expertise outperforms generalized competence.

Many real estate funds provide "immediate cash flow" through their quarterly distributions. This steady income can support my lifestyle or be reinvested to compound returns. I avoid long lockup periods so the liquidity can be accessed quickly if needed. Maintaining flexibility and targeting specialized operators have insulated me from turbulence.

KEY INSIGHTS:

- Funds provide diversity, but success hinges on the fund manager.
- Many funds used excessive leverage via bridge loans and floating rate debt.
- Conservative long-term fixed-rate loans reduced blow-up risk.
- Experienced managers who have seen economic cycles are key.
- Max leverage works great when rates fall but can amplify risks.

COMMANDMENT 6:
FIND AN INCOME AMPLIFIER

Stay committed to your decisions but stay flexible in your approach.

—Tony Robbins

"**B**ut wait, there's more!" That's how an infomercial creates an irresistible offer—by adding multiple bonuses and maybe even giving an extra product for the same price with free shipping.

If you're a typical investor and can make 8–15 percent profit per year, you would be happy enough, wouldn't you? What if you could have collateral that would guarantee you would get your principal back plus interest? You would be ecstatic, right? That's two for the price of one.

In this chapter, I'm going to introduce you to the concept of income amplifiers and what multiple income amplifiers can do for an investor when you stack them. An **income amplifier** is any mechanic or negotiated term that helps improve an investment return. Various ways are out there to structure these deal terms, and the more income amplifiers you can get, the better the investment return should be.

Before I talk about income amplifiers, though, I want to address a false belief among novice investors (and even many experienced investors), namely that the terms are the terms. That's just not the case most of the time.

TERMS ARE NEGOTIABLE

After being offered terms, I always like to go back and negotiate something different that improves the investment, whether it's just me investing or whether I'm bringing a group of investors into the deal. In some cases, a group might give me more influence, leverage, and negotiating power to get even better terms.

INVESTMENT INCOME AMPLIFIERS

A variety of investment income amplifiers are available but rarely used by the typical investor. Here is a list of the most common income amplifiers I use:

- **Negotiating preferred terms**—terms that improve the economics of the investment
- **Sidecar agreements**—an addendum or agreement with pre-negotiated preferred terms
- **Co-investment** opportunity—an opportunity to invest in a specific deal outside of a fund but alongside the fund managers
- **Equity kickers**—free equity that is given as an incentive to make an investment even better

- **Warrants**—an option to buy equity in the future at a predetermined price
- **Revenue shares**—a percentage of top-line revenue paid to an investor, typically with monthly distributions
- **Liquidation preference**—a clause in a contract that dictates the payout order of proceeds upon the sale of a company or other corporate liquidation
- **Advisory shares**—business advisors will often exchange their involvement within a company for compensation with common stock options, which can lead to equity in the company

In addition to this list, three others worthy of special attention are explained here in more detail:

- **Debt investment**—Investing in the form of a loan rather than straight equity. Debt investment allows a return of the principal investment with interest instead of an equity investment that likely has no principal return or a very long timeline if it ever does have a return (plus the possibility of some additional income amplifiers negotiated with the loan).
- **Accelerated distribution schedule**—Investing in the form of straight equity rather than a loan but with a faster repayment schedule. This amplifier gets the initial investment paid back in a much quicker time frame than what the standard distribution schedule would be based on equity splits outlined in the **operating agreement**.
- **Profits interest**—This amplifier is an equity right based on the future value of a company. From a tax standpoint, it can often be better than equity because it doesn't incur taxes during the holding period. When the profits interest is taxed, it's long-term

capital gains tax rather than short-term capital gains tax, which is taxed like ordinary income the way a warrant is taxed.

For a lot of deals in which people invest in a seed round, which is an early-stage investment in a company before it's typically profitable and showing signs of sustaining business, they invest in it for a certain amount of equity and hope the company makes it. If there's a liquidity event, they're paid based on a multiple of the value of the company when they invested and the value of the company at the time of the liquidity event. Most companies, however, don't end up having that coveted liquidity event; and most companies don't end up making it, so the investors may never see their money again.

I would much rather structure an early-stage investment differently, specifically by making it a debt investment as a loan to the company rather than a straight equity investment. Then, in addition to the debt structure, I can negotiate a smaller portion of equity or warrants to be awarded immediately as a kicker. The extra equity or warrants would then be free kickers that won't cost me a thing!

A warrant is an option to buy shares of a company at a predetermined **strike price** based on today's valuation but exercised at some point in the future—if and when the company is worth significantly more. Warrants are similar to equity but end up being more of a liquidation preference, which means you can structure them to get paid out before equity holders and often even debt holders when a company sells.

So, instead of making a direct investment for equity in a company from which you likely won't earn a return on your investment for a long time, you can use one of the structures I prefer. You can invest in equity with an accelerated distribution schedule to get your principal back quickly, or you can secure a loan with an equity kicker to make a good return and cash flow immediately and get your principal out of the deal much quicker. Plus, you still have the ability to have an upside in the company because of the equity kicker.

I recently got involved in an investment with a well-known company, The Franklin Mint, that sells coins on TV, online, and through mail-order catalogs and magazines. In the Commandment 3: Find Invisible Deals chapter, I told you about Dress Barn, a business that didn't grow with the times, didn't transition to e-commerce fast enough, and found itself in a challenging position. A similar situation occurred with The Franklin Mint.

An investment syndicate I'm involved in gathered its members and negotiated a simple-to-understand but uncommon investment structure that exemplifies the "but wait, there's more" offer. Instead of negotiating my usual 15-20 percent interest, the syndicate members decided to change things up. They agreed on a 10 percent monthly distribution of gross sales paid as a royalty (that detail will become important later), plus several more income amplifiers on top of it. Here they are:

- **Income Amplifier #1:** Negotiated a monthly distribution of gross revenue.
- **Income Amplifier #2:** Eliminated downside risk by negotiating collateral in the form of a **holding company** worth over $100 million. If the investment fails, the holding company is worth significantly more than the relatively small investment to buy The Franklin Mint, so there's a lot of protection to help avoid losing money. The value of the collateral in this example was over twenty times greater than the value of the purchase price of The Franklin Mint.

- **Income Amplifier #3:** Negotiated a 20 percent cash bonus based on the principal investment, to be paid out at the end of the three-year note term.
- **Income Amplifier #4:** Added an equity kicker of 6 percent per $1,000,000 invested. Since this is a kicker, the equity is actually free, and none of the investment went towards purchasing equity. This amount of equity to be given as just a kicker is incredible. Typically, kickers are much less, if given at all.
- **Income Amplifier #5:** Capped the total return of principal at 2X (100 percent return on investment). It was the one thing this group we invested in required. They guaranteed a maximum term of three years to double our principal investment, but we actually anticipate it will take just one to two years to double it. The cap protects the group we invested in, but it also is a nice return in a short period of time for my group of investors.

Let me break this deal down for you in terms of how it worked and what the expected return is. Imagine you as the investor.

	Cash Amount	Equity	Royalty	Cash Bonus
You Invest:	$1M	6%	10%	20%
After Royalty – You Get:	$2M			
After Year 3 – You Get:				$200K
Total Return – You Get:	$2.2M			

If this investment takes the full three years to hit the 2X return on principal plus the 20 percent bonus, it will be a 40 percent return each year with a total return over those three years at 120 percent. If it takes just two years, it will be a 60 percent return each year. Either way, contractually, the deal has a tremendous amount of upside with very little downside.

My favorite deals are like this one—with **asymmetric risk/reward**, meaning the downside of the investment is protected. If I were to lose any money, it likely wouldn't be much, but the upside has exponential growth possibilities.

When I stack multiple deals like this one together, investing gets really exciting. If, for any reason, one of the deals does go bad, I would have others that perform exceptionally well and give exponential returns, which means I'd be way ahead. I actually like to structure these deals so that even if five deals go bad and only one deal goes according to plan, I still come out ahead.

This deal is just one example of how I structure deals to create great long-term returns but also offer strong cash flow during the life of the investment. The goal is, obviously, to have as many investments produce an exponential return as possible while protecting the risk of each investment at the same time. In this example, the odds of five deals going bad are extremely unlikely because of the high degree of risk protection I negotiate into all of my investments.

There's a plot twist to how this deal unfolded that you won't want to miss. It's even more proof that applying the commandments and principles in this book can protect you in the short term while creating unexpected long-term returns and results.

THE DANGERS OF DISTRESSED ASSETS

A PROMISING PARTNERSHIP TURNED SOUR

When the Franklin Mint approached us ready for a capital infusion, I saw endless potential if we could spark a rapid transformation. This once-revered brand had lost its luster after failing to keep pace with changing consumer habits. But it still had name recognition, and our deal was designed to catalyze a swift turnaround.

Our team negotiated a highly advantageous deal giving us ample downside protection while maximizing upside if the turnaround gained momentum. The creatively structured terms included preferential access to cash flows, valuable equity kickers, and more. On paper, it was a home run deal with asymmetric risk-reward ratios in our favor.

In the early months, our unconventional investment appeared to be paying off. Nostalgia-fueled sales spiked as we leveraged the brand's heritage. However, when management made an impulsive acquisition that distracted focus, things changed.

> **Lifestyle Investor Lesson:** Even the best plans can go awry when human nature deviates from logic.

After an initial period of optimism and early wins, several compounding missteps by leadership led the company downhill into eventual insolvency.

Despite our guidance and warnings, leadership continued to get distracted. What we assumed would be a ninety-day sprint to stabilization turned into a prolonged nose dive.

As cash flows dried up, we watched momentum evaporate and key talent head for the exits. The person leading the initial turnaround efforts was abruptly let go, despite doing an admirable job. It became increasingly clear our investment would badly underperform compared to the original projections and assumptions.

When the company inevitably defaulted, we initiated prepackaged bankruptcy to contain the fallout. As the process unfolded, though, we ultimately decided to not follow through with the bankruptcy, as this would have cost us another $10 million.

Another pivot. This time, the senior secured investors pursued a strict foreclosure under the Uniform Commercial Code (UCC) Article 9. This article allows creditors to repossess a secured property if a debtor defaults on their debt.

Now that these proceedings have ended, our syndicate officially owns this company brand and all other associated intellectual property assets outright. So while the deal certainly did not transpire as originally planned, we still anticipate emerging stronger on the other side than we previously imagined.

We can now pursue opportunities to sell it to a more fitting owner who can optimize the brand's latent value.

MAKING SENSE OF A DISAPPOINTING INVESTMENT

Sifting through the wreckage, I gained several unconventional but critical insights:

- Sometimes investments don't work out the way they should "on paper." Protect against missteps with contingency plans and oversight.
- Return on investment can take many forms, each with its own time horizon. Look through multiple perspectives, especially non-obvious ones.

- Adopting a turnaround mindset requires balancing quick action with restraint and strategy, a tricky balancing act.
- Not all distressed assets are worth the effort post-investment. Vet these deals just as carefully as other investments to save yourself time, hassle, money, and frustration.

COURSE CORRECTING TO CHART A WISER PATH FORWARD

And now, I'm walking away wiser with a renewed commitment to risk reduction:

- Negotiate structures that anticipate irrational behavior and bind leadership to the agreed strategic plan.
- Institute additional oversight and set feedback loops during volatile turnarounds. Lack of visibility compounds issues.
- Develop rapid response plans addressing scenarios if investments head south. Fortune favors the prepared.
- Cut losses swiftly if turnaround stalls despite exhaustive efforts. Sunk cost fallacy makes it easy to throw good money after bad.

SIDECAR AGREEMENTS

Next, I want to introduce you to sidecar agreements and how they work as an income amplifier to add to your toolkit. A **sidecar agreement** is, effectively, a term sheet that gives a separate set of enhanced terms, ones that are better than what a typical investor would qualify for and be able to get.

I use sidecar agreements often to guarantee that I get preferred treatment when I invest. If I'm investing with a group of investors, I make sure that they also get the same preferred terms that I get. Here's how I stack sidecar agreements:

1. The first thing I do is negotiate preferred terms for the current investment. If my Lifestyle Investor Mastermind is investing with me, I negotiate terms on behalf of the whole group. Those preferred terms can include a discount in management fees or administration fees (or other fees), a discount on **carried interest,** which is a share of profits that serve as compensation to investment managers, an increase in preferred return or interest payment, an increase in profit split, or even a decrease in the minimum investment. Sometimes those preferred terms include an increase in the **hurdle rate**, which is the minimum rate of return required by an investment. My biggest focus at this stage is to negotiate terms that allow me to improve my overall return and allow me to invest at an amount I am comfortable with based on the investment.

2. Next, I negotiate the opportunity to have preferred terms and first-mover advantage on any upcoming investments. I want to be the first money in as many deals as I can while maintaining those same preferred terms. I negotiate the first right to invest in future deals so I can get access to every opportunity before anyone else and that I am not limited in how much I can participate in each investment.

3. Last, I often negotiate preferred terms on an opportunity to co-invest in additional investments. For example, let's say I'm investing in a fund, and that fund has additional investments that don't fit the criteria or would represent too large of a single investment for the fund. I would negotiate an

additional agreement to co-invest in subsequent deals, often with *even better* preferred terms than were outlined in the first sidecar agreement. These co-investments are often extremely limited and difficult to get into in the first place, but if I get them, I have even better preferred terms in place for those investments.

I will explain this last point about co-investments in more detail, but before I go on, I want to make sure you understand negotiating preferred terms. You can amplify your income by negotiating preferred terms on any deal, but you can also amplify a deal by using a sidecar agreement for preferred terms, whether you are making a direct investment or a fund investment.

CO-INVESTMENTS IN FUNDS

I've discussed direct investments in-depth already, so I'm going to spend some time here talking about investing in funds and how to amplify those investments.

Personally, I like investing in funds. Funds are a collection of many different investments inside of the same investment vehicle. The reason savvy investors like funds is because they mitigate some of the risks that exist if they only have one investment. In a fund, if one investment doesn't work out, that's okay because the other investments that do perform well will typically more than cover the deal that went bad, making the fund's overall return still strong. Good and bad investments in the same fund can balance each other out, so it's not a total loss as it would be in a direct investment that went bad.

If I can work smarter and buy assets, I can earn more.

Now let's look at an example. Sometimes, if you get into the right fund with the right people, you can negotiate a sidecar agreement. You might have money in the fund that has exposure to all the deals, but there may be a particular one-off deal you really like. Maybe you know that market or the operators really well, or you have some sort of advantage or insight to know that this particular deal is a great opportunity. Or maybe there is an opportunity to get equity or warrants for a particular investment.

In this case, you can negotiate preferred terms for just that individual investment, which is often referred to as a **co-investment**. You'll get better returns on your overall investment than if you were only in the fund. Because you're in the fund, you still get exposure to that deal, but often you may want more exposure than the fund will give you. If that's the case, and you look at a deal and know it's a slam dunk, you can negotiate preferred terms or use a sidecar agreement that already has pre-negotiated preferred terms for that single investment. This way, you can participate in some of the general partner economics of the deal for a better return on your investment, which may include equity, warrants, or an overall larger interest payment or preferred return with reduced fees.

EARN ON INVISIBLE MONEY

In the investment world, **phantom income** is the ability to earn a return from money that doesn't even exist. One example of phantom income is the appreciation you may see in a rental property from one year to the next or over a longer period of time. Robert Kiyosaki, the author of *Rich Dad Poor Dad*, talks about the phantom income you receive from having your tenants pay down and eventually pay off your mortgage, which reduces your debt and grows the value of your asset. Once your asset is completely paid off, eliminating that debt service increases your cash flow, which is another type of phantom income. Additionally, when you depreciate your assets and the income from those assets, you create phantom income because you profit more than what you pay taxes on.

The number one benefit of phantom income is that you can earn a consistent return on money that doesn't even exist—if you use it the right way. Each of the different ways to create phantom income can come with a wide array of benefits and drawbacks, depending on the situation. The phantom income I want to discuss for Lifestyle Investing utilizes specialized whole-life insurance products in a unique strategy that offers many benefits and usefulness, especially to investors.

There is a way to create a specially crafted whole-life insurance policy that is super-funded or maxed out in a creative way on the front end, so it creates exponential returns as it compounds tax-free over time. Most life insurance products you would purchase off the shelf will not work for what I am going to describe. Many life insurance agents don't even know how to create the policies I use, which involve an expert in the insurance space who specializes in creating specific whole-life policies that perform as if they were on steroids based on the way they are structured. The life insurance expert must add additional riders that help these policies perform exponentially better and in a way that is most beneficial to the client—based on the lower commissions paid to the agent and the accelerated growth and compounding of the cash values, meaning the investment dollars that are put into the policy through premium payments.

For example, most people don't know that they have access to money in their whole life policy and that they can actually borrow against it, ultimately using that same money in an investment elsewhere. In other words, the money inside the whole-life policy is still earning a return because borrowing against is not actually taking out the money, only taking a loan against that money. That loaned money, however, can be invested in another deal to earn a return on it. In other words, they can earn two returns with the same money. They earn a dividend from the whole-life policy, which has a guaranteed minimum return in most cases, but they can also earn cash flow and potential equity from those same dollars by investing in another deal that has its own return.

To amplify the return a little more, if they follow my Commandment 4, "Get Principal Back Quickly," they can maintain equity in that second investment, turn around with those same dollars, invest them again in yet another deal, and earn a third return on the same money. In that case, they would be earning a return and building equity in three separate investments—all with the same investment capital.

This example of phantom income is also an example of **fractional reserve lending** like the banks do. Fractional reserve lending takes place when the banks take your deposits and only keep a fraction of them on hand and lend out the rest—usually ten times with the same money. It seems impossible, but this really is what banks do. They invest a large portion of your deposits into high-risk **derivatives**, which is what led to the market crash in 2008. So, in my example, where I had three returns with the same investment capital, I was able to do what the banks do but on a much smaller scale and in much safer investment vehicles.

In the previous example, I utilize phantom income because I have all of my money out of the deal, I've made a profit on the first investment, and I still have equity and cash flow as if the money were still in the deal. In essence, I get to do what the banks do, on my terms, for my portfolio, and for my benefit in a very safe way. And you can do it too.

In the chapter Commandment 7: Plus the Deal, I share a real-life example of how I used my whole-life policy and earned a return in two places at the same time through a combination of arbitrage, equity, and investment income. **Arbitrage** is where you can take advantage of making a risk-free profit on the margin between two different prices or rates of return.

EXAMPLE: DRESS BARN

I've already broken down the Dress Barn deal earlier in Commandment 3: Find Invisible Deals, but I want to give you a bit more detail on how the Income Amplifier strategy worked with it and how you can turn a connection or relationship into a super-profitable cash flow investment.

MINDSET

I attended a conference with another investor, and we became friends. We started to share our network contacts. He gave me access to some high-profile investors and entrepreneurs, and I did the same for him. This deal was about knowing the right people at the right time because there were only a few people who even had the opportunity to invest in it. One of the reasons I liked this investment so much was because I would be able to get my investment principal back quickly. Another reason was that the odds of this company failing inside of the first year were really small. Even if the company failed in year two, I would have all my money out of the deal. I also believed, however, that scaling retail brands online and eliminating brick-and-mortar retail stores was the future of this industry.

STRUCTURE

Here is the structure of that deal:

- One-year note
- 20 percent interest
- Monthly distributions
- Balloon payment at one year—full repayment of investment principal
- Option to extend part or all of my note for two more years at the same 20 percent interest plus a 15 percent cash bonus at the end of the note term and an additional 10 percent warrant kicker
- Option to partially or fully convert my note to equity later, when time allowed me to evaluate the progress of the company and investment
- 3 percent equity kicker per $1 million investment
- Collateralized by the intellectual property, which was worth much more than the investment

FILTER

This example is typical of an asset that was selling for pennies on the dollar with a strong brand. The operators are high-profile people who can't afford to have a deal go bad and tarnish their stellar reputation. They also have the financial means to cover anything that could go wrong. This investment was collateralized against Dress Barn's intellectual property, including the brand name itself and a customer list of almost eight million people.

NEGOTIATION

Several items were negotiated, including the ability to extend the loan past one year if the business were performing well and having the intellectual property as collateral for this investment. Additionally, I am first in line to invest in any of the future distressed assets owned by the parent company, so I can invest in each of them to diversify my position and build a portfolio of distressed brands that are scaled online rather than in retail stores.

Most investments don't have all of these perks. The big kicker negotiated in this deal was the free equity. Rarely do investors retain equity in a company once the investment principal has been repaid. Plus, the amount of equity to be paid as a kicker is extremely high. Typically, kickers are much less—if even given at all.

THE DEAL IN REVIEW

My Lifestyle Investor Mastermind bought an extremely high-quality, almost 60-year-old brand for pennies on the dollar. If anything went wrong, we could sell it for an immediate profit based on the great deal we negotiated and the fact that several groups made offers on this asset, and at least one of the offers was for significantly more than our offer (literally millions of dollars more). However, the parent company, Ascena Retail Group, liked our timeline and team the best. Additionally, the likelihood of the company failing inside the first year when the balloon payment of the note came due was nearly impossible. We got our entire investment back, retained the free equity, and can participate in the upside of this company's growth as the operations team continues to scale its e-commerce growth.

DRESS BARN WOMEN'S FASHION RETAILER - 2024 DEAL UPDATE

2024 UPDATE SUMMARY:

- Structured one-year note with bonus profit kickers
- Exited initial investment with 20 percent plus gains in one year
- Subsequent unchecked expansion led to distress
- Bankruptcy allowed investors to take possession of the brands
- Importance of controlled growth

A while back, I invested in Dress Barn, a women's fashion brand that was acquired out of bankruptcy. The company had strong assets but got overextended with physical retail stores.

My partners and I structured the investment as a one-year note paying around 20 percent interest. We believed the brand value and e-commerce business could thrive without expensive retail leases weighing them down.

After the one-year term, we had the option to be fully repaid, extend our note, or convert to equity. Fortunately, the company executed well, and we decided to exit, locking in our strong fixed return.

Emboldened by our success, we looked at other distressed retail brands owned by the same parent company. However, this time the company expanded too aggressively without proper operational controls. As a result, they overextended themselves and performance deteriorated. They eventually filed for bankruptcy to clean up the situation.

While the rapid ascent was exciting initially, unchecked growth put the company right back into trouble. However, the bankruptcy allowed investors to take outright ownership of the underlying brands if things went well.

The one-year duration of this fashion brand with bonus profit kickers exemplified "Finding an Income Amplifier." We boosted returns substantially by negotiating preferred terms compared to a straight equity investment.

As I reflect on this deal, I'm reminded that even though an investment may look great on paper, as investors, we ultimately place our trust in human operators to execute their strategic plans and perform as expected. In this case, because we reduced the risk and took a long-term perspective, we may eventually be in a situation where we achieve an outsized return by owning the brands and then selling them to the right buyer.

KEY INSIGHTS:

- The initial investment performed extremely well.
- We exited with 20 percent plus locked-in returns in under one year.
- Subsequent overexpansion led to financial distress again.
- Bankruptcy allowed investors to take over assets.
- We saw the importance of controlled growth and proper operations.

COMMANDMENT 7: PLUS THE DEAL

You can't put a limit on anything.
The more you dream, the farther you get.

—Michael Phelps

I n the previous chapter, I opened up with, "But wait, there's more!" Every income amplifier is an extra bonus. Now, I'm going to show you how to finance a deal and the bonuses with *extremely inexpensive* and safe money. In the world of marketing, this strategy is called "selling money at a discount."

The last chapter focused on negotiating income amplifiers into a deal, which is a great way to increase the return on any investment. Technically you can have a great investment without having any income amplifiers, but I get at least one (and often multiple income amplifiers) on most of my investments.

This chapter focuses on another round of additional negotiations that may come in the form of extra income amplifiers, additional protections on your risk, or often both. These additions may happen close to the start of the negotiation or in the final hours before signing a contract to finalize an investment.

THE MYTH OF A DONE DEAL

There is a myth that once you've negotiated a deal, it's set in place. The bottom line is that the deal is not done until the contract is signed. Until that happens, you still have room to improve the overall investment terms. I don't look at deals like others do. Any time I see an opportunity, I like to take advantage of it. If I see that a company has the ability to make more concessions, or if I haven't at least attempted to ask for something I didn't think of in my first round of negotiations, I've no qualms about asking. They can always say no.

Sometimes when I ask, they're not in a position where they really need to raise money and are just playing a little offense and trying to get ahead of the game, so they're not receptive to further negotiations. But oftentimes, I'm investing in a situation where they're distressed or at least in a more urgent state, and they have a set timeframe for when they need to raise the funds, and they're often willing to make some concessions.

I constantly negotiate a deal until I feel comfortable with the terms and feel like my risk has been properly minimized or totally mitigated.

A TWO-FOR-ONE DEAL

I'm going to give you a two-for-one deal with the added benefit of having no risk. Here's how it works. I use a specially designed whole-life insurance policy (much different than off-the-shelf policies) to finance my investments and operate like a bank, but with much better terms, as I discussed in the previous chapter. I use this same bank replacement strategy, taking loans against my whole-life policy, to earn multiple returns on the same money.

I used this strategy to invest in Dress Barn as well as all of my mobile home park purchases to date, all the operating companies I have invested in (more on this at the end of this chapter and in the next chapter), and many other investments as well.

Note: Not all insurance agents are created equal, not all life insurance policies are created equal, and not all life insurance companies provide the services I'm about to describe.

The life insurance company that you want is one that uses a **non-direct recognition** dividend structure. What that term means is that the company will pay you the same dividend regardless of whether you have a loan against your policy or not. Most insurance companies use a **direct recognition** structure and pay a lesser dividend when you take a loan against your policy, which can still be good if you're earning enough of a return to create an arbitrage—but nowhere close to the arbitrage of a life insurance company that offers non-direct recognition. Often with direct recognition, an arbitrage is negative, where you can actually lose money on that transaction. So, be careful which company you choose.

People, in general, only think about life insurance for its death benefit. They pay money, die, and give their beneficiaries some income. A properly crafted whole-life policy, however, can offer you many living benefits you can utilize. The truth is life insurance is the single greatest asset protection structure that exists. People may think trusts are, but if you look at all the case law, it is evident that life insurance is the single greatest way to protect your assets from creditors.

Additionally, life insurance is a vehicle that allows your money to compound with tax-free growth and tax-free distribution upon retirement (not to mention you also have a tax-free death benefit to your heirs). You can have a policy from a top-performing life insurance company that generally pays around a 6.5 percent dividend each year with a guaranteed minimum return typically of 4 percent. Top insurance companies are currently paying dividends of 5–7 percent, which after subtracting costs associated with the life insurance, the total internal rate of return (IRR) is typically paying 4–6 percent.

These returns in life insurance are an *actual rate of return*, not an average rate of return, as was discussed earlier in the book under Myth 1. So, unlike other investments that promise an average return of 10 percent—like a financial advisor pitching an investment in the stock market—this is an actual rate of return. It's a real number and not manipulated, so the return is the return, consistent year in and year out.

Back to the two-for-one deal. If you find a great investment opportunity like the ones I've described for you in this book, you can borrow against your policy, which is used as collateral, with flexible payment terms and at an interest rate of around 5 percent. If you come upon hard times, you can actually choose not to pay back the loan, and the policy will still perform well, just not as well as if you paid back the loan. And whenever you die, the insurance company subtracts the loan amount from the death benefit so it doesn't become a burden to your beneficiaries.

USE AN ARBITRAGE

Let me give you a real-life example of how I used an arbitrage as a strategy to plus a deal. I used my whole-life policy when buying my first mobile home park. I took the same money I would've invested in the mobile home park, invested it in my whole life insurance policy first, and took a loan against that policy to invest in the mobile home park. The result? I earned two returns on the same money. Why wouldn't I want to earn two returns instead of one, especially when one of these returns is guaranteed?

Whole-life insurance has a **minimum guaranteed return** offered with most policies, but many pay more than that minimum through a dividend. Each year the insurance company assesses how well it performed on its investments and pays whichever is higher, the minimum guaranteed return or the dividend. This dividend, however, is unique in that it is actually considered a return of capital rather than a distribution that is typically taxed. So, this dividend is not taxed.

I made a 36 percent cash-on-cash return in the first year on my first mobile home park investment, but I also received a 6.5 percent dividend on the same money, which was still in my whole-life policy, since my down payment on the mobile home park was just a loan against my policy. As I mentioned earlier, there are some costs to having life insurance, so let's use an IRR of 6 percent to factor in those costs associated with paying a 6.5 percent dividend. In total, I earned a 42 percent (36 percent + 6 percent) return on my money, which I used to repay the loan against my whole life insurance policy—and then repeated the process with my next mobile home park investment. That second deal netted a 54 percent cash-on-cash return, so when I added in the 6 percent IRR that I earned on my whole-life policy, my total return was 60 percent.

Look for investments that allow tax-free growth. This is the best type of growth that exists. These vehicles allow your money to compound faster than any other vehicle. Nothing interrupts the compounding, so these returns have the strongest velocity. Both of these examples have returns that grow tax-free. And because I could depreciate the mobile home park as an asset, that profit also grew tax-free.

Note: Not many of these tax-free growth vehicles are out there, and most of the ones that do exist have low government-imposed limits, such as a Roth IRA and a 401(k) Roth.

A small cost was associated with this loan, which I will explain next, along with my rationale for it.

First, let me say that some lending institutions specialize in lending money at lower percentages than a life insurance company and will use your policy as collateral for that loan, just like your life insurance company does, when you take a loan against it, saving you an additional couple of percentage points. So instead of taking a loan through your insurance company at 5 percent interest, you can instead take a loan through one of the lending institutions that specialize in collateralizing whole-life policies. You can choose from a fixed interest option or a variable interest option.

For the deal I just elaborated on, the fixed interest rate was 4 percent, and the variable interest was only 3 percent at the time, so I chose the variable interest loan. It was close to the cheapest money I could ever find then, and I didn't see interest rates going up for quite some time (and whenever they did, I could change it to a fixed interest rate). So, instead of paying the whole-life insurance company 5 percent interest for a loan, I saved 2 percent interest by paying this specialized lending institution only 3 percent. Plus, I have the flexibility of making payments that are as little as interest-only, which creates a huge opportunity to generate significant cash flow.

Let me illustrate how this deal works so you can see what this arbitrage looks like for you. Let's say you invest in a deal that pays 20 percent interest, such as one of the investments I have illustrated in this book using the commandments, amplifiers, and kickers. You make that investment by borrowing against your life insurance policy, which is currently producing a 6 percent IRR. The interest you pay on that loan is just 3 percent, which gives you a total return of 23 percent (20 percent + 6 percent – 3 percent = 23 percent).

Let's go back to the first example I gave on the first mobile home park I invested in. That one produced a cash-on-cash return of 36 percent. Add the 6 percent internal rate of return (IRR) from the whole-life policy, subtract the 3 percent interest, and you're left with a 39 percent total return. That's free money with no risk, or at the very worst, extremely minimal risk.

Here's how the numbers look in real-world terms when I invested in a whole-life policy, borrowed the money, and invested it into the mobile home park. This deal is an example of both arbitrage and leverage—making my money work for me in two places to earn profit twice.

The Deal at a Glance

$65,000 in my whole-life policy x 6 percent IRR = $3,900

$65,000 loan from my whole-life policy x 36 percent cash-on-cash return = $23,400

3 percent interest on the $65,000 loan = $1,950

$3,900 + $23,400 – $1,950 = $25,350 net profit and a 39 percent total return

---

What if you are uninsurable, have poor health, or have any other condition that would make *your* life insurance more expensive? You can take out a life insurance policy on *anyone you have an insurable interest in*—family members, employees, or anyone you have a working relationship with where your business would be impacted if something happened to them.

The example that follows shows several ways to "plus the deal," where I added additional income amplifiers and mitigated some of the risk involved with this investment.

EXAMPLE: ORANGETHEORY® FITNESS FRANCHISE

Orangetheory Fitness is an extremely popular and successful fitness franchise. There are more than 1,300 locations in the US alone that are regularly scheduled to capacity before the doors even open. The franchise has one of the highest profit margins of all franchises, but it's virtually impossible to buy one today because they are in such high demand. Existing owners and area representatives have the first right of refusal to open new studios.

At any given time, other franchises might resemble an opportunity like this—high demand, proven record of success, low risk, and high profitability, with operators who may be stretched to their credit capacity but have access to deals unavailable to the general public. For any investor who either has access to credit or cash, it is a perfect storm opportunity

In my case, a great opportunity opened up for me to get involved as an investor with two operators who didn't have access to enough credit but were willing to put in **sweat equity**. This investment opportunity involved knowing the right people and experiencing the natural byproduct of having created strong relationships, ones I reached out to periodically and stayed connected with over the years.

I chose to enter into this particular deal with a couple with whom I'd worked in the past and had a great relationship. They found the opportunity to invest in this organization through one of their connections, but they didn't have the capital to open it by themselves. I'd already had the privilege of advising these two smart business professionals on each of their first business ventures, and we enjoyed working together. They knew I'd be a good capital partner because not only would I have the investment capital they needed, but I could also advise them, leveraging my experience from investing directly in several other operating companies over the years.

Negotiating finds ways everyone gets what they want, so everybody wins. It's collaboration, not competition.

We created a fantastic win-win situation for all parties and were able to get a Small Business Administration (SBA) loan through a local bank with a down payment of 16 percent.

MINDSET

I'd wanted to get into the franchise space with a strong brand for a while. I'd pursued Orangetheory Fitness for quite some time, but because of the high demand, it was practically impossible to get a license from them. The only way to get a license was to get one from a secondary party who wanted to sell. I had several friends who were successful owners of this franchise. I had connections who were able to help secure this license and strong operators who could run and scale the business. Additionally, private equity firms buy up large portfolios of Orangetheory Fitness franchises at extremely attractive prices, so I like investments that have an attractive exit strategy already built in.

STRUCTURE

Here is how I structured the deal:

- Equity investment of $120,000 for the down payment
- 33 percent equity in the business
- Accelerated distribution schedule of 67 percent until the loan is paid off
- 33 percent distributions thereafter, in perpetuity
- Initial equity investment of $120,000, to be repaid within one year
- Additional cash bonus of $35,000 paid to personally guarantee 20 percent of the SBA loan

FILTER

The track record on this particular brand was impeccable. No franchise owner at that time had ever shut down, and the company was one of the fastest-growing brands in the US and internationally. Additionally, the systems that could be created for this franchise (and the systems already in place) allowed for owners to be able to automate and repeat and thus scale at a high level. The terms my partners gave me were great: low-risk, high-returns with monthly cash flow payments, and an accelerated distribution schedule, which gave me access to my capital quickly for additional investments.

NEGOTIATION

I negotiated from a minority equity position into an equal partner by contributing more capital without doing any more work. I negotiated an accelerated distribution schedule for a faster return of my investment, with two-thirds of the distributions going to me monthly until I had my full investment returned. I was able to monetize the minority portion of the personal guarantee I agreed to with the bank by being compensated with an additional cash bonus that was added to the accelerated distribution schedule. In the end, I only have a small 20 percent personal guarantee backing this loan because I was able to negotiate that total down with the bank—even though I am an equal partner on the deal and have a much higher net worth than both of my partners.

THE DEAL IN REVIEW

This deal is a perfect example of a lifestyle investment where your money works for you—no operations or time invested (so your most valuable resource, time, is preserved), monthly cash distributions, and long-term equity with fantastic opportunities for a substantial future exit and additional franchises. The only risk for an investment such as this one is if the franchise itself had some significant brand-damaging news or took a massive hit from a shift in the current economic climate. (Despite the 2020 stay-at-home measures, this investment was still profitable because of its powerful business model and brand.)

Additionally, I recently invested in the purchase of another operating company with these two business partners, and the location is really close to our Orangetheory Fitness studio. We have had such a great time working together that we wanted to expand our portfolio together. I am again the capital partner, and one of my two partners from our fitness franchise has started running operations for the new business while my other partner continues to run operations for our Orangetheory Fitness studio.

Based on the strong financials, strength of the brand, premier location, and excellent operators running the business, it was a great investment. But I also found several ways to "plus the deal." I utilized an accelerated distribution schedule and doubled my overall percentage paid out, so my principal investment was paid back quickly over the first year of owning the franchise. My partners and I used profits from that franchise to purchase another business with even better cash flow than the Orangetheory Fitness franchise. Additionally, I was able to convince the bank to reduce the personal guarantee from 100 percent to 20 percent, which helped mitigate most of the risk in this investment.

ORANGETHEORY FITNESS FRANCHISE - 2024 DEAL UPDATE

2024 UPDATE SUMMARY:

- Partnered with two operating partners to invest in this franchise
- Negotiated accelerated distributions to get capital back quickly
- COVID significantly impacted fitness industry revenues
- Upside available as equity partner if sold
- Got principal investment returned to reduce risks

Given the popularity of Orangetheory Fitness, I partnered with two operating partners to invest in a franchise location. We knew the demand would be there if we could secure a territory. One partner had experience in fitness, while the other ran sales and marketing. I came in as the capital partner to fund the buildout and provided strategic advice to help optimize the studio's performance.

We structured the investment so I received two-thirds of the distributions until my capital was repaid, which only took about a year. After that, the distributions reverted to an even split among the three partners.

For the next couple of years, the studio performed well and produced consistent profits. However, when COVID-19 hit, we faced the same headwinds as most fitness concepts and revenue declined. Thankfully, by receiving my invested capital back quickly, my downside risk was protected. While business is rebounding, we may ultimately sell the studio based on the tenant opportunities within the retail center we've located.

If we sell, I would still participate in any profits as an equity partner. Despite COVID's dampening impact, I'm glad we were able to get our capital out early to mitigate risks.

I "Plussed the Deal" by negotiating a disproportionate share of distributions until my capital was repaid. This reduced my risk while still allowing me to participate in the franchise upside as an equity partner over time.

Additionally, I originally had negotiated a personal guarantee to just 20 percent, but I also negotiated for it to be completely removed after a few years. At this point, I have no personal guarantee remaining, which is another great way to de-risk a deal.

As another example, by leveraging my personal balance sheet, I've secured equity in deals without needing to invest capital. I recently provided a partial personal guarantee for three KidStrong fitness locations with the same partners without having to contribute any cash.

In exchange for guaranteeing a maximum 20 percent portion of the notes, I received 25 percent ownership in all three KidStrong studios. Over time, I've negotiated my personal guarantee percentage down so it eventually declines to 0 percent while retaining the equity. I share even more on this technique of negotiating personal guarantees so they're reduced and eventually removed in Commandment 9.

Despite COVID's dampening impact, I'm glad we were able to get our capital out early to mitigate risks on the original fitness franchise. Maintaining flexibility while optimizing leverage has continued to open new doors.

KEY INSIGHTS:

- Structuring to get invested capital back quickly reduces downside risk.
- COVID had a severely negative impact on the fitness industry, but commercial real estate still has promise.
- Aligning incentives with operating partners from the start makes all the difference.
- By retaining equity, upside is still available after principal is returned.

COMMANDMENT 8: CUT OUT THE FAT

Beware of little expenses; a small leak will sink a great ship.

—Benjamin Franklin

How do you feel when you find out you've overpaid for something? Let's say you go out and buy a ring at a nice jewelry store for $7,000 and then go to Costco and see the same ring for $3,200—except it's bigger and of higher quality.

If you're a collector of rare or treasured items, you know the value of a highly connected person who searches far and wide, makes phone calls, finds what you want for you, and saves you 40 percent on a deal. You would gladly pay this person a healthy commission, and probably an upfront fee because of the value of this service. And you would go back to this person again and again. You value the relationship you have with this person on multiple levels.

Let me apply this story to the world of investments. First, let's look back. Then, we can look forward.

You've read the previous chapters and know about many of my investments. For my first three mobile home parks, I did the deal without a broker, and I did seller financing for part or all of the purchase price. At that time, I had more time than I had money. I sourced the deal, took my time to negotiate terms, and by cutting out the broker, saved myself a bunch of fees in commissions—all of which translated into an extra $100,000 in my pocket. Through seller financing, I was able to negotiate a small down payment of 15 percent at 5 percent interest for ten years, enabling me to have immediate cash flow and net profit before improving the asset and increasing rents.

Best of all, the loan I negotiated was a non-recourse loan, so the worst thing that could happen if the investment didn't work out or I fell upon hard times was that the seller would receive the asset back, and my inability to make the loan payments wouldn't affect my credit score. If I'd used a bank, I would've had to guarantee the loan with personal assets, and the default would've negatively affected my credit score.

Later on, when I had more money than time, I learned to use middlemen and brokers to my advantage. I was happy to pay them a fee to save me the time from doing what I did in the first portion of my career.

THE RELATIONSHIP RESOURCE

Here are a few bullet points on the resources you can use in making great deals when you have the money and wish to preserve your time.

- Great **brokers** will bring deals you don't know about and introduce you to a network you don't have access to, which will save you decades of time.
- Great **financial advisors and insurance professionals** can introduce you to financial products you've never thought of or heard about because they're obscure.
- Great **bankers and financial institutions** will introduce you to financial vehicles and instruments that are equally obscure and inaccessible without their connections.

When you find these resources, you add the highest quality, precision tools of all to your investment toolbox—relationships. When combined with your other tools, they can give you access to big deals, more leverage, better terms, and ideas and concepts that you would never learn anywhere else.

This entire book and all the tools I've exposed you to have taken me over ten years to acquire. I've invested almost $1 million in my personal growth and paid hundreds of thousands of dollars in legal and professional fees, education, training, and coaching. These resources have helped me create an investment portfolio in the tens of millions of dollars. That outcome wouldn't have happened, however, if it weren't for the fact that I've cultivated

Investing, growing wealth, and net worth become a game.

a league of superheroes who can tackle almost any opportunity or deal.

PARASITIC MIDDLEMEN

In all relationships, some are healthy for you and some are just not. The same is true for investment relationships, so be cautious. Look for relationships that are amplifiers or partners in business, not parasitic middlemen. The fastest way to make money is never to spend it unnecessarily in the first place.

Costco, Sam's Club, and Walmart all figured out how to cut out the middlemen and keep more profit, generate more volume, and give their customers more products for less money. Amazon figured out how to cut out the middlemen *and* get their products into your home in under a day.

I had to learn, and you will, too, the difference between a relationship resource and a parasitic middleman. When you cut out the parasitic middlemen, you become a powerhouse. You win.

Let me give you a list of the biggest sources of business parasites that add "fat" and cause discontent—sources (not resources) that cost you money and can create unprofitable deals due to fees and commissions:

- Financial advisors
- Brokers
- Insurance salespeople
- Fund managers
- General partners
- Money raisers
- Banks and financial institutions
- In general, all middlemen

Disclaimer: I love many of the professions I just listed above—if the terms and agreements are structured correctly. I have many friends who are financial advisors, brokers, lenders, and insurance salespeople who do great work on behalf of their clients. But not all financial advisors, brokers, lenders, and insurance salespeople are created equal.

How can you discern fat from muscle? Here's my time-tested *Cut Out the Fat* toolkit and system that creates dividends and income without exception. Use each of these tools to unlock the best deals and avoid the "fat."

FIND THE FAT

1. Do They Win When You Lose?

Brokers and financial investments have hidden fees; and many mutual funds, 401(k) plans, and insurance policies are loaded with excessive fees, fine print, and exceptions that leave you holding the bag. These "professionals" are getting new cars, bigger mortgages, and boats without you knowing how they get paid. Opaque deals never work in your favor.

2. Do They Have Skin in the Game?

Find partners who will do performance-based deals instead of fee-based services. An exception is if you're working with fiduciaries, for example—professionals with decades of experience who charge a simple fee for services and are completely transparent with any commissions or additional fees they receive.

In the financial services industry, the vast majority of financial services representatives, agents, and brokers are *not* fiduciaries—they don't have to make decisions that are best for their clients, and they actually make decisions that are best *for themselves*. Legally, all they have to do is provide you with a product that is "suitable." That extremely low standard is not one to subject your financial future to. Only a small percentage are actually fiduciaries, which is disturbing.

3. Do They Practice What They Preach?

Would you trust an overweight nutritionist or personal trainer? The same is true for your financial advisors. Do they invest in the thing they're selling you themselves, or are they offering it to you because there's an extra commission on that particular product? Do they even invest? What's their history? What's their net worth? Look for congruency and character in the people you trust with your money.

4. Where Can You Save Time or Money?

What's more important and valuable to you right now—your money or your time? Your answer may change, depending on where you are in life at that moment, and will determine how and where you can *cut out the fat.*

Let me share an investment nightmare story. In the financial world of Wall Street, brokers and financial advisors are taught to use the term *average rate of return.* Imagine for a moment: if someone came to you and showed you the following:

- Year one, you lost 50 percent
- Year two, you gained 50 percent
- Year three, you lost 50 percent
- Year four, you gained 50 percent

What do you think the average rate of return would be? Most people would say at a glance that you have a 0 percent average rate of return.

But let's plug in some real-life numbers. We'll call these "Wall Street numbers." Let's pretend you invested $100,000.

- Year one, you lost 50 percent, which means your account has $50,000, not including brokerage fees.
- Year two, you gained 50 percent, which brings you up to $75,000 because it's half of what's left.
- Year three, you lost 50 percent, which brings your account to $37,500.
- Year four, you gained 50 percent, which brings your account to a total of $56,250.

That's a *minus* 43.75 percent rate of return!

The reality is, your account total would be even lower because you paid brokerage fees, hidden fees, and were subjected to other shenanigans along the way.

What makes this a *terrible* deal for you is that your financial advisor gets paid no matter what. That financial advisor and the executives at ScrewU Financial have brand-new Bentleys, and they're sending their kids to private schools on your money.

Sometimes brokers save me time, money, and energy. When that's the case, I'm happy to pay them a fee or commission. When they're not doing that, then they should not be entitled to that money. If they're offering me value, I will gladly incentivize them. But if they're offering a service I can do myself just as well, why would I include the added expense? It may not make sense for me to hire someone else to do something that I'm already able to do better or faster. Conversely, if they have more expertise than I do, hiring them allows me to do the main things I'm good at, and I'm happy to pay for their services.

Remember what I said about a fiduciary? That's the kind of relationship you're looking for. Having some experience or partnering with someone who knows how to ask great questions will make and save you a fortune.

SKIN IN THE GAME

Here's an example of skin in the game, adding more detail on the example in the previous chapter. As I mentioned previously, I invested in Orangetheory Fitness because former coaching clients brought me the deal. They didn't have the money to do it (I did), and I didn't have the time (they did). They were happy to provide all the sweat equity. For them to have skin in the game, they invested their entire life savings of $15,000. It was a comparatively small amount to my investment of $120,000, but it represented everything they had, and it was their sole opportunity to get out of the rat race and become entrepreneurs.

In this situation, I have long-term equity, and my partners have a vested interest in the success of the organization. And from my point of view, because they committed their time and resources, the work ethic they bring to the operations practically guarantees success. I also drew from my large network of advisors and professionals, because my partners didn't have the money, time, or expertise to pay for or build those relationships. It was a win-win-win.

UNNECESSARY FAT

Here's an example of cutting out the fat. Earlier in Commandment 5, "Create Cash Flow Immediately," I shared my story of acquiring my first three mobile home parks. I had a tremendous amount of success with my first two parks, and the third park was the investment that would allow my passive income to exceed my earned income. The first two parks were purchased with seller financing, but the third park was a unique situation. It was an invisible deal because it was an off-market deal where the buyer cold-called the owner of the property to see if he would sell the park. The two parties signed a contract. They avoided the unnecessary fat of a broker or realtor.

I have a strong network of business professionals, experts, and friends. In this case, the buyer who put the park under contract was a good friend of mine. He decided he didn't want to purchase the park, so he asked me if I wanted to buy it instead. I liked the property and decided to buy the assignment from him, so I was able to get a contract without paying a broker or realtor.

An **assignment** is when someone has a property or asset under contract for purchase, such as with a **purchase sale agreement (PSA),** but instead of closing the transaction, they decide to transfer the rights of the contract to another person. To put it simply, the buyer has the right to execute and close the agreement or assign it to someone else. And once the contract is assigned, that assignee assumes all the terms of the contract.

In this instance, the seller had no say in who bought the property because they were bound to the original contract—not the original buyer they were under contract with, and the contract has language allowing assignments. All the contracts I use also allow assignments.

I had several professionals vet this deal, all of whom loved it. Also, my friend had already done a tremendous amount of due diligence on the deal, so there wasn't much work left for me to do. So, I proceeded and bought the assignment for $20,000 from my friend. I was happy to give my friend a **finder's fee** for all the value he added by doing the work to find and vet the park, and I also was happy to incentivize someone who enabled me to get the deal without having to do the work myself, in essence buying my time back. Additionally, if I had gone through a broker, I would have paid at least double the amount I paid to my friend as a finder's fee. It was a win-win for my friend *and* me.

There's more I want to point out about this deal. My friend did a great job negotiating a really good deal on this park, but as you know from the previous chapters, I have many strategies I use to get an even better deal than most. I went back to the owners of the park and renegotiated additional terms, and I was able to lower the price by over $100,000. I was also able to get them to agree to sell me all the personal property associated with the park, including mobile homes and tractors and their massive shed lined with tools, for an additional $50,000 discount. So, all in all, I reduced the total sale price by over $150,000 on what was already a good investment.

A big myth is that there's really only one way to invest, and you need a money manager and exposure to the stock market. I'm not saying those are bad things—but they're not the *only* things. Having some stock market exposure can be good, but I wouldn't put all my eggs in one basket. I like to be diversified, and I also like to have a little more control and influence on the majority of my investments.

To the best of my ability, I want to cut out all middlemen so my family and I get the profit, or I split the profit with my partners. Alternatively, if they perform well, I make sure the middlemen get some profit that they typically don't earn. If someone earns it by directly adding value, I'm happy to pay for it. I've worked with a number of great brokers, and I'm happy to pay their fees, but if I can avoid a financial institution and go with seller financing, I'm taking that option every time. If I can invest in a way where I don't have to pay a percentage to money managers who make money whether I make money or not, I cut that out as well.

PROFIT FROM KNOWLEDGE

The secret to cutting out the fat is knowing what questions to ask and when to ask them. You learn this by making mistakes over decades *or* by investing in a coach who can save you precious time and hundreds of thousands— or millions—of dollars. Mentorship is the perfect shortcut.

You're going to make mistakes and lose money at some point. Seek the lessons. Learn.

In general, if you look at the fees paid on any account for money that's being professionally managed, you'll be surprised to learn what is being charged. When a much larger part of my investment portfolio was exposed to the stock market and I had someone actively managing it, I recall looking at my statement and feeling like I was punched in the gut. It said I had an average rate of return, which was 7 percent. I thought, *That's cool. I should have made some good money with such a strong average rate of return.* But when I dug a little deeper, I realized I actually *lost* money. My *actual* rate of return was different from my *average* rate of return. I actually lost money with a positive average rate of return!

Even though the average return over the previous five to ten years earned a positive percentage, a down year somewhere in that stretch of time caused me to lose money. Just because the other years had a high percentage and averaged out to make my overall average return percentage look good didn't mean I was actually making money. I had that eye-opening experience, and I felt like I had been duped. I felt like I had been misled. The information shared with me really made it look like I was making money. I felt totally deceived. That is when I first learned that a tremendous amount of misinformation and manipulation are the norm in the financial services industry and conventional investment world.

At that point, I realized that people in that world are really looking out for themselves more than they are me; worse than that, I saw that the person who managed my money still made money even when I lost money. Those bits of information didn't sit well with me. That moment was a turning point in my investing career, where I decided to take matters into my own hands and get serious about my financial education, and I started investing myself.

PROFIT FROM RELATIONSHIPS

Besides learning how to *cut out the fat*, it's really important to be intentional about who you are spending time with—and focus on spending quality time with people you admire most and want to do life with. You really become like the people you surround yourself with, so it's important to choose those relationships wisely. I enjoy meeting people, and I spend a significant amount of time meeting with other investors and entrepreneurs. Talking to investors and business owners is where I learn new strategies that I'm able to employ.

Besides meeting new people, I'm also part of several investment groups. I want to meet like-minded people, but I also want to meet people who think differently than I do—people who play the game of life at a higher level than I do. I'm constantly challenging myself to rise above the status quo, to hold myself to a higher standard, to challenge myself to continue to grow both personally and professionally, and to "level up" my game on a regular and consistent basis. By the latter, I mean finding ways to get better at what I do through mentors, peer groups, books, and podcasts.

Being intentional with these relationships also helps me when I mentor and advise business owners and entrepreneurs. I'm able to show up with years of investment expertise I've tapped into through relationships I've developed over time. I combine and share that expertise along with all the reading, studying, and hands-on experience I've gained independently. In other words, my insatiable desire to learn and grow and my passion to share that knowledge with others combine in ways that profit everyone.

My approach to investing translates perfectly in the next couple of investment opportunities I'll discuss. The first one is about investing in operating companies in general. The second one focuses on a specific investment in a portfolio of software companies that already have some strategic buyers in place who are courting them.

OPERATING COMPANY INVESTMENTS

The next example is one most people have never considered investing in. And, even if they had, they likely wouldn't know how to structure such an investment. Hidden in plain sight are tons of income multipliers. What are they?

You can make a lot of money investing in businesses with little or no capital by increasing the value of that business and getting paid while you do it. When the business sells, you can get a huge payout that multiplies your income. Once you start investing and seeing deal patterns, finding income multipliers by solving problems becomes easier and easier with a combination of your experience, network, advice, and relationships. You can walk into a deal with a little bit of cash or access to capital, a great team, an amazing network, and your experience. With you and your expertise on board, the business can increase its revenue, profit, and desirability to be acquired. Everyone wins. After a time, you can make money over and over again with little personal effort.

Additionally, the money you make on these deals can be negotiated and structured without a broker, fund manager, general partner, investment advisor, or financial institution. You can use these professionals when it makes sense, and you can also reduce expenses when you invest directly in a company without using these professionals.

EXAMPLE: INVESTING IN OPERATING COMPANIES

I have several examples of investments in operating companies from the last ten years that you can use to model deals for yourself. Some are in companies that my friends own, and some are companies owned by people I have never met who've heard about me through word of mouth. An **operating company** is any business that produces goods or services and has regular operations, revenues, expenses, and a team, even if it's just a one-person team in the beginning. An operating company is different from a holding company that just owns the assets of operating companies.

The size of the operating companies I invest in generally ranges from small- to medium-sized businesses with gross sales of $500,000 to $30,000,000, although I have had a few that were much larger as well. Each investment is unique, and each company has different needs, so there is no consistent investment amount or structure. Sometimes the businesses just need some sort of loan to help scale the company and hire more people. Other times, they would like some advice on how to scale, manage a growing team, hire high-level executives to help run the company, create a hiring and training process, create additional systems they can implement, improve, and innovate their advertising and marketing efforts, and other challenges. Though no deal is the same, I do have a standard framework I use for each of these investments.

MINDSET

For years I have invested in operating companies and have also consulted and advised some of these companies on how to scale. I'm constantly reading business books and talking with other successful entrepreneurs about creating standard operating systems (SOPs), scaling, and utilizing unique structures to fund growth. I am always "sharpening my ax" and reinventing myself to offer the maximum amount of value for anyone I work with. Often, people work with me just to gain access to my network, which I am happy to offer. I think it's a great idea for most business owners.

At this point in my career, my favorite deals revolve around giving a loan with some additional kickers and connecting the business owners with my network of professionals and experts so they can scale their companies without needing any of my time. This way, my capital can work for me, and I can earn a great return while enjoying the lifestyle I worked hard to create. I love earning a great return, especially when it doesn't involve any of my time! Once you begin, your network and value will grow at an exponential rate as well.

STRUCTURE

Here is a typical operating company deal structure, though the terms vary based on the investment, and not all terms apply to each investment:

- Two- to three-year loan at 8–15 percent interest (I always give my friends an amazing deal, which is why I have a much wider range with a lower starting point on the interest rate)
- Interest-only payments for one year (I can be flexible here, but I want to create a comfortable loan repayment for the businesses I invest in and reduce risk)
- Principal and interest payments for the rest of the loan term
- Monthly payments for the term of the loan
- Loan collateralized against accounts receivable, real estate, inventory, equipment, intellectual property, stock, and other assets worth significantly more than my investment (in the case of a liquidation, I know I can get my investment back)
- Often have them sign a personal guarantee to secure the loan
- In some cases, instead of a loan, negotiate an equity investment with an accelerated distribution schedule to get principal back over a quicker time frame with monthly distributions
- Top line **revenue share** of 0.5–10 percent (depending on how involved they would like me to be)
- Equity of 0.5–10 percent (depending on the scope and responsibilities they request)

FILTER

Some of these companies had been in business for over twenty years at the time I invested and had a strong track record of consistent revenue and profit. On these investments, my downside is still really low because many of these companies are consistent performers. They aren't necessarily growing or growing at the rate the business owner wants, and the odds of maintaining their current production or growing that production are high. I like investments where I can cap the downside risk but have the opportunity to also participate in a big upside return.

NEGOTIATION

Most of these deals don't involve too much negotiating because the business owners come to me through referrals and already know the terms I used with other business owners. There is always still some element to the negotiation, though, especially when entrepreneurs want more than just a loan. Sometimes I structure revenue shares on the gross income because I prefer terms that provide monthly cash flow over the life of the business. Other times, I structure equity in the company, especially if plenty of opportunity exists for distributions or the company has the potential to grow quickly with an extremely high valuation in the future. Sometimes we agree to both a revenue share and equity.

I also know that I can get into a senior secured debt position with a first lien on that asset to mitigate some of the downside risk. Again, I am in the safest investment position and will be the first person to be paid back, which is the most important position to be in when investing. In Commandment 1: Lifestyle First, I talked about hard money loans, which is another example of being in the first lien position. My goal is always to create a win-win scenario between a business owner and me.

THE DEAL IN REVIEW

"In the land of the blind, the one-eyed man is king!" What that proverb means is that if you walk in with some experience doing deals like these, word will spread, and soon you'll get requests to help other business owners. The more deals you do, the faster you'll grow your value and gain experience, which gives you more leverage. Every business owner becomes a mentor to you.

The feedback I often hear from business owners, business partners, and other entrepreneurs is that the loan or investment I gave them was helpful to scaling their business, but my advisory capacity and my network connections turned out to be far more valuable to them than the loan or investment. In other words, the connections I make and the creative ideas I'm able to share on how to scale are worth more to them than the loan or investment. The way I advise and the ideas I share are unique, and the relationships I bring to the table end up becoming valuable strategic partnerships across many brands and professions. This capacity will organically and naturally happen for you too.

Remember, when you're just starting out, you probably have more time than money, so the fastest way to *cut out the fat* is by doing a few more things yourself. That's what I did when I started because time was a lot less expensive than money. Also, in every situation, you want to understand *how people get paid* so that you can negotiate in a way that requires that the other party has

Learn and gain an education from every investment. Ask: "Teach me why you made this investment decision."

"skin in the game" (risk) and is providing as much value as possible.

Finally, keep in mind that the biggest mistake new investors make is not asking enough questions to find out where the fat actually is and how everyone makes money. In my experience, the best thing you can do is ask a lot of questions, find out where the fat is, and negotiate a deal where vendors, brokers, and bankers only win when you win—and they get paid *after* they fulfill their promises. Once you start making a lot more money and have more assets, you'll find that you're willing to pay a little extra to work with these experts in some deals because you can do even more deals, which more than makes up for the increased expense. In addition, the sizes of the deals you'll be doing will increase, and you'll have partners and employees who give you leverage so you can continue to remain profitable while protecting your time.

INVESTING IN OPERATING COMPANIES - 2024 DEAL UPDATE

2024 UPDATE SUMMARY:

- Invested in accelerator providing startup portfolio diversification
- Favorable terms and milestone warrants provide upside
- Revenue/equity structures avoid unnecessary fees
- Early traction signals promise across several companies

Over the last decade, I've enjoyed partnering with a range of promising operating companies across multiple industries. My involvement ranges from pure capital provider to an active advisor and network connector.

I like to structure these investments with debt or equity upfront and additional revenue share and equity kickers once key milestones are achieved. This optimizes my return potential while incentivizing the operating team.

Recently, I invested in an accelerator platform that provides exposure to over two hundred amazing startups. We receive equity upfront in each company at favorable valuations. As the companies hit growth milestones, we have the right to invest more at the same valuation through warrants. This provides built-in upside if the startups succeed, while our downside is protected if they languish.

Though early, multiple portfolio companies already have tremendous traction. The platform's robust deal flow and rigorous vetting also provide built-in diversification.

Importantly to note, this platform plans to invest in another 800+ companies, bringing the portfolio to 1,000+ startups in total. Our investment includes all new companies the accelerator platform backs going forward.

Overall, this accelerator has proven to be a phenomenal model to participate in the growth of emerging companies while mitigating risk. I'm extremely energized by the early signs I'm seeing.

In fact, I've invested in another accelerator where each of the first eleven companies has awarded us free warrants. Rather than a portfolio model, this accelerator creates a new fund for each startup cohort.

Rather than solely invest capital, I cut out the fat by structuring revenue and equity shares. I avoid unnecessary middleman fees this way while incentivizing my partners to build valuable companies.

KEY INSIGHTS:

- Invested in several accelerators providing diversified emerging company exposure
- Favorable upfront valuations reduce downside risk.
- Milestone-based warrants allow upside participation if companies grow.
- Multiple portfolio companies showing exciting early traction.
- Accelerator model simplifies startup vetting and provides inherent diversification.

EXAMPLE: SOFTWARE PORTFOLIO

The last example I shared was more of an overview of the way I invest in operating companies as a whole because each investment is different, and the terms vary. Here I want to walk you through an example of a specific company I invested in and some of the unique terms I negotiated. This company has a different structure than my last example, but the deal still incorporates most of the other commandments covered in this book. If you ever have an opportunity to invest in an operating company like this one, you'll have more options for what to look for and how to structure the investment.

MINDSET

I invested in a company that is an incubator for software companies and strategically invests in equity positions in those companies. An **incubator**, sometimes called an **accelerator**, is an organization designed to accelerate the growth and success of early-stage companies through an array of business support resources and services offered at below-market prices. This company's specific niche is SaaS (software as a service) companies, which are software licensing companies. I like the SaaS industry because it has some of the highest multiples on exits in the business world. In this context, a **multiple** is a performance measurement found by a simple calculation of multiplying a specific item on a financial statement by another number to determine the total value of the asset.

Typically, multiples are applied to **EBITDA** (Earnings Before Interest, Taxes, Depreciation, and Amortization), which is one way of measuring a company's profit. However, SaaS companies often sell for a multiple of revenue, which means the exits are much bigger because the value is based on top-line revenue before subtracting expenses. SaaS exits can have multiples of eight to twenty times annual recurring revenue (ARR) or even more! **Annual recurring revenue**, or **run rate**, is the annual revenue from a business's existing subscriptions. Companies in high growth can even sell based on **monthly recurring revenue (MRR),** which investors find even more predictable.

The larger the run rate and current month-over-month growth, the higher the multiple. Most businesses typically have a multiple of one to four times EBITDA. So, not only are the multiples for SaaS companies higher than most other businesses but the multiples are also taken on top-line revenue as opposed to EBITDA or profit. I like having a portion of my investment portfolio allocated to technology such as SaaS companies for the large upside potential.

STRUCTURE

At the time of the investment into this particular incubator, there were seven portfolio companies that were valued at $16,000,000. I was able to get a 36 percent discount on the valuation of the company for my investment. The portfolio has since increased in value, so that negotiated piece was a major win. I also negotiated a warrant structure of 1 percent per $100,000 (0.5 percent per $50,000) in the parent company into perpetuity. This piece of the deal means that every time any one of the seven portfolio companies sells, my investor group gets a piece of the action regardless of how long it takes for a company to sell.

The plan was to have one of the portfolio companies sell every six to twelve months so there would be multiple liquidity events. Also, I negotiated the same warrant structure on all additional portfolio companies the parent company acquires to get an ownership interest in each new acquisition for the next five years. For clarity, the investment in the first seven portfolio companies is in perpetuity. It's only any additional portfolio company beyond those seven that is tied to the shorter five-year term.

If my Lifestyle Investor Mastermind doesn't earn a minimum of a 2X multiple on our investment by the end of that five-year term, the portion of the agreement specifically related to earning warrants on any additional portfolio companies automatically renews for another full year until the 2X minimum is hit. So far, three additional portfolio companies have been acquired and added to our investment. We were automatically awarded the same warrant structure for these three new portfolio companies as the previous seven, now making a total of fifteen portfolio companies in this investment, with more to be added.

FILTER

Most of the time when you invest in software companies or venture capital funds that invest in software companies, it is a long-term hold, meaning you likely won't see a return on your investment for seven to ten years or more. That time frame is too long for me to wait to get my investment back or to realize a return because I want to put the same money to work multiple times at once. For example, if I get my principal back within two years of each investment, I can make at least five different investments during that ten-year timeframe with the same money while earning at least five different returns—and potentially have at least five different equity positions.

In this particular investment, the likelihood of an exit within the first year was really good. As long as you choose wisely and negotiate terms the way I'm showing you, the likelihood of an exit within the first year or two is really good for you too. In addition, there are multiple opportunities for a liquidity event, so there could be several returns over the life of this investment and possibly even on an annual basis.

NEGOTIATION

In order to reduce the risk, I negotiated a couple of strategic deal terms. The first was a put option plus 20 percent interest. If my investor group doesn't like the direction the company is headed, we can get our investment back at any time with a 20 percent interest payment for the duration the money was invested. The second negotiation was a first liquidation preference so that the first exit would pay our principal investment back in full, regardless of how much the sale price was. Even if the sale was less than the amount to cover our investment based on the warrants, we have a contractual guarantee that we are first in line to get our full investment paid back before anyone else in the company can take out any money. Also, if the owner raises more money, we are still in the first position to be paid.

THE DEAL IN REVIEW

I like an investment that has big return potential and multiple exit scenarios with strong downside risk protection. This scenario is extremely friendly to the investor. Within the first year, it is likely I will earn at least my principal investment back and then have all my money out of the deal to participate in the upside for years to come. Even if only one company sells out of the ten current portfolio companies, I still make my investment back with a good return on top of it. If two or more companies exit, however, I could have an exponential return. The likelihood of two or more companies selling is really good because already some notable strategic buyers have inquired about purchasing several of these portfolio companies.

Additionally, the owner is already in discussions to add several more companies to the current portfolio. It is possible that the total portfolio could grow in size to thirty plus companies that my Lifestyle Investor Mastermind will have warrant coverage on. If the investment doesn't perform for any reason, we can execute the put option plus 20 percent interest for a great return.

The bottom line is, this incubator was a great investment opportunity to *cut out the fat* and invest in a way that the owner has plenty of skin in the game, and the deal has total alignment with everyone involved, including the investors.

> **2024 UPDATE:** This company is in the process of being acquired by a public company. Their portfolio companies are growing and expanding, with multiple acquisitions in motion.

COMMANDMENT 9: USE LEVERAGE TO YOUR ADVANTAGE

Success is 80 percent mindset and 20 percent skill.

—Tony Robbins

I hear people say they don't have the money to invest in real estate. That's a total myth. *You don't need to have the money.* I've learned that when you have a good deal, the money shows up from a variety of sources. Investors want a good deal. If you can find one, it's really easy to raise money from them. Sophisticated investors will recognize a good deal and want in.

I like using banks as a source of funds for my investments, but only when they benefit me with favorable terms. When they don't, I cut them out of my deal.

In some instances where I'm buying real estate or investing in other assets, I'll use a bank. Traditionally banks use a **recourse loan**, which means if I default for any reason, they can come after my assets. With those loans, you want to be careful and know what you're signing. In many instances, the asset itself is a high enough value that there may not be additional recourse. If things go south, hopefully, the bank will take the asset, and you can move on. Legally, however, the bank has the right to come after all your assets until they get paid back in full.

If you work with a bank on a real estate deal, you can typically purchase an asset with a down payment of just 20–25 percent. It's a great way to increase your net worth and have an asset that produces income purchased predominantly with other people's money. In addition, you get appreciation on that asset and can improve it to make even more money on a cash flow basis by charging more rent. Plus, the whole time, you've got tenants in your real estate who are paying you to rent your property. You can pay the mortgage down by using the renters' money.

This is just one example of how you can have an asset grow and only have to put down 20-25 percent to purchase it—or even less if you can negotiate a seller-financed deal or find the right bank that will work with you. You can collateralize a loan for better terms so you don't spend as much money, and you get an asset with intrinsic value. Because you can own it for so little down, your leverage is magnified.

Another reason some people don't invest in real estate is because they think it is too great of a risk. That is a total myth as well. The truth is, they don't invest because they don't understand it well enough and haven't committed the time to learn it. I don't buy anything based on the *hope* that it appreciates; I buy assets because *I know for a fact* that the cash flow starts today.

Real estate investing isn't difficult to learn, especially real estate rentals. I often review the same deals people choose to pass on because they think the deals are too risky. When I do, I often realize *I can get in this deal for virtually no risk and negotiate better terms because all those people who looked before me looked at the first offer someone made to them without any negotiations.*

In those situations, the only party who would benefit was the seller, so the buyers passed without negotiating further. A deal isn't a good deal until both the buyer and the seller benefit. I go in on those same deals people walk away from and negotiate better terms that make money with almost zero risk. Success comes from how you structure the deal and how you negotiate, all with a mindset of both parties winning. The investor

> The mind is the limit. As long as the mind can envision the fact that you can do something, you can do it, as long as you really believe 100 percent.
>
> —Arnold Schwarzenegger

benefits from building that asset class and gaining more equity, and the seller wins by getting a price and terms they feel good about. All parties win.

LENDING OPTIONS

Let's discuss for a moment all the different lending options available, what risks exist with each, and how to use each type of leverage to your advantage.

The first two loans are direct lending options, which means that the loan funding happens directly with the end lender.

1. **Seller finance**. This is my favorite direct lending option. It is much faster than traditional lending products, and often you can negotiate the best terms. This loan is *non-recourse* typically, which means if anything goes wrong, the lender can only take back the specific asset in the contract and cannot come after your other assets. The borrower is not personally responsible for the repayment of the loan. That is a very good protection I like to have in place.

2. **Traditional bank loans.** I prefer small local banks because you typically have more negotiating power. These banks are looking for loans they can write and often know the local real estate market better than a bigger bank. Most of these loans are *recourse* loans, which means the bank can come after any asset you have to get repaid in the event of a default. The primary options here are SBA loans and conventional loans. An SBA loan is partially guaranteed by the government, but you need to jump through many more hoops to get that loan, and it can take a longer time to close. Most of the loans I do with banks are conventional loans, and the length of the note usually varies from three to ten years.

The next two loans are secondary market lending options, which means the loans are bought and sold between lenders and investors. These are non-recourse loans.

1. **Conduit loans, also known as commercial mortgage-backed security loans**. These loans typically have Wall Street investment firms originating them. The loans themselves are eventually bundled and sold in the secondary market to other

investors. These loans have a lower interest rate than traditional bank loans and can often offer a longer term for the note. Most of these terms are ten years. These loans are often assumable, so if you sell the asset, someone else can take over the current loan for you, releasing you from your loan obligation. That aspect of the loan can be attractive to a new buyer, especially if the interest rate is below market rates.

The downside of conduit loans is the lack of flexibility once a loan is written. These loans are designed for more of a long-term hold, so you wouldn't want to use them if you were just planning on flipping the property within a few years. Also, you have several fees to consider. There are fees if you sell or refinance the property early, called **defeasance;** or if you prepay the loan, the fee is called **yield maintenance**. Often there are fees to allow a new buyer to assume the loan. Generally, the fee to set up a conduit loan is 1 percent paid upfront at the time of closing.

2. **Agency loans**. These loans are issued by one of the government-sponsored agencies such as the Federal National Mortgage Association (**Fannie Mae**) and Federal Home Loan Mortgage Corporation (**Freddie Mac**). These loans are also bundled and sold on the secondary market to other investors. These loans have many of the same pros and cons as conduit loans, such as being non-recourse and having a similar fee structure, but the main benefit to these loans is you can often get a 30-year fixed-interest loan. For investors whose strategy is to buy and hold, these loans are highly desirable.

HOW TO USE DEBT TO YOUR ADVANTAGE

Another successful Lifestyle Investor strategy is to buy assets and hold them forever and never sell them. If you need cash, you can just borrow against these assets and pledge them as collateral. You can pledge your real estate, your stock, and your whole life insurance as collateral, among other assets. I have used this strategy to my advantage over the years.

Most people don't know that their stock can be pledged as collateral. Let's say you own $1,000,000 of Amazon stock. Currently, you can go to your local bank and get an $800,000 loan at the London Inter-Bank Offered Rate (LIBOR) plus fifty **basis points** (0.5 percent) for a total of 0.65 percent interest. **LIBOR** is the benchmark interest rate that global banks use to lend to one another. There is no tax treatment on getting one of these loans because they are not taxable.

Let's take this example one step further. If you have $1,000,000 of stock and need $100,000 of it to live on, you can sell $100,000 in stock and be charged anywhere from 25-50 percent in taxes depending on your income. In this case, you could end up having as little as $50,000 left over after taxes to live on. You would actually have to sell $200,000 to be able to have closer to that $100,000 you need to live on. You would then have only $800,000 in stock left. If you sell $200,000 a year for five years in a row, you will eventually spend all of your stock down to zero (except for the gain it makes). In the sixth year after doing so, you are out of money and need to find another way to get your $100,000 to live on.

Here is a better way. Currently, you can borrow instead against your $1,000,000 in stock and pay as low as just 1 percent interest or less. Let's say you borrow $101,000 ($100,000 plus $1,000 in interest) against your stock to get the $100,000 to live on. In this example, since you have a loan and aren't selling your asset, you would not owe tax on the stock because you have no income or capital gains associated with it.

Additionally, you can do the same for as long as the stock continues to increase in value. If the asset goes up 10 percent per year, then you can borrow against it into perpetuity at the amount it appreciates. In other words, if you have $1,000,000 in stock and it goes up by 10 percent per year, that is $100,000 per year it increases so you can borrow against that amount each year to live on.

You can do something similar with real estate as well. If real estate appreciates 7–10 percent per year (and potentially more in strong markets), you can go to the bank and refinance the real estate and pull out that debt to live on tax-free. There is no capital gain because you didn't sell anything, and you have no income from it because you are just borrowing against it. The liability offsets the asset. Plus, the real estate can be handed down to your heirs so that they can do the same thing in perpetuity and hand it down to their heirs.

This example shows what every sophisticated real estate investor does. As the government continues printing more money, your real estate will continue to increase in value because as the supply of money expands, so will your assets.

Let's say you have $10,000,000 in real estate and you can borrow $8,000,000 against it. You wouldn't want to sell the real estate because you would pay taxes. Instead, you would just keep borrowing against it for tax-free income. As you continue to refinance equity out of your real estate, besides having income to live on, you can use that same income to buy more real estate that you can borrow against and pull more cash out of to live on. You can literally never make any money your entire life if you follow this plan and live off the debt you pull out of your assets.

In order for this strategy to work, you need a low-interest loan environment and a strong relationship with some good bankers. You also want the monetary supply to continue to expand so your assets continue to increase in value. You can then use leverage to acquire even more assets and then borrow against those assets.

Rather than generating income that you will have to pay taxes on, you can own real estate that appreciates without being taxed, ideally holding it forever, as Warren Buffett says to do. All of this is possible even if your real estate doesn't produce cash flow, although I prefer cash-flowing assets to add even more optionality to your lifestyle and finances.

You can use this same strategy of borrowing against your assets utilizing whole-life insurance as well, with potentially even greater upside than these last two examples of using stock and real estate as collateral to take out tax-free loans to live on.

HOW LIFESTYLE INVESTING WORKS

This next example utilizes several of the strategies from this chapter and is a perfect example of Lifestyle Investing. Throughout this book, I've been using examples of mobile home park investments because they are real deals that sparked my success, have generated a lot of money, and are non-obvious investments. I'd like to illustrate this example through the lens of leverage. I'm doing this so you can see there is consistency, continuity, and discipline in the investments I've made. Once you start finding deals, I encourage you to apply the same level of discipline and incorporate all of the principles, filters, and commandments throughout this book.

EXAMPLE: MOBILE HOME PARK

This particular mobile home park deal I found by cold calling the owner close to five years prior to purchasing it. I developed a relationship with the owner, his wife, and their daughter who helped run the day-to-day operations of the business. I kept in touch regularly over the years because I wanted to remain top of mind with them. Plus, the mobile home park was right down the street from two of the other parks I owned, so I would stop by in person periodically when visiting them.

I knew that the owner would sell the park eventually because he was getting older, but because he'd built the park himself, he was so emotionally attached to it that it was difficult for him to let it go. Eventually, the owner died, but the family remembered me. When it came time to sell, I was at the top of their list.

MINDSET

I love investing in mobile home parks for a variety of reasons. If you buy them the right way, they have very little risk. It's easy to get financing on them because they have one of the lowest default rates in all of real estate, which lenders love. You can buy them with any one of several options—seller, bank, conduit, and agency financing—with just a 20 percent down payment and great terms. These parks produce cash flow on the first day you own them. It's also easy to make improvements, which immediately increases the value and produces even more cash flow.

Affordable housing will always be in great demand and is virtually recession-proof. Everyone needs a place to live, and a mobile home park is the cheapest housing available and provides more amenities than Class C apartments. Mobile homes have a yard, no one above them, and no adjoining wall transferring noise at all hours. They can eventually have the American dream of home ownership with only the expense of the lot rent, which is just $280/month on average in the US. There is no housing cheaper than that.

For you, there are massive tax benefits because you own real estate.

STRUCTURE

Here is how I structured this deal:

- Purchase price of $2,700,000 and structured financing with a local bank
- 20 percent down payment of $540,000
- Ten-year note at 5 percent interest for the remaining $2,160,000
- Amortized at 25 years (payments based on a 25-year loan)
- Monthly cash flow (with that low of a mortgage payment, I had considerable monthly cash flow starting the very first month of ownership)
- Additional loan of $150,000 added to the main note so I could repave the roads and amortize that expense over the same 25 years (a strategic way to do **capital improvements** is by using bank capital and not your own capital and with no down payment and only a small monthly payment—with huge tax advantages)
- Park appraisal for much more than the purchase price, so I knew I was buying the property way under value and was able to eliminate almost all my risk (I did buy the park for the seller's asking price, though, so it was a win-win scenario)

- Profit in that first year of $224,000 (cash-on-cash return that first year was 41 percent)
- Profit the following year of $326,000 (we improved the property and billed back water and sewer charges to the residents)
- In two years, profited $550,000 (down payment was only $540,000)
- In year three, continued to improve the property and increased rents (the park rent was still priced way under market, so profitability continued to increase)
- Due to the great relationship established with the local lender, I negotiated a loan modification to structure better terms and pull out close to $1,000,000 of equity from the park one year after purchased (a **loan modification** is similar to a refinance but it's much cheaper and infinitely faster, as it only took a couple of days to finalize)

FILTER

This deal originally made sense to me because it was an off-market deal where I was able to work out a price directly with the owners. I knew I was getting the park way under value, so it would be easy to get a loan on the property. I knew the cash flow from this park alone would cover all my expenses, current lifestyle, and beyond. This purchase would allow me to achieve my goal of not needing earned income ever again, and it was the catalyst to many more additional deals with strong cash flow. The additional cash flow that exceeded lifestyle expenses was then reinvested into more cash-flow-producing assets to compound the overall return of that single investment.

NEGOTIATION

Many of the deal points had to be negotiated to get this great of a deal. While I was in the final stages of negotiation and finalizing the purchase sale agreement, the sellers decided they wanted to use a broker to sell the park. Originally, it was just the sellers and I working together. Once the broker entered the equation, he wanted to increase the purchase price by $300,000, so the first negotiation was to get that price back down to the original price. Then there was considerable negotiation with the bank to get great terms.

I always get terms from at least three different banks whenever I decide to get financing. That way, I can put the banks up against each other and negotiate even better terms. I have found that when lenders know several banks are competing for my business, they are competitive with their terms because they don't want to miss out on providing me the loan I need. Once the deal was done, I negotiated the extra loan to repave the roads and then the loan modification to get even better terms, which were already great at that time, but I was able to pull close to $1,000,000 in equity out of the deal. I could then turn around and invest that money into several more cash flow-generating assets.

THE DEAL IN REVIEW

This example is yet another one about leverage and phantom income, as I discussed in Commandment 6: Find an Income Amplifier. I earned cash flow on nearly $1,000,000 that didn't exist when I first bought the park. Just the cash flow alone on that phantom income is earning me close to $150,000 a year now. The bottom line is that it was a great deal for a plethora of reasons, and it's a property I still own today.

The best and fastest way to get and use leverage is to borrow someone else's money or do a seller-financed deal with a low down payment (or no down payment at all) with no recourse. What you're effectively doing is transferring wealth to yourself with no risk or cost. If you can find a way to improve that asset without writing a check, you improve and increase equity and increase cash flow as well.

Here's an example. You could find an asset and do seller financing with a low down payment or no down payment or use one of the financing options I discussed in this chapter. Perhaps you could find a service provider or partner willing to make improvements on your property for a small percentage of income, and then you could find a property manager who would also work for a small percentage of income. This scenario is a no-cash transaction with no risk.

<callout>You can always grow and improve. I don't ever want to arrive. I want to continue the journey. </callout>

The best part of using leverage is that it's just a negotiation and an exercise in creativity. All anyone can say is no, but most of the time you can land the deal by asking great questions—and having someone to model who's done a similar deal in the past paves the way. Finding a mentor or a mastermind can be so powerful. Just one idea can pay for itself by 10X in a single transaction.

MOBILE HOME PARKS - 2024 DEAL UPDATE

2024 UPDATE SUMMARY:

- Among highest returning investments ever
- Grew portfolio through additional acquisitions
- Added institutional management to scale
- Assets proved profitable even during recessions
- Used leverage to accelerate growth

Many years ago I reached out to an owner of a mobile home park near some properties I already owned. He had built the park himself years before and was emotionally attached to it.

Despite his reluctance to sell, I made sure to stop by periodically to build rapport. After years of patience, the owner died, and his family finally decided it was time to sell. Because I had nurtured the relationship, I was at the top of their list.

We negotiated an off-market deal for the property at a substantial discount to intrinsic value. The low basis meant I could earn strong cash flow from day 1. And there were clear opportunities to add value and grow the bottom line.

In the first year alone, we generated over 40 percent cash-on-cash returns by improving operations, and that was just the beginning. Fast forward to today, and that single park has produced millions in profit over the years since acquiring it.

The success of that third park gave me the confidence to continue acquiring additional communities. Now our portfolio has grown to over 1,500 lots and we partnered with an institutional operator to scale the platform.

Beyond the returns, mobile home parks proved to be one of the most stable assets, with occupancy remaining high even during recessions. As more institutional capital enters the space, values have grown substantially.

I used extensive leverage to my advantage to acquire mobile home parks. The leverage magnified equity returns manyfold while the assets' cash flows protected my downside. This allowed me to scale rapidly.

KEY INSIGHTS:

- Mobile home parks generated strong profits even during recessions.
- Portfolio growth and institutional management enhanced efficiencies.
- Emotional sellers and off-market deals can yield bargains.
- Segment continues to attract growing institutional attention.

NEW DEAL EXAMPLE: DOG TRAINING COMPANY

Here's a deal that didn't make it into the 2020 version of *The Lifestyle Investor,* but is a perfect example of what can happen when you combine multiple Commandments with my Core Principles of Lifestyle Investing. This shows how you can structure and negotiate your investments in a way that's a win for everyone involved.

OVERVIEW

I had the opportunity to partner with my friend John to purchase a dog training company. At the time, John was working in corporate America making $65,000 a year. Meanwhile, the owners of this dog training company were paying themselves $75,000 a year. I saw this as the perfect opportunity to help John ditch the rat race and step into a business where he could make more money off the bat and also earn some sweat equity upside.

This deal came about through good old-fashioned relationships and intentional networking. I had introduced John to the concept of buying a business rather than starting one from scratch since acquisitions can have an established track record. He learned about this company through a connection that led to the owners. We moved quickly to put in an offer and secure the deal.

When we first took over, the business totally cratered. The seller was shady, the staff bailed, and there was no training program like we were promised. But through overhauling systems, hiring strong leaders, and booking out months of training appointments, we got this business producing over $100,000 per month in just a few months. We ended up selling at 1 year and 1 day for over 11X the return.

MINDSET

My mindset going into this deal follows Commandment 1, "Lifestyle First," and Commandment 2, "Reduce the Risk." I wasn't doing this to make the most money possible: I wanted to help my friend John exit his corporate job for good. Even though I could have taken far more equity, I let John have the majority stake so he could reap maximum rewards.

I also knew that with proper systems and leadership in place, a dog training business would be recession-proof. People love their pets and will spend money on them even in tough times. The huge demand for dogs and training coming out of COVID made this look like a smart bet. And with a proven model in place, our downside risk seemed minimal, even if we had to overhaul things initially.

STRUCTURE

- Purchased for $500,000 with $100,000 down
- At the time, business had $160,000 EBITDA
- Purchased at a 3X EBITDA multiple
- Structured 80 percent loan with 20 percent down payment
- Split ownership 60 percent (John) / 40 percent (me)
- Gave John majority equity so he could have the maximum reward and be "pot committed" to making this work
- Owner's salary of $75,000 accounted for in existing EBITDA

FILTER

The criteria I used to evaluate this deal made it really appealing to me. With COVID trends showing a massive increase in pet and dog ownership, I knew demand for training would be high. We had the chance to purchase this business at an attractive 3X EBITDA multiple. Having my friend John as a strong corporate operator to lead the transition also gave me confidence.

My maximum downside was capped at my $100,000 investment, but the upside potential was huge. The deal structure allowed for distributions in the short term, so I could get my capital back quickly. And I would retain long-term equity for residual cash flow. Based on these factors, it was clear this deal could produce strong returns with minimal risk.

NEGOTIATION

There were several elements of this deal I negotiated for preferred terms. Although I could have taken the majority of equity, I gave my operating partner John 60 percent ownership to align everyone's incentives.

I also negotiated with John for an accelerated distribution schedule of 80 percent of the cash flow so I could get my $100,000 principal investment back in less than four months, which completely de-risked the deal for me. Then we reverted back to the 60/40 equity split for distributions.

Given my relationships with banks, I was able to personally guarantee financing at favorable rates. In this case, I negotiated a partial personal guarantee, so I was only on the hook for 20 percent of the banknote.

Something important to consider is that over time, personal guarantees fall off. You may not realize this, but you can negotiate the terms of a personal guarantee with banks. I've often been able to reduce personal guarantees to half after one to two years and eliminate them completely after three to four years.

This leaves me with no more personal liability. Reducing and eventually eliminating personal responsibility was an important negotiating point for me in this and other deals.

I also negotiated the deal terms with John to include a salary bump from his corporate job along with significant equity upside. My goal was structuring a win-win partnership where John could build wealth by owning a business instead of just collecting a paycheck.

These negotiated elements made the deal work well for all parties.

THE DEAL IN REVIEW

This investment reinforces the value of stacking my commandments and core principles. It provided passive income and aligned with my lifestyle and my operating partner's lifestyle (Commandment 1). The business was likely to thrive even in tough times, which reduced my risk (Commandment 2). We found an invisible opportunity to buy a business in a booming industry with plenty of demand (Commandment 3). And I negotiated terms to get my principal back in less than four months (Commandment 4). Finally, it produced immediate cash flow (Commandment 5).

And, as I mentioned above, although I could have been more aggressive, I structured this deal so my operating partner John had the majority of equity. My priority was creating an opportunity to help him build wealth through business ownership. This exemplifies the long-term, win-win partnerships I try to structure. A decade later, John continues to partner with me on new investments because of the generosity on the front end of this deal.

COMMANDMENT 10:
EVERY DOLLAR OF INVESTMENT
GETS A RETURN

An investment in knowledge pays the best interest.

—Benjamin Franklin

What if I told you I could give you a guaranteed 5,000 percent return on your investment *and* get your initial investment back in just two months? And if you chose *not* to do it that way, you would lose your investment for sure? In times of war, soldiers are told to prepare for the worst. That's because *when you prepare for the worst, it never happens.* (I'll tell you what this investment is at the end of this chapter.)

MYTHS ABOUT KNOWLEDGE

Some people believe they can't invest because they don't know about investing. Another myth. You can learn. In fact, once you own investments, you're quickly *forced* to learn about them. I found ownership to be the fastest way to learn.

Ordinary people think that if they're not an expert, they can't do something. That's a total myth too. You can hire experts for everything. I work with a team of advisors who are infinitely smarter than I am on many different topics. That's why I work with them and why I'm excited to have them on my team. When I talk to a professional, I let them know upfront that I'm not hiring someone to do all of the work for me. Anyone can do that. I am hiring them to teach me all the nuances associated with why they make the decisions they make.

The first place to invest is in yourself and your education.

I also only hire professionals who are the foremost experts in their craft. I want to learn what they know so I can draw upon that knowledge in the future. This approach ensures that I get the highest level of education in working with them. There's more. Not only do I get an incredible education from these experts that I can use in the future, but I can also avoid paying for that same work in the future once I understand the *how* and *why* behind it.

Imagine if you hired someone to educate you. You would want to know *why* they made certain decisions because you're not paying for the *service*; you're paying for the *education*. That mindset has really benefited me. Because I've paid close attention and asked my attorneys, CPAs, and tax strategists tons of questions in every one of my deals, I come into all new deal negotiations with that background and expertise. In addition, because I can do so much of the pre-work myself, I might need less of their time, which can mean lower legal bills when I do use them.

EXPERIENCED ADVISORS

I take great joy in paying for top-notch legal and professional services. I used to be bothered by paying so much in legal and professional fees until I understood how much work and effort it would take me to figure those things out on my own. Now I see that I earned an incredible return from hiring the best and brightest minds to help me. It is the happiest money I spend when it's the right fit.

In my experience, the best type of primary attorney to hire is one who specializes in bankruptcy. They see the world as it falls apart; they understand what the breakup process typically looks like and the real risks that exist. Because of this perspective, they can add specific elements to your contracts to protect you and your partners at the beginning.

I truly believe it makes sense to outsource anything that's outside your core competencies once you find an expert who will teach you what they're doing.

Real knowledge is to know the extent of one's ignorance.

–Confucius

My advisors are brilliant, and they have years of expertise in fields I know little to nothing about. Hiring them saves me so much time and headache for something I couldn't even do as well as them—even if I made it my full-time job. Plus, they may think about things completely differently than I do and offer insight I would never have had on my own. My advisors also help me pay attention to my blind spots and are much more detail-oriented than I am personally so they ensure small details don't slip through the cracks.

Besides helping me make a better return on my investments and structure my deals to perform as intended, they also help me to not make poor investments. When I think about the education and expertise I want help with the most from my advisors, I think about how they can continue to add value to me based on them helping me make better overall returns, protecting me from losing money, and helping me minimize my tax exposure. My legal professionals have made me an incredible return on my investment with them because of focusing on these key areas.

Sometimes getting into a deal is really opening the door for future deals. It's letting people know you're there to play and will be first in line when they have the next appealing deal. A huge part of investing is networking and establishing relationships. Then, it's making sure you do what you say you're going to do. If you say you're going to invest in something and fund it, it needs to be funded exactly when and how you said it would. Leave a good impression wherever you go.

One other point on finding the right advisors. Some people don't realize the importance of working with people you actually really enjoy spending time with and learning from. I first interview all professionals I work with so they understand how important education is to me. I also make sure we'd be a good fit and that I'd actually enjoy working with them. If not, I cross them off my list. I want to work with people who are experts, but I also must enjoy working with them. Therefore, my vetting process for selecting experts is important to my success.

Gaining knowledge in investing is also about modeling success. When I find someone doing something that works, I'm going to copy it. There's a good chance that once I educate myself more with that particular model, I'm going to innovate and make it better. It doesn't mean I necessarily will do what they do better, but it does mean I can at least replicate what other successful people are doing.

I'm a big fan of immersion learning, so I enjoy boot camps, conferences, and seminars. I've attended countless of these events over the years for various investment topics and projects. I'm also a fan of reading. I read at least a book or two a week. Reading is probably my top way to learn outside of hands-on experience. I'm also happy and excited to enlist the help of mentors. I've had many mentors in my life; most often, the relationship begins with simply asking a person to step into that role. And by the way, I'm happy to pay for that mentorship; I've invested in various mentorships over the years because I know that the return is tenfold, twentyfold, or maybe even more.

CASHFLOW Quadrant: Rich Dad's Guide to Financial Freedom by Robert Kiyosaki was a pivotal book that taught me how to think about where in the CASHFLOW Quadrant I fall in terms of being an employee, self-employed, business owner, or investor. Early on in my entrepreneurial career, I thought I was a business owner because I was running a small business; but really, I wasn't a business owner yet. I was self-employed. As Robert Kiyosaki explained in *CASHFLOW Quadrant*, if a business owner can stop running his or her business for more than a year and it grows during that time without them, then it is an actual business and not a sole proprietorship. In other words, a true business owner has systems and teams that run the business, so it operates successfully without the owner's involvement. If I would have left town for an extended period, then my business would have fallen apart.

That big realization taught me that I had to create a better business that didn't rely on me to function and scale, which is a challenging task most entrepreneurs never achieve. My biggest realization, however, was understanding that what I thought I wanted was to be a business owner but actually, I wanted to be an investor instead. Only as an investor would I truly be able to separate my time from my income.

At that point, my focus became how to move to the *investor* side of Kiyosaki's CASHFLOW Quadrant to invest in or buy businesses rather than start and run businesses. I spent many intentional years moving toward that investor goal.

So, what's that 5,000 percent return I shared at the beginning of this chapter that could repay itself in just two to three months? *The biggest and best investment you'll ever make is increasing your knowledge and capabilities by investing in a great business coach.*

A BUSINESS COACH

A great business coach can prevent you from making stupid mistakes, such as hiring the wrong people, and help you build a better team around you in record time. You don't have to learn what they know. They can bring you into deals and opportunities that you couldn't find yourself and help you structure deals and think about different ways to negotiate.

Think about it like this—if you could go back in time twenty years and invest in Apple® and Google®, would you do it? A couple of thousand dollars would be worth tens of millions (or more) now. A great coach is like going into a time machine. Nobody can ever foreclose or bankrupt your brain or take your knowledge and experience from you. When you hear about billionaires who've lost all their wealth multiple times over their careers, this secret is why they're able to reinvent themselves over and over again.

Here's the short version of how an investment opportunity came together and why this example is an important story for you to think about.

EXAMPLE: SINGLE-FAMILY HOME MAINTENANCE COMPANY

I had invested in a single-family home maintenance company with two business partners through another business we owned together. The parent company that made that investment wanted to raise money through a **Series A** investment, typically the first significant round of venture capital financing. **Venture capital** is a form of private equity and a type of financing that investors provide to startup companies believed to have long-term growth potential.

I had previously sold some of my equity in that parent company and was being paid in installments, but the unpaid balance of the note still owed me looked like debt on their books, which made it difficult for them to raise money through a Series A investment. During this time, a conflict arose between my two partners who ran the operations of the parent company and the owners of the maintenance supply company. After multiple attempts to renegotiate between the parties, it looked like the maintenance supply company we had invested in didn't want to pay us what they contractually owed, which meant we might have to litigate to get paid.

I really wanted to make sure this situation could be solved amicably, so I stepped in and negotiated a deal. I forgave the balance of the note the parent company still owed me to clear up the debt getting in the way of raising their Series A. This deal was in exchange for the full rights of the **royalty agreement** in place from the original investment in the single-family home maintenance company. The royalty agreement was based on top-line revenue on gross sales; however, I reduced the overall amount the maintenance company would pay to help create a better cash flow scenario for those two owners and their company. It was a true win-win-win for all three parties involved.

MINDSET

I invested time with my attorney, analyzing my investments and cash flow. He connected me with many of his colleagues at his law firm to get expert recommendations on several of my current ventures. During a brainstorming session, we saw a huge opportunity with that parent company that could help solve the conflict my partners were having with the maintenance company. It was an outside-the-box opportunity and solution—a perfect example of the power of having such a strong, creative, and strategic legal team that thinks differently than you do. I learned some unique contractual mechanisms and some creative ideas to facilitate brokering a much better situation and deal for all parties. I likely would not have come up with them on my own.

STRUCTURE

Here is the structure of the agreement:

- $0 investment (but I did forgive a note that the parent company owed me close to $500,000 dollars)
- Offer to help the maintenance company negotiate out of a contract they had and create a new and better contract for them to avoid litigation
- Percentage of top-line gross revenue
- Monthly distributions
- Warrants on the gross sale proceeds if the maintenance supply company ever sold
- First liquidation preference if the company did sell

FILTER

This deal was a great investment because it's in a booming industry with unlimited growth potential, it didn't require much time or capital from me and would create a monthly income stream to cover my family's lifestyle and ultimately buy me more time. I was also able to help the maintenance company out of a sticky legal situation they were in and renegotiate deal terms to benefit them. Looking ahead, I know I can be a resource to them as they continue to scale. It was a win-win scenario for all parties involved.

NEGOTIATION

I negotiated a percentage of top-line revenue with a monthly distribution, which is always one of my favorite investment structures. I was able to negotiate additional warrants if they chose to sell in the future, and that right is based on gross sale proceeds rather than net sale proceeds, which is a very important distinction. It's similar to the difference between a top-line revenue share model and a profit share model, where a revenue share will produce more income than a profit share because it's prior to expenses being taken out. The same is true for gross sale proceeds producing a better return than net sale proceeds. I was also able to secure a minimum guaranteed return on the revenue share proceeds in case the owners sold the company earlier than planned.

THE DEAL IN REVIEW

Once you've accumulated enough knowledge, assembled a great team of advisors and professionals, and gotten involved in enough deals, you'll be able to find tremendous opportunities to negotiate and even renegotiate deals in a way that benefits multiple parties and provides long-term cash flow and equity painlessly. Without the knowledge and experience of others and getting into the game, however, opportunities like this win-win investment will never appear.

All of these learned skills require taking a first step, making a commitment, and pursuing your dream.

SINGLE-FAMILY HOME MAINTENANCE COMPANY - 2024 DEAL UPDATE

2024 UPDATE SUMMARY:

- Negotiated revenue share provided over $2M despite minimal capital
- Company achieved significant growth through bootstrapping
- Home services/maintenance is a highly valuable sector
- Strategic advice more beneficial than capital for founders
- Minimal ongoing time requirements

When I first advised a single-family home maintenance company on their growth strategy, I negotiated a modest revenue share in lieu of heavy involvement. This aligned incentives while allowing me to stay focused on other projects.

Frankly, I assumed it would provide some supplemental cash flow but didn't expect much. However, within a few years, distributions from my tiny revenue share grew to over $45,000 per month.

To date, I've received over $2 million in cumulative distributions without ever having to contribute capital. The company's commitment to reinvesting profits allowed them to grow quickly.

Their services fall into an extremely valuable niche: property maintenance and repair. Private equity firms aggressively acquire companies in this space with their own proprietary software for 10–20X EBITDA multiples.

For the founders, access to my network and growth strategy advice proved more valuable than capital. By aligning interests early on, the revenue share provided exponential returns despite minimal ongoing time investment.

This deal exemplifies how pursuing unique structures beyond just capital can yield outsized upside. Even more so, identifying emerging sectors primed for consolidation can produce phenomenal returns over time.

Though I provided minimal capital, I ensured that every invested dollar got a return through the revenue share and equity upside. Beyond the financial return, I gained invaluable knowledge about their operations and growth strategies.

KEY INSIGHTS:

- My negotiated revenue share provided over $2,000,000 in distributions.
- Home maintenance and repair is a highly valuable consolidating sector.
- Strategic advice and connections were more beneficial than capital.
- Minimal time required beyond initial strategic involvement.
- Unique deal structures and emerging niches can generate massive upside.

OUTSMARTING THE VENTURE MARKET

The typical way a venture fund operates is based on several rounds of funding before a liquidity event, which means it can reasonably take ten to twelve years to fully realize a yield.

Naturally, I wanted to figure out how to shorten this timeline. Here are a few principles I follow when investing in venture capital deals:

1. Diversify across multiple funds and 100+ seed investments.
2. Target the highest growth Series A to Series B phase.
3. Access discounted secondary shares post-Series B.

Lifestyle Investor Lesson: Most experts agree that you need fifty to one hundred seed investments to receive just one positive return. Optimize your seed investments accordingly.

This strategy stack gives me an edge over individual VCs when investing in high-risk, high-reward venture deals. Through experience and deliberate strategies across stages, sectors, and fund structures, I aim to maximize the upside while minimizing downside risk.

To diversify risk in the early, pre-VC stage, I invest in specialized funds that construct portfolios across 600+ seed and pre-seed startups. This breadth spreads exposure across sectors, geographies, and founders to avoid concentration risk. Given the long odds at this nascent phase, volume is key—and with at least 600 seed bets, winners can more than offset inevitable flameouts. I let the fund's experienced investment team handle the heavy lifting on sourcing and due diligence to access the most promising emerging start-ups nationwide.

A major advantage of this strategy is being able to write off losses from failed startups while taking up to $10 million or 10X the investment in tax-free gains on winners under Qualified Small Business Stock (QSBS) regulations. This optimizes the upside while mitigating downside risk.

I also leverage creative channels like accelerators to gain pre-VC exposure to startups. I've mentioned the portfolio accelerator with 200 plus early-stage companies, many already profitable. This provides broad early access to minimize risk. As they add 800 plus startups over the next five years, my exposure to early winners compounds.

What about after startups raise a Series A round? I've learned the optimal time for outsized yet shorter-duration gains is from Series A to Series B. This is when valuations often surge five to ten times over just two to three years as market traction validates the model. At this stage, I tap specialists who have proven models for identifying the most promising Series A companies poised for hypergrowth.

These groups typically invest early in a startup's Series A Extension, then exit a couple of years later in the secondary market after the Series B round closes. This is when valuations normally peak before returning to steadier growth trajectories. By concentrating capital in this brief window of maximum acceleration between A and B rounds, outsized returns can be captured.

After startups complete Series B and later rounds, risks decrease substantially as the company typically has an established product and business model. I partner with seasoned secondary players to purchase founders' and employees' shares, often after Series B at favorable valuations. Their diligence filters for profitable, de-risked companies with strong growth prospects. Buying post-Series B stakes at discounts to true value is a path to generate outsized returns with lower risk.

I also spread capital across sector-focused funds in high-conviction areas like AI, cloud software, digital health, fintech, biotech, and blockchain. This diversity by sector reduces correlated risks. Within each sector, I'll invest in five to six top funds to further spread exposure. Before doing this, I scrutinize fund economics, fees, carry structure, and incentives to ensure optimal alignment.

For US-based sectors where America retains a competitive advantage—like AI, autonomous tech, and biotech—I strategically concentrate more capital into top VC funds and startups poised to lead globally. This targets assets positioned to outperform.

Of course, I review track records on relevant benchmarks before investing in new managers or follow-on funds. It's key to learn from failures and emphasize funds that demonstrate improving performance over time. Patience and long hold periods give time to compound outsized returns.

Additionally, I'll fund riskier early-stage venture investments using steady cash flows from proven 12–15 percent income streams. This insulates my lifestyle if an emerging bet flames out. And when one hits? I'll recycle those gains to fund the next five seed investments—rapidly cascading returns.

Once reliable income surpasses my monthly lifestyle target—let's use $25,000 per month, as this was my target when I first started—100 percent of the surplus becomes investable. Compare this to the early career scramble to save 10–20 percent of wages. The psychology flip is profound. With abundance and discipline, I can commit 80 percent of this surplus to compounding and 20 percent to causes. As your reliable income grows, you can adjust these figures to compound your wealth even faster or multiply your philanthropic efforts based on your goals.

Cascading cash flow lets me take bold risks across one hundred seed investments, turbocharge gains when winners emerge, and pay it forward—that's the heart of sustainable wealth creation.

By being selective, strategic, and diversified, I aim to leverage startups' steep growth trajectories while safeguarding against risks. With the right expertise and deliberate approach, Venture Capital can generate tremendous upside. These principles allow me to participate in a way that follows the core investment principles I apply throughout the rest of my portfolio.

PRINCIPLES FOR HACKING VC

Based on hard-learned lessons, I've identified strategies to reduce risks and maximize upside when investing in venture capital funds and startups. Here are key principles I follow to boost returns and limit risks:

- **Fund higher-risk VC investments using steady cash flow streams.** Build up monthly or quarterly cash flow funds first, then deploy those distributions into riskier VC bets. If an emerging investment fails, lifestyle is protected, and cash flow continues.
- **Diversify intelligently across sectors, stages, and geographies.** Don't put all your eggs in one basket. Spread capital across early-, mid-, and late-stage funds. Disperse investments across high-conviction sectors (mine are SaaS, AI, biotech, and fintech). Mix exposure by geography between startup hotbeds like Silicon Valley, New York City, Austin, Boston, and the Southeast. Mitigate risk through thoughtful diversity.

- **Leverage micro-VC platforms for early-stage access with dilution protection.** Gain entry to nascent startups alongside top-tier VCs via platforms like AngelList. Negotiate pro-rata rights to avoid dilution in follow-on rounds. Invest directly in companies on favorable terms you dictate.
- **Target the Series A to Series B phase for maximum value acceleration.** This is the steepest part of the growth curve, where valuations often surge 5–10X in just two to three years. Concentrate capital in this brief window of hypergrowth to maximize gains.
- **Access discounted secondary shares post-Series B for lower risk and higher return.** Purchase founders' and employees' shares at favorable valuations after risks diminish. Leverage secondary specialists to filter for profitable, mature startups.
- **Scrutinize VC fund economics, fees, and carry structure to align incentives.** Negotiate investor-friendly terms for follow-on investments. Insist on performance versus benchmarks before committing additional capital.
- **Review track records versus benchmarks before investing.** Reference against year, sector, and stage to gauge top performers. Require funds to demonstrate learning from failures.
- **Prepare for long hold periods to let winners compound over five to ten years.** Be patient and allow underlying value to build. Avoid premature exits.

There's a reason venture capital is risky: it requires highly specialized experience, relationships, and deliberate tactics to outperform the odds. As individual investors, we can play the VC game in a way that limits risks.

As with any Lifestyle Investor deal, it starts with your mindset and then how you filter, structure, and negotiate the opportunity. While I've shared the companies and funds I've done business with above, it's critical you do your own research and make decisions based on your own due diligence, investment principles, and gut instincts.

After a full day strategy session that seemed like just ten minutes with one of my favorite private coaching clients (let's just call him JJ), we enjoyed a celebratory dinner. We had worked together in building a perfect portfolio that matched his lifestyle investing goals. After only working with him for ninety days, he's already invested in close to ten deals, each in the multiple six and seven figures. One of the benefits of working with really smart Lions like JJ is that I learn as much from my clients as they learn from me.

The day after that strategy session together, here's what I wrote in my journal.

Yesterday was a fun strategy session with JJ. I am so impressed with JJ and his desire to learn and his ability to retain information. He is incredibly smart and is dialed in on so many levels. I enjoy how deep of a thinker he is and how strategic he is. I feel like he is thinking so many steps ahead of most people. His knowledge of intellectual property is impressive, and he is offering so much value to the company he most recently invested in and is really helping them scale. He not only had a big strategic exit in his first company, but he is setting up this next company to have an even bigger exit and is offering so much wisdom to the executives and other owners. I'm excited for round 2 today and to get into the details on many specific strategies I use. I think JJ is going to benefit tremendously from our time together and our new friendship. I'm also enjoying learning his perspective and insights as well. This is going to be a fun year and beyond for us!

At the beginning of this book, I told you that being wealthy has everything to do with having a wealthy mindset. I can't stress it enough. A wealthy mindset means living in a wealthy ecosystem of abundance-minded, coachable thinkers who can spot mutually beneficial opportunities where everyone wins. Investing isn't a zero-sum game.

I have the greatest satisfaction in knowing that I'm truly teaching someone to fish by sharing these principles and commandments that work. I have the privilege of changing people's mindsets and providing fantastic financial returns. Every dollar of investment gets a return, especially when you're investing in your personal growth and your Lifestyle Investor mindset.

PART THREE

THE CALL

NEXT STEPS

*Success isn't overnight. It's when every day you get
a little better than before. It adds up.*

—Dwayne Johnson

Now that you've discovered the *10 Commandments of a
Lifestyle Investor,* are you ready to do the work? Becoming
a Lifestyle Investor is about creating the life you dream,
a life of abundance, but it's also about helping others
through that abundance. Once you've mastered this lifestyle,
you create a ripple effect inside your circle of influence that
can change lives and impact hundreds, thousands, or even
millions of people.

Not everyone who reads this book will expend the time
and energy it takes to shift their mindset. Every person
has some baggage related to money. I believe everyone
is conflicted about money at some level. Either you are

conflicted and realize it, or you're conflicted, unconscious, and unaware.

Before you go on, here's what I recommend you do:

1. Stop reading and write out what *you* believe about money. Get specific.
2. Now go back through the commandments and complete any response you skipped.

My goal is that you dog-ear this book because you refer back to these commandments often. Mark it up. Use it to jot down thoughts, questions, and ideas. Better yet, start a journal and watch your progress as you implement these strategies and become a Lifestyle Investor Lion.

FIRST THINGS FIRST

Have you identified people who are smarter than you in certain areas that can help you become a Lifestyle Investor? What about a coach? Make a list of these people.

Next, figure out your stripped-down, bare necessities living expenses. Think about it this way. If you were injured and couldn't work for three months, what money do you need in the bank to ensure your family survives? Write this out using actual numbers. Take that three-month figure and multiply it by four. That's the annual amount your family needs to survive. And if you break it down monthly, it shows you the amount of cash flow you need coming in each month to cover your basic expenses. It doesn't look as formidable as you thought, right?

Do this same exercise with your current lifestyle, if you haven't already, so you know what it costs you to live each month. Now you can figure out how much cash flow you need each month to become financially free. That's what your freedom looks like.

FREEDOM FORMULA

Now, review your personal freedom formula. What needs to happen to fulfill your top priorities? It's time to take action if you want to become a Lifestyle Investor.

1. How much will you allocate to make your first investment?
2. How much monthly cash flow will that investment provide for you?
3. What are some investment opportunities that interest you?
4. Evaluate your portfolio against the 10 Commandments. Where do you rate (5/10, 7/10, 10/10)?
5. Find a deal that aligns with all of the commandments.
6. Network with people you might know who invest or join my private Lifestyle Investor Mastermind community to access vetted deals. Build a network of other Lifestyle Investors who share the same values and goals you do.

INVEST IN EDUCATION

Harvey Mackay famously says, "Our lives change in two ways: through the people we meet and the books we read," which fits nicely with the characteristics of a perfect Lifestyle Investor Lion. Lions have the desire to learn, the right education, and the drive to figure out how to become financially independent and wealthy.

If you want to earn more, surround yourself with like-minded, abundance-minded people. As Tony Robbins teaches in his life events, "Take the top five people you spend your time with, add their incomes, divide by five, and that's probably what you earn." Lions also hire a coach, join mastermind groups, read books by people they admire, and network their way into meeting them.

Consider how many total years you're going to be making financial decisions. Even one year in a group like the Lifestyle Investor Mastermind will change the way you make those decisions for decades.

REMEMBER THE BASICS

Here's a short review of the basics of building wealth:

1. Building wealth is a skill set, just like any other. So many ways to create wealth exist, and it's impossible to capitalize on them all—but you need to have enough of an education and skill set to recognize an opportunity when it presents itself or to find an opportunity that is invisible to most people. If you took all of my wealth away today, I could build it back in a fraction of the time because I know how to do it. It's part of my skill set, and I believe other people can develop the same skill set.

    The moment money is in the deal, people want to learn.

2. Building wealth is more about consistent behaviors and using a system than having a one-time exit event. I have never had a big payout. Instead, I have been consistent with small returns adding up over time. Understanding consistency is good when you invest so you don't take the approach of trying to hit a home run with each investment. Hitting many

singles and doubles adds up over time. Triples are nice but unnecessary.

3. Invest in yourself first. As you invest first in your mind, body, and spirit, you create more opportunities that otherwise would not have existed if you hadn't been. A rich man without his health will spend all his money to gain it back.

MINDSET

A Lifestyle Investor Lion is:

- Willing to learn
- Hungry for a better life
- Growth-minded
- A giver, not a taker
- Ready to invest in themselves and others
- Coachable
- Open to constructive criticism
- An action-taker

STRUCTURE

A Lifestyle Investor Lion will:

- Arrange their life to have time to take action on what they're learning
- Adjust their schedule to create margin
- Learn and grow in their investment knowledge
- Leave their comfort zone
- Surround themselves with like-minded people and other investors

FILTER

A Lifestyle Investor Lion possesses certain criteria, that is the willingness to:

- Invest in themselves first
- Invest actual money
- Model other successful investors
- Make financial decisions based on their financial education
- Pull the trigger on the right investments

NEGOTIATION

A Lifestyle Investor Lion takes these actions:

- Looks for the win-win in every opportunity
- Gives and contributes meaningfully to the community at every opportunity
- Serves others as a producer, not a consumer, in every opportunity
- Approaches every opportunity with a growth-minded partnership
- Seeks to 10X every opportunity

START NOW

You can become a Lifestyle Investor Lion at any age or life stage. One of my clients recently told me that his thirteen-year-old granddaughter wanted to start a business. As he listened to her, he realized he could teach her to become a lifestyle investor just as he was becoming one himself. And that's what he did. She invested her savings and followed her grandfather's instruction (and took out a small loan from him that must be repaid).

Today, that granddaughter earns $125 a month from her investments. That amount is a lot of money for a thirteen-year-old, so her grandfather is teaching her how to break up the cash flow she earns into savings, new investments, and repayment of the loan she owes him. Because he taught her the benefits of being a Lion, she certainly will also spend some of that money on fun things she desires.

That story embodies the actions and attitude I love. One person learns to be a Lifestyle Investor and takes that knowledge to teach another. What's especially exciting for me to see is the impact this family's actions will have on future generations of family and friends.

Whatever your age, you can choose to become a Lifestyle Investor. It's all about adopting the correct mindset and getting started on the journey.

FINAL THOUGHTS

Imagine what life will feel like when you design your perfect day, rate your most important Freedom Values, create an inspiring Freedom Vision, and take your first step toward adopting a Lifestyle Investor mindset. Review the "Mindset Is Everything" chapter to prepare your mind to take action on your dream.

Here's my dream for you: See opportunities you've never seen before and build the life you desire to live. I encourage you to take the next six big steps.

1. Reread your Freedom Vision from Commandment 1: Lifestyle First

Right now is the best time to anchor a vision and a dream for what you want as a Lifestyle Investor. You're closer than you think to achieving financial freedom, monthly cash flow, and passive income.

2. Access Bonus Content from the Lifestyle Investor Mastermind

Watch some of the most powerful moments from the Lifestyle Investor Mastermind Education calls at *LifestyleInvestor.com/Gift*. You'll get expert wisdom on tax strategy, whole life insurance policies, estate planning, investment criteria, and different asset sectors. Be sure to also download the Lifestyle Investor Workbook, which is purpose-built to complement this book and help you turn your insights into action.

3. Listen to *The Lifestyle Investor Podcast*

Start performing at your highest level. Get tips and principles to learn how to think and invest to limit risk, maximize repeatable returns, and achieve lifestyle goals using passive income cash flow strategies. You can find the podcast at *LifestyleInvestor.com/Podcast*.

4. Take a 60-second quiz to find out your #1 Investor Blindspot

If you're reading this book, it's because you're looking for practical, tactical resources and tools to give you a shortcut to becoming a Lifestyle Investor. The truth is that there are four blind spots when it comes to investing that can hold you back from growing your wealth. Take the short quiz at *LifestyleInvestor.com/Quiz*. Knowing your blind spot as an investor is the first step in making changes that support your lifestyle goals.

5. **Schedule a free strategy session with the Lifestyle Investor Team**

If you're serious about becoming a Lifestyle Investor, you desire to learn and build a cash flow portfolio, and you want access to my network of experts and advisors, you can save yourself decades of time in our community. Our strategy sessions typically cost $500 because, as the saying goes, "When you pay, you pay attention." During these calls, it's common for people to get major clarity, insights, and breakthroughs that affect their finances and lifestyle. In appreciation for you reading this book, I'd like to waive our fee and offer this strategy session at no charge. Head to *LifestyleInvestor.com/Strategy* to schedule a free, personalized consultation call with my team to explore the best options for the results you want. It's one of the best, low-risk ways you can experience the value of the Lifestyle Investor mindset and community. Ready? Set? GO!

GLOSSARY

10 Commandments. The ten investment criteria I use when making investing decisions.

Accelerated Distribution Schedule. Increasing the speed with which an equity investment is repaid to the investor. Typically, this would include distributing a larger percentage of profits than what the typical equity splits are in a partnership for a limited period until the initial investment is repaid.

Accredited Investor. An individual or business entity that is allowed to invest in certain investment opportunities based on satisfying at least one requirement regarding their income, net worth, asset size, governance status, or professional experience.

Actual Rate of Return. A formula that reflects the actual gain or loss of an investment over a certain period compared to the initial investment's cost. This is the preferred way to measure actual returns on investments because it isn't based on an average percentage but rather on the actual investment return compared to the original cost. Beware of "average" rate of return, which can be misleading.

Actuary. A professional who assesses and manages the risks of financial investments, insurance policies, and other potentially risky ventures.

Agency Loan. A loan that an agency of the federal government may make available to an investor. *See also* Fannie Mae and Freddie Mac.

Alternative Investments. A financial asset that does not fall into one of the conventional stocks, bonds, or cash categories. Examples include: Private equity, venture capital, hedge funds, real estate, art and antiques, and commodities.

Amortization. The gradual repayment of a debt over a period of time, such as monthly payments on a mortgage loan. Often, the amortization is based on a greater number of years than the actual loan term to lower monthly payments to create greater profitability and cash flow.

Amplifier Stack. Negotiating multiple income amplifiers on the same deal for even greater projected returns.

Angel Investor. A high net-worth individual (also known as a private investor, seed investor, or angel funder) who provides financial backing for small startups or entrepreneurs, typically in exchange for ownership equity in the company. Often, angel investors are found among an entrepreneur's family and friends. The funds that angel investors provide may be a one-time investment to help the business get off the ground or an ongoing injection to support and carry the company through its difficult early stages.

Annual Recurring Revenue (ARR). A financial metric that shows the annual revenue from business products or services. In this book, ARR refers specifically to revenues of existing subscriptions, also commonly referred to as annual run rate.

Arbitrage. The purchase and sale of an asset in order to profit from a difference in the asset's price between markets. It is a trade that profits by exploiting the price differences of identical or similar financial instruments in different markets or in different forms. Arbitrage exists as a result of market inefficiencies and would, therefore, not exist if all markets were perfectly efficient.

Asset Cash Flow. The aggregate total of all cash flows related to the assets of a business. This information is used to determine the net amount of cash being spun off by or used in the operations of a business.

Asset Class. A group of investments that exhibit similar characteristics and are subject to the same laws, regulations, and market forces.

Assignment. The transfer of an individual's rights or property to another person or business. This option exists in a variety of business transactions. For investors, the most prominent example occurs when a purchase sale agreement (PSA) is assigned; the assignee has an obligation to complete the requirements of the contract. Other business transactions are also known as an assignment.

Asymmetric Risk/Reward. *Asymmetric risk* is the risk an investor faces when the gain realized from the move of an underlying asset in one direction is significantly different from the loss incurred from its move in the opposite direction. *Asymmetric reward* is the reward an investor may achieve when the gain realized from the move of an underlying asset in one direction is significantly different from the loss incurred from its move in the opposite direction.

Average Rate of Return. A formula that reflects the percentage rate of return on an investment or asset compared to the initial investment's cost. Be careful because this average can be misleading and doesn't necessarily reflect the actual rate of return. See the definition for the actual rate of return.

Balloon Payment. A larger-than-usual one-time payment at the end of the loan term.

Basis Points (BPS). Common unit of measurement for interest rates and other percentages in finance. One basis point is equal to 1/100 of 1 percent, or 0.01 percent.

Beneficiaries. Any person who gains an advantage and/or profits from something. In the financial world, a beneficiary typically refers to someone eligible to receive distributions from a trust, will, or life insurance policy.

Bridge Loan. Short-term financing used until a person or company secures permanent financing or removes an existing obligation. Bridge loans are short-term, typically up to one year.

Capital Improvements. Any addition or alteration to real property that meets one of the following conditions: It substantially adds to the value of the real property or appreciably prolongs the useful life of the real property.

Capital Partner. All partners who have contributed capital to the partnership. Often, this phrase is referring to the partner that contributed the most capital to a partnership.

Carried Interest (Carry). A share of the profits of an investment paid to the investment manager or general partner of private equity or hedge fund investments. This compensation is received regardless of whether they contribute any initial capital.

Cash Bonus. A lump sum of money awarded to an investor, either periodically or at the end of a specified investment period, as an incentive to invest. Most cash bonuses are paid once at the end of the term, but they can vary from investment to investment. Sometimes, cash bonus incentives are attached to the performance of the investment or company on an annual basis. These bonuses can range from a few hundred dollars to millions of dollars, depending on the terms and the growth of the company.

Cash Flow. The amount of income earned from investments and other assets.

Cash Flow Investing. Cash flow derived from assets or investments paid on an ongoing and regular basis. Typically, distributions or interest payments are paid quarterly or monthly.

Cash-on-Cash Return. A rate of return often used in real estate transactions and other income producing assets that calculates the cash income earned on the cash invested in that asset. Cash-on-cash return measures the annual return the investor made on the asset in relation to the amount of cash invested. It is considered one of the most important real estate return on investment calculations.

Co-Investment. A minority investment in a company made by investors alongside a private equity fund manager or venture capital firm. Equity co-investment enables investors to participate in potentially highly profitable investments without paying the usual fees charged by a private equity fund. Equity co-investment opportunities are typically restricted to large institutional investors who already have an existing relationship with the private equity fund manager, and they are often not available to smaller or retail investors.

Collateralize. The use of a valuable asset to secure a loan. If the borrower defaults on the loan, the lender may seize the asset and sell it to offset the loss. Collateralization of assets gives lenders a sufficient level of reassurance against default risk. It also helps some borrowers obtain loans if they have poor credit histories. Collateralized loans generally have a substantially lower interest rate than unsecured loans.

Collectible. An item that is worth far more than it was originally sold for because of its rarity and/or popularity. The price for a particular collectible usually depends on how many of the same item is available as well as its overall condition. Common categories of collectibles include antiques, artwork, coins, historical documents, wine, toys, comic books, and stamps. People who amass collectibles take a lot of time to collect them and usually store them in locations where they will not be ruined.

Commercial Mortgage-Backed Security Loan (CMBS Loan). A commercial real estate loan that is backed by a first-position commercial mortgage. Loans such as these are held and sold by commercial and investment banks or conduit lenders. CMBS loans are for properties such as apartments, hotels, warehouses, offices, retail, or any other real estate that is used in connection with a company or business in need of such a space.

Concentration Risk. The level of risk in a portfolio arising from concentration to a single counterparty, sector, or country. The risk arises from the observation that more concentrated portfolios are less diverse; therefore, the returns on the underlying assets are more correlated.

Conduit Loans. A means of raising capital from Wall Street financial institutions for private real estate investments, among other types of investments.

Cooking the Books. A slang term for using accounting tricks to make a company's financial results look better than they really are. Typically, it involves manipulating financial data to inflate revenue and deflate expenses in order to pump up earnings or profit, which makes the company appear more valuable than it really is.

Correlated Asset. An asset whose value is tied to the larger fluctuations of the traditional markets, such as the stock market.

Crowdfunding. The practice of funding a project or venture by raising small amounts of money from a large number of people, typically via the internet. Crowdfunding is a form of crowdsourcing and alternative finance.

Cryptocurrency. A digital or virtual currency designed to work as a medium of exchange that is secured by cryptography, which makes it nearly impossible to counterfeit or double-spend. Many cryptocurrencies are decentralized networks based on blockchain technology—a strong distributed ledger enforced by a disparate network of computers. A defining feature of cryptocurrencies is that they are generally not issued by any central authority, rendering them theoretically immune to government interference or manipulation.

Deal Flow. A term used by investors, investment bankers, and venture capitalists to describe the rate at which business proposals and investment pitches are being received.

Deal Structure. The agreement reached in financing an acquisition. The deal can be unleveraged, leveraged, traditional debt, participating debt, participating/convertible debt, or a joint venture, among other things.

Debt Investment. A financial transaction of loaning money to an institution or organization in exchange for the promise of a return of principal plus interest, as opposed to a conventional equity investment through buying common or preferred stock.

Deed of Trust. An agreement between a lender and a borrower to give the property to a neutral third party who will serve as a trustee. The trustee holds the property until the borrower pays off the debt. During the period of repayment, the borrower keeps the actual or equitable title to the property and maintains full responsibility for the premises unless expressly stated otherwise in the Deed of Trust. The trustee, however, holds the legal title to the property.

Default. Failure to fulfill an obligation, especially with regard to repayment of a loan.

Defeasance. A provision in a contract that voids a bond or loan on a balance sheet when the borrower sets aside cash or bonds sufficient enough to service the debt.

Depreciation (Depreciating an Asset). An accounting method of allocating the cost of a tangible or physical asset over its useful life or life expectancy. Depreciation represents how much of an asset's value has been used up. Depreciating assets helps companies earn revenue from an asset while expensing a portion of its cost each year the asset is in use. Not taking it into account can greatly affect profits.

Derivatives or High-Risk Derivatives. Investment instruments that consist of a contract between parties whose value derives from and depends on the value of an underlying financial asset. Like any investment instrument, varying levels of risk are associated with derivatives. Among the most common derivatives traded are futures, options, contracts for difference, or CFDs, and swaps.

Direct Recognition. A company in which the earnings rate on cash value is affected both positively and negatively when the cash value is used as collateral. In a *non-direct recognition* company, the earnings rates on loaned cash value are totally unaffected by loans against cash value.

Diversification. A risk management strategy that mixes a wide variety of investments within a portfolio. A diversified portfolio contains a mix of distinct asset types and investment vehicles in order to limit exposure to any single asset or risk. The rationale behind it is that a portfolio constructed of a mix of assets will, on average, yield higher long-term returns and lower the risk of any individual holding or security.

Due Diligence. An investigation, audit, or review performed to confirm the facts of a matter under consideration. In the financial world, due diligence requires an examination of financial records before entering into a proposed transaction with another party.

Earned Income. Income derived from active participation in a trade or business, including wages, salary, tips, commissions, and bonuses. This is the highest taxed income.

EBITDA: Earnings Before Interest, Taxes, Depreciation, and Amortization. One way of measuring a company's overall financial performance.

Equity Investment. A financial transaction where a certain number of shares of a given company or fund are bought, entitling the owner to be compensated ratably according to his ownership percentage. Typically referred to as shareholders' equity (or owner's equity for privately held companies), an individual or company invests money into a private or public company to become a shareholder.

Escrow Collateral. All the borrower's rights, title, and interest in and to the Escrow Property, the Escrow Account, and the Escrow Agreement.

Fannie Mae. A United States government-sponsored enterprise (GSE), the Federal National Mortgage Association

(FNMA), commonly known as Fannie Mae, is, since 1968, a publicly traded company. Founded in 1938 during the Great Depression as part of the New Deal, the corporation's purpose is to expand the secondary mortgage market by securitizing mortgage loans in the form of mortgage-backed securities (MBS), allowing lenders to reinvest their assets into more lending and in effect increasing the number of lenders in the mortgage market by reducing the reliance on locally based savings and loan associations (or *thrifts*).

Fiat Currency. Government-issued currency that isn't backed by a commodity such as gold. Fiat money gives central bankers greater control over the economy because they can control how much money is printed. Most modern currencies, such as the US dollar, are fiat currencies.

Fiduciary. A person or organization that acts on behalf of another person or persons, putting their clients' interests ahead of their own, with a duty to preserve good faith and trust. Being a fiduciary requires being bound both legally and ethically to act in the other's best interests. It also involves trust, especially with regard to the relationship between a trustee and a beneficiary, always having the beneficiary's best interest at heart.

Filters. Criteria used to sort through and narrow down investment opportunities. Using filters to screen investments saves significant time and creates greater efficiency.

Finder's Fee. A commission paid to an intermediary or the facilitator of a transaction. Also known as *referral income* or *referral fee,* it is awarded because the intermediary discovered the deal and brought it to the attention of interested parties. The presumption is that without the intermediary, the parties would not have found the deal; thus, the facilitator warrants compensation.

First-Lien Position. The highest priority debt in the case of default. If a property or other collateral is used to back a debt, first-lien debt holders are paid before all other debt holders. This debt holds less risk than a second-lien debt.

Fractional Reserve Lending. A system in which only a fraction of bank deposits is backed by actual cash on hand and available for withdrawal, done theoretically to expand the economy by freeing capital for lending.

Freddie Mac. A stockholder-owned, government-sponsored enterprise (GSE) chartered by Congress in 1970 to keep money flowing to mortgage lenders in support of homeownership and rental housing for middle-income Americans. Freddie Mac, also known as Federal Home Loan Mortgage Corp (FHLMC), was established to purchase, guarantee, and securitize mortgages to form mortgage-backed securities.

Freedom Formula. Time + Money + Relationships + Impact = Lifestyle Investor Freedom

General Partner. One of two or more investors who jointly own a business or asset and assume the day-to-day role in managing it. A general partner has the authority to act on behalf of the business without the permission of the other partners but has unlimited liability for any debt.

Hard Money Loan. A loan that is secured by real property and considered a loan of "last resort" or short-term bridge loan. It is primarily used in real estate transactions, with the lenders generally being individuals or companies and not banks.

Holding Company. A business entity, usually a corporation or limited liability company (LLC). Typically, a holding company doesn't manufacture anything, sell any products or services, or conduct any other business operations. Rather, holding companies hold the controlling stock in other companies.

House Money. For this book, it refers to money invested that you have no risk on because you have already gotten your original investment back, so any additional return is icing on the cake.

Hurdle Rate. (1)* The rate investment managers must earn in their funds before they receive incentive-based compensation. (2) The minimum rate of return on a project or investment required by a manager or investor.

*Allows companies to make important decisions on whether or not to pursue a specific project. Describes the appropriate compensation for the level of risk present. Riskier projects generally have higher hurdle rates than those with less risk. To determine the rate, the following areas must be taken into consideration: associated risks, cost of capital, and the returns of other possible investments or projects.

Income Amplifier. Any mechanic or negotiated term that helps improve an investment return. Various ways exist to structure these deal terms; in general, the more income amplifiers, the better the investment return.

Incubator. An organization designed to accelerate the growth and success of entrepreneurial companies through an array of business support resources and services offered at below-market prices.

Internal Rate of Return (IRR). A performance measure used in financial analysis to estimate the profitability of potential investments. Return on Investment (ROI) measures the total return from start to finish, whereas IRR identifies the annual return.

Invisible Deals. A deal typically not known to the general public, and if it is known, it is likely not accessible;

difficult to get access to due to exclusivity but can be deals in emerging markets, new technology, or disruptive trends.

Kicker. A right, warrant, or other feature added to a debt obligation to make it more desirable to potential investors, such as equity participation.

LIBOR. The benchmark interest rate that global banks use to lend to one another.

Lien. A legal claim against an asset used to secure a loan that must be paid when the property is sold. Liens can be structured in many different ways. In some cases, the creditor will have a legal claim against an asset but not actually hold it in possession, while in other cases, the creditor will actually hold on to the asset until the debt is paid off. The former is a more common arrangement when the asset is productive since the creditor would prefer that the asset be used to produce a stream of income to pay off debt rather than just held in possession and not used.

Lifestyle Investor. Someone who has intentionally built a great life and is able to support their lifestyle with passive income they earn from investments rather than earned income from their job or business.

Limited Partnership (LP). Exists when two or more partners conduct a business in which they are liable for an amount not exceeding their investment. The general partner oversees and runs the business, and limited partners do not partake in managing the business; however, the general partner has unlimited liability for the debt, and any limited partners have limited liability up to the amount of their investment. (A limited partnership is different from a limited liability partnership or LLP.)

Liquidation Preference. A clause in a contract that dictates the payout order in case of a corporate liquidation event, such as the sale of a company, initial public offering (IPO), or other liquidation payout. Typically, a company's debt holders get their money back first ahead of preferred stockholders, who are ahead of common stockholders in the event that the company must be liquidated.

Liquidity Event. An acquisition, merger, initial public offering, or other event that allows founders and early investors in a company to cash out some or all of their ownership shares. Considered an exit strategy for an illiquid investment—that is, for equity that has little or no market to trade on. Founders of a firm naturally push toward a liquidity event, and the investors along the way—venture capital firms, angel investors, or private equity firms—hope for or expect one within a reasonable amount of time after initially making an investment. The most common liquidity events are initial public offerings (IPOs) and direct acquisitions by other companies or private equity firms.

Loan Modification. A change made to the terms of an existing loan by a lender. It may involve a reduction in the interest rate, an extension of the length of time for repayment, a different type of loan, or pulling out available equity in the form of cash.

Long-Term Capital Gains Tax. A tax applied to assets held for more than a year. Long-term capital gains tax rates are 0 percent, 15 percent, and 20 percent, depending on income. These rates are typically much lower than the ordinary income tax rate.

Lost Opportunity Cost. The benefit foregone by choosing another course of action, also known as opportunity cost. Lost opportunity is sometimes measured by the lost contribution margin (sales minus the related variable costs).

Mindset. A way of thinking, an attitude or opinion, especially a habitual one.

Minimum Guaranteed Return. The minimum return guaranteed on select permanent life insurance products.

Monthly Recurring Revenue (MRR). A financial metric that shows the monthly revenue from business products or services (in this book, it refers specifically to revenues of existing subscriptions). Also commonly referred to as monthly run rate.

Multiple. A performance measurement found by a simple calculation of multiplying a specific item on a financial statement or an investment by another number to determine the total value of the asset or investment.

Murphy's Law. An adage that states, "Anything that can go wrong will go wrong."

Negative Arbitrage. The opportunity lost during the purchase and sale of an asset when there was not a profit in the difference in asset prices between markets. It occurs in a trade where, instead of making a profit by exploiting the price differences of identical or similar financial instruments, the prices change in a way that the trade creates a loss.

Negotiation. A strategic discussion that resolves an issue in a way that both parties find acceptable.

Non-correlated Asset or Uncorrelated Asset. An asset whose value isn't tied to the larger fluctuations of the traditional markets, such as the stock market.

Non-Direct Recognition. A strategy by insurance companies in which the earnings rate on cash value is unaffected by any loans against the cash value. Unlike *direct recognition*, there is no cost with a lower dividend when a loan is taken out against the policy.

Non-Direct Recognition Company. A company in which the earnings rate on cash value is unaffected by any loans against cash value. In a direct recognition company, the earnings rates on loaned cash value are affected both positively and negatively when the cash value is used as collateral.

Non-Recourse Lending. A loan secured by collateral, usually property. If the borrower defaults, the issuer can seize the collateral but cannot seek out the borrower for any further compensation, even if the collateral does not cover the full value of the defaulted amount. (The borrower does not have personal liability for the loan.)

Off-Market Investments. An investment that has not been advertised publicly for sale, so there is no competition or less competition to buy the asset.

Operating Agreement. A key document used by an LLC because it outlines the business financial and functional decisions, including rules, regulations, and provisions. It governs the internal operations of the business in a way that suits the specific needs of the business owners.

Operating Company. A business that produces goods or services and has regular operations.

Passive Income. Income received from investments and other assets that require little to no effort to earn and maintain. This is one of the lowest taxed incomes.

Personal Guarantee. An individual's legal promise to repay credit issued to a business for which they serve as an executive or partner.

Phantom Income. For the context of this book, it is the ability to earn a return from money that doesn't even exist.

Points. Also known as *discount points*, fees paid directly to the lender at closing, often in exchange for a reduced interest rate.

Ponzi Scheme. A fraudulent investing scam promising high rates of return with little risk to investors. The Ponzi scheme generates returns for early investors by acquiring new investors. It is similar to a pyramid scheme in that both are based on using new investors' funds to pay the earlier backers.

Preferred Return. A profit distribution preference whereby profits, either from operations, sale, or refinance, are distributed to one class of equity before another until a certain rate of return on the initial investment is reached.

Principal. The original sum of money borrowed in a loan or put into an investment. It can also refer to the face value of a bond.

Private Equity. An alternative investment class that consists of capital and is not listed on a public exchange. It is composed of funds of investors who directly invest in private companies or who engage in buyouts of public companies, resulting in the delisting of public equity.

Private Placement Memorandum (PPM). A legal document provided to prospective investors when selling stock or another security in a business. It is sometimes referred to as an *offering memorandum* or *offering document*.

Profits Interest. An equity right based on the future value of a partnership awarded to an individual for their services to the partnership. The reward consists of receiving a percentage of profits from a partnership without having to contribute capital.

Pro-Rata. A Latin term used to describe a proportionate allocation. It translates literally to "in proportion," which means a process where whatever is being allocated will be distributed in equal portions.

Public Equity. A stock that is bought and sold through a public market such as the New York Stock Exchange or the London Stock Exchange. Companies often offer the investor the right to buy either "common" or "preferred" stock.

Purchase Sale Agreement (PSA). The document received after mutual acceptance of an offer. It states the final sale price and all terms of the purchase.

Put Option. A contract giving the owner the right, but not the obligation, to sell—or sell short—a specified amount of an underlying security at a predetermined price within a specified time frame. This predetermined price is called the *strike* price. Put options are most commonly traded on underlying assets, including stocks, currencies, bonds, commodities, futures, and indexes. Put options can also be negotiated on investments in real estate and private equity deals as a protection against the risk of capital exposure if a deal goes bad. A put option can be contrasted with a call option, which gives the holder the right to buy the underlying at a specified price, either on or before the expiration date of the options contract.

Quick Principal Back. A strategy in which an investor focuses on getting their initial principal investment back as quickly as possible.

Real Estate Fund. A mutual fund that primarily focuses on investing in securities offered by public real estate companies.

Real Estate Investment Trust (REIT). A company that owns, operates, or finances income-generating real estate. Modeled after mutual funds, REITs pool the capital of numerous investors. They make it possible for individual investors to earn dividends from real estate investments without having to buy, manage, or finance any properties themselves.

Recourse Lending. A loan that can help a lender recoup the investment if a borrower fails to pay and the value of the underlying asset is not enough to cover the debt. A recourse loan is a form of secured financing. It lets the lender go after the debtor's other assets that were not used as loan collateral or take legal action in case of default in order to pay off the full debt.

Return on Investment (ROI). A performance measure used to evaluate the efficiency of an investment or compare the efficiency of a number of different investments. The ROI tries to directly measure the amount of return on a particular investment relative to the investment's cost. The benefit (or return) of an investment is divided by the cost of the investment to calculate ROI. The result is expressed as a percentage or a ratio.

Revenue Share (Rev Share). The distribution of the total amount of income generated by the sale of goods or services between the stakeholders or contributors. It should not be confused with profit shares. As with profit shares, only the profit is shared; that is, the revenue left over after costs have been removed.

Right of First Refusal. The right of a party to match the terms of a proposed contract with another party. Also known as the *first right of refusal.*

Royalty Agreement. A legal contract between two parties where one party agrees to pay the other party fees of some sort, typically based on a percentage of gross or net revenues derived from the use or performance of an asset.

Run Rate. The financial performance of a company based on current financial information as a predictor of future performance. It functions as an extrapolation of current financial performance and assumes current conditions will continue. Technically, the run rate can also refer to the average annual dilution from company stock option grants over the most recent three-year period recorded in the annual report (not how the term is used in this book.)

Series A Money. The first venture capital funding for a startup (also known as Series A financing or Series A investment). Series A refers to the class of preferred stock sold. The Series A funding round follows a startup company's seed round and precedes the Series B funding round.

Securities and Exchange Commission (SEC). An independent federal government regulatory agency responsible for protecting investors, maintaining the fair and orderly function of the securities markets, and facilitating capital formation. It was created by Congress in 1934 as the first federal regulator of the securities markets.

Seed Round. The first official equity funding round for a startup company.

Seller Finance Loan. A real estate agreement in which the seller handles the mortgage process instead of a financial institution. The buyer signs a mortgage with the seller instead of applying for a conventional bank mortgage. Also called *owner financing* or *seller carry*.

Senior Debt. Money owed by a company that has first claims on the company's cash flows. Also known as *Senior Note*, it is more secure than any other debt, such as subordinated debt (also known as junior debt). Senior debt is usually collateralized by assets. The lender is granted a first lien claim on the company's property, plant, or equipment in the event that the company fails to fulfill its repayment obligations.

Short-Term Capital Gains Tax. A tax applied to profits from selling an asset held for less than a year. Short-term capital gains taxes are set up so that in federal tax brackets, the investor pays at the same rate they pay ordinary income taxes.

Sidecar Agreements. A contract or agreement with pre-negotiated terms better than what most investors received in a particular investment or fund, among other definitions; a special set of enhanced terms that improve the investment for a single investor or, more commonly, a group of investors.

Software as a Service (SaaS). A method of software delivery and licensing in which the software is accessed online via a subscription rather than bought and installed on individual computers.

Solvency Ratio. A key metric used to measure an enterprise's ability to meet its debt obligations often used by prospective business lenders. Solvency ratio indicates whether a company's cash flow is sufficient to meet its short- and long-term liabilities. The lower a company's solvency ratio, the greater the probability that it will default on its debt obligations.

Standard Operating Procedure (SOP). An established or prescribed method to be followed routinely for the performance of a designated operation or in a designated situation.

Stock Pledge. The transfer of stocks against a debt in the form of a legal agreement. The debtor pledges the stocks as an asset against the amount of money taken from a lender and promises to return the amount. The debtor pledges the stocks as security against the debt. According to the law, after the payment of the obligation, the lender must return the stocks to the debtor. The agreement then stands void.

Strategy Stack. Combining multiple, non-obvious approaches to earn an even greater return with low risk.

Strike Price. The set price at which a derivative contract can be bought or sold when it is exercised. For call options, the strike price is the price at which the security can be bought by the option holder; for put options, the strike price is the price at which the security can be sold.

Structure. The relationship between the specific investment terms in an agreement.

Sweat Equity. A person or company's contribution toward a business venture or other project. Generally, not monetary and, in most cases, comes in the form of physical labor, mental effort, and time. Commonly found in real estate and the construction industry as well as in the corporate world—especially for startups.

Syndication. A partnership between several investors to combine skills, resources, and capital to purchase and manage a property they otherwise couldn't afford.

Venture Capital. A form of private equity and a type of financing that investors provide to startup companies and small businesses that are believed to have long-term growth potential. Venture capital generally comes from well-off investors, investment banks, and other financial institutions able to provide it.

Volatility. A statistical measure of the dispersion of returns for a given security or market index. In most cases, the higher the volatility, the riskier the security. Volatility is often measured as either the standard deviation or variance between returns from that same security or market index.

Warrant. An option that gives the right, but not the obligation, to buy (or sell) a security—most commonly an equity—at a certain price before expiration. The price at which the underlying security can be bought or sold is referred to as the *exercise* price or *strike* price.

Wealth Optimization. A process that focuses on improving overall wealth by supporting and optimizing each individual component of wealth, such as health, relationships, purpose, and finances.

Whole-Life Insurance. Coverage for the life of the insured. In addition to paying a death benefit, whole-life insurance also contains a savings component in which cash value may accumulate. These policies are also known as "permanent" or "traditional" life insurance. Whole-life insurance policies are one type of permanent life insurance. Universal life, indexed universal life, and variable universal life are others. Whole life insurance is the original life insurance policy.

Yield Maintenance. A prepayment penalty that allows investors to attain the same yield as if the borrower made all scheduled interest payments up until the maturity date. It dictates that borrowers pay the rate differential between the loan interest rate and the prevailing market interest rate on the prepaid capital for the period remaining to loan maturity.

Visit *LifestyleInvestor.com/Gift* for a downloadable version.

RESOURCES

A detailed list of all the books I've read related to all things money, investing, lifestyle, personal development, and personal growth is available to you. The list is extensive (I average 70 to 150 books per year) so I have not included it here but made it available to you at *LifestyleInvestor.com/Goodreads*.

Here's a list of my top twenty-five books that I recommend every Lifestyle Investor listen to or read (I happen to like audiobooks):

1. *Rich Dad, Poor Dad* by Robert T. Kiyosaki

2. *Rich Dad's CASHFLOW Quadrant: Guide to Financial Freedom* by Robert T. Kiyosaki

3. *Tax-Free Wealth: How to Build Massive Wealth by Permanently Lowering Your Taxes* by Tom Wheelwright, CPA

4. *Berkshire Hathaway Letters to Shareholders* by Warren Buffett

5. *The Millionaire Fastlane: Crack the Code to Wealth and Live Rich for a Lifetime!* by MJ DeMarco

6. *Killing Sacred Cows: Overcoming the Financial Myths That Are Destroying Your Prosperity* by Garrett B. Gunderson

7. *What Would the Rockefellers Do? How the Wealthy Get and Stay That Way, and How You Can Too* by Garrett B. Gunderson

8. *The Holy Grail of Investing: The World's Greatest Investors Reveal Their Ultimate Strategies for Financial Freedom* by Tony Robbins and Christopher Zook

9. *Money Master the Game: 7 Simple Steps to Financial Freedom* by Tony Robbins

10. *Unshakeable: Your Financial Freedom Playbook* by Tony Robbins

11. *The Hands-Off Investor: An Insider's Guide to Investing in Passive Real Estate Syndications* by Brian Burke

12. *The Creature from Jekyll Island: A Second Look at the Federal Reserve* by G. Edward Griffin

13. *What Has Government Done to Our Money?* by Murray N. Rothbard

14. *The Case Against the Fed* by Murray N. Rothbard

15. *The Bitcoin Standard: The Decentralized Alternative to Central Banking* by Saifedean Ammous

16. *The Internet of Money* by Andreas M. Antonopoulos

17. *Think and Grow Rich* by Napoleon Hill

18. *Becoming Your Own Banker: The Infinite Banking Concept* by R. Nelson Nash

19. *Currency Wars: The Making of the Next Global Crisis* by James Rickards

20. *The Little Book of Common Sense Investing* by John Bogle

21. *Set for Life: Dominating Life, Money, and The American Dream* by Scott Trench

22. *The Intelligent Investor* by Benjamin Graham

23. *The 4-Hour Work Week* by Timothy Ferriss

24. *The Richest Man in Babylon* by George S. Clason

25. *Roths For The Rich* by Will Duffy

Download this resource at *LifestyleInvestor.com/Gift*.

ABOUT JUSTIN DONALD

The magazine, *Entrepreneur,* calls Justin Donald the "Warren Buffett of Lifestyle Investing." As the founder of The Lifestyle Investor and a master of low-risk cash flow investing, Justin's ethos is to "create wealth without creating a job." He excels at simplifying complex financial strategies, structuring deals, and disciplined investment systems that consistently yield profitable results.

After twenty-one months of investing, and before his thirty-seventh birthday, Justin's investments generated sufficient passive income for him and his wife Jennifer to leave their jobs. Following his straightforward investment system and 10 Commandments of Lifestyle Investing, Justin negotiated deals with over three hundred companies, multiplied his net worth to over nine figures, and continues to maintain a family-centric lifestyle.

Justin's extensive entrepreneurial experience includes owning several profitable real estate-related businesses, one of the largest mobile home park portfolios in the US, various additional rental property portfolios, Orangetheory Fitness and KidStrong franchises, and multiple successful operating companies. One notable venture is Stellar, a residential maintenance and rehab company that Justin co-founded, that recently completed its Series B funding round, led by Alerion Ventures and S3 Ventures, the largest venture capital firm in Texas.

Justin routinely publishes his wisdom on lifestyle investing as a member of the Kiplinger Advisor Collective. He has also been a SXSW investor judge and a keynote speaker for organizations like Keller Williams and Entrepreneurs Organization. He is a member of Tiger 21 and serves on the board of Front Row Foundation International. Through his Lifestyle Investor Mastermind, Justin now consults and coaches entrepreneurs, executives, and successful media personalities on lifestyle investing. He hosts *The Lifestyle Investor Podcast*, with the aim of helping listeners consistently generate repeatable returns. Justin has also appeared on hundreds of podcasts and shared prominent stages like Texas Rangers Stadium with renowned leaders like Richard Branson, Robert Kiyosaki, Sam Zell, Ron Paul, and Kevin Harrington.

In January 2021, Justin released his #1 *Wall Street Journal* and *USA Today* bestselling book, *The Lifestyle Investor: The 10 Commandments of Cash Flow Investing for Passive Income and Financial Freedom*. The book is now in the top 1 percent of all books ever sold, with all proceeds donated to the Tebow Foundation and Love Justice International, two nonprofits that combat human trafficking in over fifty countries.

Justin and Jennifer are dedicated philanthropists who contribute to various causes privately and through their church, with a primary emphasis on fighting human trafficking among other humanitarian efforts. Additionally, they sponsor several children through Compassion International. The Donalds reside in Austin, Texas, and love adventure-based international travel with their cherished daughter.

Connect with Justin

Website: LifestyleInvestor.com

Email: Support@LifestyleInvestor.com

LinkedIn: LinkedIn.com/in/JustinWDonald/

Facebook: LifestyleInvestor.com/FB

Instagram: Instagram.com/JustinDonald/

X (Twitter): X.com/jwdonald1

GO FURTHER TOGETHER

COMMUNITY | CASH | CONNECTIONS

The Lifestyle Investor® Mastermind includes these benefits:

- ▶ Achieve the lifestyle of your dreams with passive investing
- ▶ Find the best investment deals that support your lifestyle
- ▶ Get tools, templates, and resources to negotiate better deals with low risk
- ▶ Access real investment opportunities not available to the public
- ▶ Learn how to deconstruct new and current investments to model yourself
- ▶ Create a plan and protect your assets
- ▶ Multiply and optimize capital
- ▶ Increase your Investor IQ
- ▶ Access, communicate, and close better deals with investors
- ▶ Exclusive visits with entrepreneurs, founders, and CEOs
- ▶ Network and connect with abudance-minded lifestyle investors

Apply today to begin your journey to become a high-performance lifestyle investor at
LifestyleInvestor.com/Mastermind

ABOUT THE LIFESTYLE INVESTOR

Imagine an exciting new life in which you're able to earn passive income, amass long-term equity, and achieve total financial freedom without having a job.

If you knew you could make this transformation through low-risk cash flow investment principles that resulted in passive income streams and significant wealth creation, would you be intrigued?

The path by which you can journey to this destination is put before you with eye-opening clarity in Justin Donald's much anticipated new book. *The Lifestyle Investor: The 10 Commandments of Cash Flow Investing for Passive Income and Financial Freedom* reveals cash flow investing strategies and principles that show you exactly how to:

- Put your lifestyle first
- Reduce your investment risk
- Find deals invisible to the public

- Create immediate cash flow
- Get your principal back quickly
- Replace your job or business with passive cash flow streams

In addition, you'll discover how to "plus" your deals, use financial leverage to your advantage, and make sure every dollar you invest generates a return.

Justin illustrates the Lifestyle Investor mindset by sharing real-world case studies of the investments of entrepreneurs and executives who've manifested complete freedom in their lives.

Enjoy the Passive Income Masterclass®

Join Justin for a guided tour of the Lifestyle Investor® system:

- Manage your fears, and become a great Lifestyle Investor
- Negotiate the best possible deals so you generate immediate cash flow and long-term equity
- Stack multiple Lifestyle Investor® strategies to increase your overall return while decreasing your risk
- Spot invisible deals normally ignored by typical investors
- Structure investments and returns to decrease taxes and increase your net worth
- Partner with investors and dealmakers to save decades of time and hundreds of thousands (or millions) you would have otherwise lost
- Receive tools, templates, documents, and resources that you can use and model (and save tens of thousands or more on legal and professional services fees)
- Many other strategies and techniques to lower your risk and increase your chances of success for achieving financial freedom as a Lifestyle Investor

Join the Lifestyle Investor Masterclass at
LifestyleInvestor.com/Masterclass

Bring the investment world's next Warren Buffett to speak at your event.

Audiences throughout the world are eager to hear from Justin Donald for one simple reason: they're extremely interested in learning how to build a portfolio of low-risk investments that generates passive income without a job!

- Stop trading time for money
- Rapidly learn Lifestyle Investing® principles
- Optimize passive investment strategies that will allow you to earn income while you sleep and go on vacations

Justin will engage, captivate, and motivate your audience who want to blend passive wealth creation with a prosperous, rewarding lifestyle. Discover relevant, actionable strategies anyone can use.

Book Justin for your next event today.
Visit LifestyleInvestor.com/Speaking

THE LIFESTYLE INVESTOR REVIEWS

Justin clearly shows us how wealth and freedom can co-exist. His 10 Commandments are required reading for anyone aspiring to become a Lifestyle Investor.

—Kary Oberbrunner
Author of *Unhackable, Day Job to Dream Job,* and *Elixir Project*

He's a man of faith, honesty, and integrity—and that's what I love about Justin Donald.

—Clint Buckelew
Realtor with Buckelew Realty

I spent the better part of twenty years as a highly successful options trader on the floor of the Chicago Mercantile Exchange, always trying to live by the concept of risk-adjusted returns. When I first started reading *The Lifestyle Investor,* it became apparent that I had not applied that same philosophy to my personal investing. I'm so thankful for Justin sharing his easy-to-follow strategies in this must-read book. He's opened up a new world of opportunity for me that I never knew existed!

—Cal Callahan
Investor and Host of *The Great Unlearn* Podcast

Justin Donald is intelligent, savvy, and has remarkable insights around entrepreneurship and investing. Justin provides incredible value, whether it be analyzing a potential deal or simply being a sounding board for strategic business decisions.

—Nick Najjar
Entrepreneur and Investor

Justin changed the direction of my life, and without his strategies, I would be at least a decade away from financial independence. Instead, my family enjoys an abundant lifestyle with predictable, indestructible monthly cash flow.

—Adam Sobieski
Investor

Justin is one of the few people I turn to when I have financial questions. He willingly shares what he knows and truly desires to see other people grow in wealth and freedom. When it comes to financial advice, I lean on Justin.

—Brent Lindberg
Entrepreneur and Founder of Fuseneo

Justin's love for life is contagious. He brings excitement and energy to every conversation you have with him, whether he is sharing his passions for food and travel, how to be intentional with your spouse and kids, or painting a bigger picture on the value of investing in yourself and your future. What I love and appreciate about Justin is that he not only eagerly engages you in these topics, but he also has a plan of attack. Justin marries his passions and dreams with the steps needed to accomplish them. I encourage anyone to hone in on the methodologies that he puts into place. You will experience a deeper understanding of who you are, what you want to accomplish, and a plan on how to get there.

—Brian Rhame
Consultant

In a world where financial success and freedom seem hard to achieve, *The Lifestyle Investor* by Justin Donald is a game-changer. As Justin's close friend, I've seen his incredible journey to becoming a top lifestyle investor. His passion for helping others reach their financial goals shines through in this book. Justin reveals how to create cash flow and build wealth without the usual risks and complexities in finance. He's living proof that it works! This book stands out because Justin truly wants to help you live your dream life. His clear, engaging advice is perfect for everyone, regardless of their financial experience. From the moment you start reading *The Lifestyle Investor*, you'll feel inspired to take charge of your financial future. It's a must-read for anyone aiming to create lasting wealth and happiness. I fully endorse *The Lifestyle Investor* by Justin Donald as the go-to guide for financial freedom, and I'm sure it'll change your life and how you think about wealth creation, just like it did for me.

—Erik Van Horn
Founder of Scalable Franchise and
Host of the *Franchise Secrets* Podcast

As a mentor to entrepreneurs, I help business owners build million-dollar businesses in record time. Justin Donald does the same for investors; he helps people like us build passive income in a fraction of the time it usually takes. Financial freedom takes most people a lifetime, but I've seen Justin create life-changing results in just a few years. He has a unique ability to find great people, great deals, and great ideas. He is a trusted resource for many—myself included—when it comes to generating a truly abundant life.

—Ryan Moran
Founder of Capitalism.com

The Lifestyle investor is pure gold. Justin's concepts are insightful and easy to implement.

—Preston Smiles
7-figure Conscious Entrepreneur and Author of *Love Louder*

This is a must-read if you are looking for a book that will expand your view of what is possible when it comes to building wealth!

—Geoff Woods
Chief Growth Officer, Jindal Steel & Power, and Co-Founder and President of The ONE Thing

When I hear the word "investor," I often think of Justin Donald for obvious reasons. Justin has made investing a part of his lifestyle and taught many others to do the same.

—Dan Fleyshman
Founder of Elevator Studio

I am a very experienced passive investor by anyone's definition, as my passive income easily covers all my expenses and allows me to travel and do just about anything I want. HOWEVER, after reading Justin's book and learning his methodology, I was blown away. Even after investing for well over a decade myself, I found nugget after nugget of valuable info on almost every page. I can't recommend this book enough!

—Hans Box
Co-Founder of Box Wilson Equity

This book and Justin's website resources will revolutionize your views on investing and money. *The Lifestyle Investor* provides a roadmap to financial independence and a life of your choosing. In a simple and engaging way, Justin teaches cash flow investing and shares his proven methods that boosted his net worth to millions. He teaches you how to maximize resources, create a monthly income-generating portfolio, and develop a successful investor mindset. Justin's approach is values-driven and devoid of ego. He also covers strategies to optimize taxes in an implementable way.

—Rich Christiansen
Bestselling Author, Prolific Entrepreneur,
and Founder of Legado Family

For a generation that has become obsessed with personal choice and freedom, most people lack the skills to put money to work for them, so they can build the lifestyle of their dreams. For those who do not want to rely on and wait for a forty-year, buy-and-hold strategy to bear fruits, *The Lifestyle Investor* teaches you the principles and tactics to accelerate your path to financial freedom while you take back control of your time and schedule.

—Sam Marks
Host of *Invest Like A Boss* Podcast

The depth of Justin Donald's knowledge of investments and business makes him uniquely qualified to be a thought leader in this space.

—JP Newman
CEO and Founder of Thrive FP
Host of *Investing on Purpose* Podcast

The advice he's given me has always been helpful; some of his suggestions I had never heard before. When I share it with other high-performing people I respect, it seems they hadn't heard of it before and are impressed. I've put some of it to use and get great results.

—Aimee Mueller
Life Coach and Inspirational Speaker at AmieeMueller.com

Justin Donald is among the most inquisitive and curious people I have ever met. As a friend, we can have conversations that are engaging and thought-provoking. As an investor, these same traits manifest themselves as rigorous analysis and due diligence that is as deep as it is broad.

—G. Bantayehu
Real Estate Developer of Bantayehu Development

Justin has personally helped me transition from a successful career to a full-time investor. The vast industry knowledge he has through multiple sectors, the ability to bring in experts, analyze deals, and incredible deal flow make him unique.

—Ryan Casey
Investor, Sales and Business Consultant,
Core Values Index Certified Practitioner

Justin has the unique ability of distilling complex topics down into actionable steps, making financial freedom both attainable and fun in the process. This is the book I wish I had ten years ago but will remain on my bookshelf as a timeless resource.

—Phoebe Mroczek
Host of the *Unbecoming* Podcast

Made in United States
North Haven, CT
11 October 2024

58757745R00211